Domestic Affairs

AMERICAN PROGRAMS AND PRIORITIES

by James H. Duffy

SIMON AND SCHUSTER · NEW YORK

Designed by Irving Perkins
Manufactured in the United States of America
1   2   3   4   5   6   7   8   9   10

Library of Congress Cataloging in Publication Data

Duffy, James
  Domestic affairs.

  Includes bibliographical references and index.
  1.   United States—Social policy.   2.   United States—
Economic policy.   3.   United States—Politics and
government.   I.   Title.
HN65.D83   309.1'73   78–12581

ISBN   0-671-22871-4

Permission to reprint from the following is gratefully acknowledged:

"Major Public Initiatives in Health Care," by Herbert E. Klarman, and "Some Lessons of the 1960's," by Eli Ginzberg and Robert M. Solow, in *The Great Society: Lessons for the Future,* edited by Eli Ginzberg and Robert M. Solow, copyright © 1974 by National Affairs, Inc., Basic Books, Inc., Publishers, New York.

Acknowledgments

Writing this book simply would not have been possible without the assistance of the following:

My editor, Alice Mayhew, who had faith in the whole undertaking from the beginning and helped greatly in bringing into focus what I was trying to say;

My agent, Lois Wallace, who offered many practical suggestions;

My good friends, Louis Begley, Robert Dujarric and John F. Hunt, who read the manuscript and offered useful and helpful comments;

My extraordinarily patient secretary, Marian Rees, who typed (and retyped) the manuscript without complaint;

The staff of my firm's law library, which performed a number of helpful tasks;

My friends and teachers of many years ago, Alpheus Thomas Mason and Paul D. Tillett, Jr., who made clear that writing a book was not only a possible but perhaps even an honorable thing to do.

The Firestone Library at Princeton University served as a hospitable home-away-from-home, where much of my work was done. If Princeton is "the best old place of all," as I firmly believe, the magnificent Firestone Library is surely the best spot within that place.

Finally, a word and a salute to my wife, Martha, who unerringly knew when to be quiet and when to speak up as the book progressed.

J.D.

For my parents, Phyllis and Bill Duffy

Contents

Preface

This book is an outgrowth of my personal feelings of discouragement after the 1972 elections. Despite evident domestic problems in America —probably more evident to someone living in New York City—domestic affairs received short shrift in that campaign. Senator McGovern exploited to the full his courageous opposition to the Vietnam War, but one can only agree with his Republican opponents that his treatment of purely domestic issues was ill-prepared and "fuzzy." And President Nixon continued in that campaign to break, as Jonathan Schell has described it, "the unity of word and deed which makes political action intelligible to the rest of the world."[1] Nixon was "fuzzy," too, but in a manner calculated to appeal to negative racial and social feelings in ways that would not have been acceptable if done directly.

Reflecting on the 1972 campaign, I began a systematic effort to inform myself on current social and economic issues, a process somewhat neglected over the years since college, in the course of a busy law practice.

An attack of hepatitis in early 1975 kept me out of saloons for an extended period and the steroids used to treat my infection had the interesting side effect of producing an overabundance of energy. The combination of extra time and energy enabled me to reflect further on domestic affairs and to start putting my thoughts in writing.

As long as I can remember, I have believed in the necessity for programmatic solutions to social and economic problems, although, after almost twenty years as a lawyer (and taxpayer), I am now more attracted by programs that stand a decent chance of working efficiently.

Another belief, which this project has tempered greatly, has been that the social programs in this country can be financed from the fruits of steady, noninflationary growth in the national economy. This was Adlai

Stevenson's belief in the 1950s, and it is one that I shared. The cold reality today appears, at least on the basis of recent experience, to be that our economy is not going to grow at a rate adequate to produce a dividend big enough to finance the cost of an extensive range of social programs.

Confronted with this reality, one has to consider not only what the problems are, but how they should be ranked in terms of priorities. This exercise demands a sharper definition of both the problems themselves and the proposals for their solution.

The process of delineating priorities has become more acute with the so-called taxpayer rebellion, first evidenced by the adoption of Proposition 13 in California in 1978. What the press has called "Proposition 13 Fever" may not represent the totally negative reaction against government spending that it purports to be. But it certainly does signal the need for public officials to explain the reasons—and the priorities—for their spending proposals.

This book starts with a reach back thirty years to a look at the Economic Bill of Rights proposed by Franklin D. Roosevelt in 1944 as the basis for continuing and extending the New Deal after World War II. The "rights" set forth by FDR serve as useful reference points in measuring American social and economic progress since 1945,* in order to identify areas that should be the subject of our major priorities in 1979.

Roosevelt's agenda reflected the do-everything-at-once enthusiasm of the New Deal. While this approach appeals to my programmatic instincts, it is, I am afraid, an unrealistic way of looking at our current problems.

The President and Congress have always had to make distinctions and to set priorities, at least to some degree. Now that performance of these functions has become a matter of more urgent necessity, it is clear to me that the capacity of the President and Congressmen to deal with issues, both institutionally and personally, has become extremely relevant to any discussion of domestic affairs; abstract consideration of desirable policies would not be worth much without a look at the realities of what we can reasonably expect from the Executive Branch and the Congress.

I have not attempted a textbook study of the capabilities and limitations of the Federal government. But I have tried to assess what we can

* See Chapters One to Three.

and cannot realistically expect from our national institutions and the men and women who staff them.

In so far as the Congress is concerned, I have attempted two in-depth studies of Congressional activity as it relates to aid to secondary education in the entire postwar period* and to national energy policy in the single year 1975.†

With the passage of the Elementary and Secondary Education Act in 1965 and its subsequent extensions, aid to education has ceased to be at the top of the social and economic agenda, although, as I point out, much remains to be done to strengthen ESEA and to make it more effective. Yet the two-part aid-to-education story—the period leading up to the passage of ESEA in 1965 and its subsequent implementation by the Congress—illustrates that the Congress has had difficulty in coming to grips with the problem of improving American secondary education.

There is hardly a more fundamental issue in our society—or in any other society—than the way accumulated knowledge is transmitted from one generation to the next and how young people are prepared for roles in an increasingly complex world. It is a rare citizen who does not have views, and very strong views, on how the educational process should be carried out by our schools. The expression of these views, coupled with emotional overtones of race and religion, created pressures on the Congress that resulted first in delay and then in compromise in meeting educational needs. The story says much about the limitations of Congress as an instrument of social change.

Aid to education involved both economic and social questions, but it is fair to say that social concerns predominated. By contrast, the question of a comprehensive national energy policy has involved primarily a clash of powerful economic interests—oil and gas producers, automobile manufacturers (and the automotive unions) and the utilities and other large industrial consumers of energy among them. For this reason I chose energy policy as an issue in which economic considerations predominate.

When writing the chapter on Congressional involvement with the energy issue in 1975, I was confident that a comprehensive energy policy would be enacted by the Congress in 1977 or early in 1978. But, instead, the failure of 1975 was played out once again, demonstrating

---

* See Chapters Four and Five.
† See Chapter Six.

that issues involving poor people and welfare are not the only ones approaching intractability, and illustrating once again the limitations of Congress as a crucible for fusing major national policy. Rather than document the legislative failure on energy matters in 1977 and 1978, I have chosen to leave the description of the earlier controversies of 1975; the issues were much the same and the reasons for Congressional failure appear to me, at least, to have been somewhat sharper the first time around.

A quite different approach seemed appropriate in looking at the Presidency. While the voice of the Executive Branch is not always one, there is more likely to be a greater coherence and unity of viewpoint than in the Congress. Normally the voice of the Executive Branch is that of the President, and normally it is a voice conditioned by the President's political background as a Republican or Democrat. (Even Dwight Eisenhower, without a history of partisan involvement, readily embraced traditional Republican positions when he became President.) Accordingly, I have tried to survey briefly the contrasting approaches of Republican and Democratic Presidents to social and economic issues. Whether our postwar Presidents have been classified as quiescent or activist, effective or ineffective, there has been a common thread uniting the Republicans on the one hand and the Democrats on the other.*

Two chapters deal with institutional changes in the Congress and the Presidency.† These changes include such formal reforms as a fundamental restructuring of the budget process in Congress and more subtle and informal alterations of the Presidency after Vietnam and Watergate. These are changes that have begun to affect the handling of domestic issues and are surely going to have an effect in the future.

Having explained some of the inclusions in this book, I should perhaps explain some of the omissions, at least a part of which were deliberate. I have not, for example, discussed the role of the Supreme Court, on the theory that, in general, the Court is not today central to the making of social and economic policy. Its decisions can and do have great political impact and social consequences, but except for its decisions regarding education, the Court has not materially affected the principal social and economic issues that are discussed. The decisions of the Supreme Court (and some state court decisions) concerning education—and desegregation and school finance in particular—are

---

* See Chapters Eight and Nine.
† See Chapters Seven and Ten.

reviewed in the context of how they were interrelated with the actions of Congress on aid to education.

I have also deliberately excluded foreign-policy and defense issues from the scope of this book. This is a purely artificial exclusion, particularly at a time when defense programs continue to take a healthy share of each dollar of Federal expenditure (24 cents), when defense procurement decisions affect employment, and when our foreign-policy initiatives in shoring up the dollar and in dealing with OPEC have profound consequences for the domestic economy. This exclusion was made not out of any neoisolationist conviction that such issues can be ignored, but for the very practical reasons that the scope of this book had to stop somewhere and that foreign-policy and defense issues have been and are being ably analyzed by others.

Finally, it should be evident that I have written this book as a Democrat, though I have tried to be fair and objective in looking at both Republicans and Democrats. If I have failed, I can only repeat what Lyndon Johnson said some twenty years ago:

> I believe there is always a national answer to each national problem, and, believing this, I do not believe that there are necessarily two sides to every question.[2]

One · The Economic Bill of Rights

This Republic had its beginning, and grew to its present strength, under the protection of certain inalienable political rights—among them the right of free speech, free press, free worship, trial by jury, freedom from unreasonable searches and seizures. They were our rights to life and liberty.

As our Nation has grown in size and stature, however—as our industrial economy expanded—these political rights proved inadequate to assure us equality in the pursuit of happiness.

We have come to a clear realization of the fact that true individual freedom cannot exist without economic security and independence. "Necessitous men are not free men." People who are hungry and out of a job are the stuff of which dictatorships are made.

In our day these economic truths have become accepted as self-evident. We have accepted, so to speak, a second Bill of Rights under which a new basis of security and prosperity can be established for all—regardless of station, race, or creed.

Among these are:

The right to a useful and remunerative job in the industries or shops or farms or mines of the Nation;

The right to earn enough to provide adequate food and clothing and recreation;

The right of every farmer to raise and sell his products at a return which will give him and his family a decent living;

The right of every businessman, large and small, to trade in an atmosphere of freedom from unfair competition and domination by monopolies at home or abroad;

The right of every family to a decent home;

The right to adequate medical care and the opportunity to achieve and enjoy good health;

The right to adequate protection from the economic fears of old age, sickness, accident, and unemployment;

The right to a good education.

All of these rights spell security. And after this war is won we must be prepared to move forward, in the implementation of these rights, to new goals of human happiness and well-being.

America's own rightful place in the world depends in large part upon how fully these and similar rights have been carried into practice for our citizens. For unless there is security here at home there cannot be lasting peace in the world.

—FRANKLIN D. ROOSEVELT,
Message on the State of the
Union, January 11, 1944

Franklin Roosevelt's Economic Bill of Rights represented his vision of a post-World War II domestic program for the United States. Speaking at a time when the American people were purposefully united in winning that war, Roosevelt easily assumed that this unity of purpose could be transferred to peacetime.

"The American people are prepared to meet the problems of peace in the same bold way that they have met the problems of war," FDR told a 1944 campaign rally in Chicago. He went on to say:

Last January, in my message to the Congress on the State of the Union, I outlined an Economic Bill of Rights on which "a new basis of security and prosperity can be established for all." . . .

Some people—I need not name them—have sneered at these ideals as well as the ideals of the Atlantic Charter, the ideals of the Four Freedoms. They have said that they were the dreams of starry-eyed New Dealers—that it is silly to talk of them because we cannot attain these ideals tomorrow or the next day.

The American people have greater faith than that. I know that they agree with these objectives—that they demand them—and they are determined to get them—and that they are *going* to get them.

The American people have a good habit—the habit of going right ahead and accomplishing the impossible.

We know that, and other people know it. Today, there are those that know it best of all: the Nazis and the Japs.[1]

As we shall see, America has not stood still since 1944; very real social progress has been made over the last thirty-four years. But Roosevelt's Economic Bill of Rights could still serve, with an addition or two (inflation and a national energy policy come readily to mind), as the heart of an agenda for our basic social and economic problems in 1979.

Why should this be so? There are several reasons. It is hard to imagine any real disagreement with Roosevelt's broadly stated premises; they are, as he said, "self-evident." But this does not rule out disagreement over the priorities accorded to particular programs and the means for carrying them out. "The right to a decent home" may be an abstract proposition supported in principle by all but a few cranks; the right to a home subsidized by the government or the right to a home in an exclusively zoned suburb may be propositions not so readily embraced and not so "self-evident."

Americans are notoriously generous, but along with this generosity runs a basic strain of independence and individualism. "We have become confirmed," as Woodrow Wilson once said, "in the habit of acting under an odd mixture of selfish and altruistic motives."[2]

Achieving a consensus on almost any subject—particularly those with economic consequences—is never easy in a nation of more than 217 million people of widely varying and often conflicting ethnic, regional and educational viewpoints, not to mention varying levels of economic achievement and expectation or Wilson's "odd mixture" of "selfish and altruistic motives." The United States is not Sweden, a compact, homogeneous country with a population roughly equivalent to that of New York City. In a sprawling nation like the United States, with its great diversities, the setting and implementing of social and economic priorities are bound to be fought over intensely. There is scarcely an issue in American domestic politics that does not involve serious potential conflict among competing interests and positions.

As James Madison predicted in *The Federalist,* the Federal government will never be able to remove the *causes* of "faction"* or the interplay of competing interests, but the diversity of the country—the diversity of the various "factions"—will at least theoretically be such that no group can improperly impose its will on the nation as a whole. This is one of the great strengths of the American Republic, but it also means that relatively straightforward approaches to social and economic problems

* By a "faction" Madison meant "a number of citizens, whether amounting to a majority or minority of the whole, who are united and actuated by some common impulse of passion, or of interest, adverse to the rights of other citizens, or to the permanent and aggregate interests of the community." Federalist No. 10, *The Federalist* (New York: Modern Library, 1937), p. 54.

must give way to compromises worked out among competing factions—often compromises that dissipate the thrust of the solution undertaken.

Along with the social progress that has been made since 1944 has come a realization that reform does not mean only the enactment of new legislation, but a capacity to deal with great complexity as well. Mandating a medical-assistance program for the elderly is relatively easy; administering such a program without waste or corruption and without pushing the cost of health care upward is infinitely more difficult. This increasing complexity of America's social and economic problems—and the increasing realization that they are complex—has served to deter and delay solutions. With the Medicare and Medicaid experience fresh in mind, for example, it is most unlikely that a comprehensive national health policy will be adopted soon in the United States.

Increasing awareness of complexity and the marshaling of diverse viewpoints in support of social programs has not made the task of our political leaders easier. Nor has the pressure from the popular media to simplify issues—to make the explanation of proposals and arguments compatible with multisecond television-news "picture opportunities" and with the standards of a daily press more and more interested in such features as "Buying Fish—The Fresher the Better."

These pressures toward simplicity have all but destroyed the Presidential campaign as a forum for meaningful debate. The shadow of "Thomas Elusive Dewey, the candidate in sneakers,"[3] is cast over our political campaigns, with voters most recently asked to choose between a candidate (Governor Carter) advocating "a government as good as its people"[4] and one (President Ford) who warned that "a government big enough to give us everything we want is a government big enough to take from us everything we have."*[5]

Franklin Roosevelt optimistically foresaw a postwar era in which domestic concerns would predominate. Yet that postwar era had scarcely begun before the Cold War started, followed by Korea and Vietnam. Domestic issues were inevitably sidetracked, as the attention of the country and the allocation of its resources were directed toward international and defense problems. Indeed, it was not until 1976 that the Gallup Poll showed (for the first time since 1936) domestic issues

* The lack of programmatic substance in Presidential campaigns is not to suggest that there is a lack of detail. The televised Carter-Ford debates in 1976 were replete with bone-numbing recitals of statistics. These recitals may have demonstrated the candidates' presumed capacity as technocrats, but they certainly did not add up to coherently expressed policies.

—inflation and unemployment—predominant in voter thinking in a Presidential campaign year.[6]

The competing demands of foreign and defense policies, while very real during most of the years since World War II, have also constituted a severe temptation to our Presidents and potential Presidents. It has become much easier to talk about apartheid in South Africa than desegregation in South Boston. The "lush melon of foreign policy,"[7] as the late David Bruce called it, had, and apparently continues to have, a great lure for politicians as they sweep around the world on headline-making trips, at the expense of time and energy that might be devoted to domestic concerns.

Franklin Roosevelt also could not have foreseen the profound distrust of government that has grown up in America in recent years. McCarthyism, Vietnam and Watergate contributed their share, as did economic policies that led to record unemployment and inflation at the same time. Public distrust and the feeling that government does not really work are not conducive to major policy initiatives.

Finally, despite the much touted "knowledge explosion" and the computer revolution, one must reckon with the profound ignorance that we have, and that our government shares, as to the answers to very fundamental questions. Take only three examples:

1. Will American consumers drive their cars less if gasoline prices are increased?
2. What is the most effective method of teaching a child to read?
3. Do public-service jobs provide meaningful work experience which makes recipients employable in the private sector?

For all the reports and studies that have been made, the answers to such questions remain obscure, with attendant consequences for efficient social planning and spending.

Roosevelt was aware of those who sneered at his Economic Bill of Rights, who felt that it was "silly to talk of them, because we cannot attain these ideals tomorrow or the next day." Certainly there are a great many who sneer today, a great many who have reached the conclusion that our economic and social problems are intractable and insoluble.[8] Fortunately this attitude, fostered by a few rather silly academics, is not yet pervasive. Whether out of cowardice or from conviction, most of our political leaders have shied away from such a stand. They may have misframed the questions and given unsatisfactory answers, but to their credit they have not told us that either raising questions or seeking answers is pointless.

Starting with this marginally hopeful fact, the chapters that follow attempt to do four things: (1) to measure the social progress of the United States since World War II (Chapters Two and Three); (2) to examine the response of the Congress (Chapters Four, Five and Six) and of the President (Chapters Eight and Nine) to social and economic issues; (3) to offer some comments on the current institutional problems and approaches of the Congress (Chapter Seven) and of the Presidency (Chapter Nine); and (4) to suggest a reworking of Roosevelt's postwar agenda to fit our situation in 1979 and the years immediately ahead (Chapter Eleven).

Two · Report Card: A Third of a Century

If we could first know where we are, and whither we are tending, we could then better judge what to do, and how to do it.
> —ABRAHAM LINCOLN, Speech at
> Springfield, Illinois,
> June 16, 1858

In his first Message to Congress after the Japanese surrender in 1945, Harry S. Truman strongly endorsed and reiterated FDR's Economic Bill of Rights. He urged Congress to "make the attainment of these rights the essence of postwar American economic life."[1]

In 1945, President Truman and the Congress were accountable to a national constituency of 140 million people, including 97 million adults over twenty-one (as "adult" was then defined), as compared with a current population of over 217 million, including almost 153 million adults over eighteen (the current legal definition of "adult" as adopted in most states in the late 1960s and early 1970s).

The age distribution of the national constituency was also different in 1945, with a lower percentage both of the aged (over sixty-five) and of the young (under twenty-five) than there is today. In 1945, 40 percent of the population were under twenty-five; an estimated 43 percent have not reached twenty-five today. And in 1945, those who were sixty-five years old and over made up 7 percent of the population, as compared with about 11 percent today.

If Harry Truman were addressing Congress in 1979, would he be urging the Economic Bill of Rights as the basis for his economic program? In large part one guesses that the answer would be yes, for a third of a century after Truman's 1945 Message the "economic truths" of Roosevelt's formulation have not necessarily been attained. Following is a brief survey of what has been accomplished.

The right to a useful and remunerative job in the industries or shops or farms or mines of the Nation.

With a substantial portion of the labor force off at war, and with domestic industry operating at full capacity to meet defense requirements, unemployment stood at a mere 1.9 percent of the civilian labor force in 1945. Traumatic memories of the jobless rates in the 1930s— 23.6 percent in 1932; 24.9 percent in 1934; 14.6 percent in 1940— were now mixed with newer expectations of full employment.

> When we have reconverted our economy to a peacetime basis [Truman said in his 1945 Message], we shall not be satisfied with merely our pre-war economy. The American people have set high goals for their own future. They have set these goals high because they have seen how great can be the productive capacity of our country. The levels of production and income reached during the war years have given our citizens an appreciation of what a full production peacetime economy can be.

The New Deal substantially lessened, but did not solve, the country's unemployment problem. Truman knew this, and he knew also that wartime employment levels could not be sustained in peacetime without government assistance. As a Senator, he had stated in 1944 that it should be national policy for the Federal government to supplement the civilian economy when it did not provide sufficient jobs; in other words, as FDR had said, there should be a "right" to a job.

Senator James E. Murray (Democrat, Montana) introduced a bill in 1945 mandating the Federal government to manage the domestic economy so as to foster jobs in the private sector and, failing private-sector performance, to step in and provide job opportunities for everyone in the labor force who desired them, so that "all Americans able to work and seeking work have the right to useful, remunerative, regular, and full-time employment."[2]

By the time Senator Murray's bill had worked its way through Congress, there was no mention of "full employment" and no commitment on the part of the Federal government to provide jobs for all those seeking work. Instead, the policy of the Federal government was declared to be "to use all practicable means consistent with its needs and obligations and other essential considerations of national policy . . . to promote maximum employment, production, and purchasing power. . . ."

Watered down though it may have been, the Employment Act of 1946 was Harry Truman's principal legislative accomplishment as President. Despite his personal disappointment, Truman praised the act when he signed it, and described its purposes this way:

> Democratic government has the responsibility to use all its resources to create and maintain conditions under which free competitive enterprise can operate effectively—conditions under which there is an abundance of employment opportunity for those who are able, willing, and seeking to work.
>
> It is not the Government's duty to supplant the efforts of private enterprise to find markets, or of individuals to find jobs. The people do expect the Government, however, to create and maintain conditions in which the individual businessman and the individual job seeker have a chance to succeed by their own efforts. That is the objective of the Employment Act of 1946.[3]

Lip service has been given to the employment objectives of the 1946 Act since its adoption. The notion was even abroad that the Act by some magic was working, since civilian unemployment in the years 1947 through 1974 ranged from a low of 2.9 percent in 1953 (again boosted by defense production for the Korean War) and a high of 6.8 percent in the recession year of 1958.

The inability of the Act to achieve the noble objectives that Truman stated for it became clear as unemployment in 1975 approached levels that were the highest since the Depression.

"It has been patently obvious for some time," Senator Jacob K. Javits (Republican, New York) said in 1975, "that, notwithstanding the commitment to maximum employment in the Employment Act of 1946, the Nation has not had at any time a full employment policy or anything approaching it."[4]

If every member of the labor force has a right to a job, that right was less than "self-evident" to 6,100,000 workers, or 6.1 percent of the civilian labor force, in May 1978. Although this rate reflected a drop from the post-Depression high of 9.1 percent reached in February,

March and June 1975, it was still disturbing by almost any standard and well in excess of the 4 percent rate that American economists have generally regarded as the maximum rate compatible with the concept of "full employment."

In nine of the years since adoption of the Employment Act of 1946, unemployment has been at an annual rate below 4 percent. But that goal and the goal expressed in the Economic Bill of Rights have not been achieved since 1969 and now appear to be remote, let alone being cruel jokes for certain groups, among which unemployment is not only above 4 percent, but above the national average of 6.1 percent as well.

To Roosevelt's "industries, shops, farms and mines" as sources of jobs, the present-day interpreter of the Economic Bill of Rights would have to add government as an employer. In 1949, government at all levels employed 7.2 million workers, or 15.2 percent of the combined total of government and private-industry employees; by 1975 government employees numbered 13 million, or 20.6 percent of the combined government–private-industry total.

From 1949 through 1975, the nation's population, the number of employees in private industry and the number of employees of the

AVERAGE ANNUAL EARNINGS

	Private Industry	*Federal Government (not including military)* *	*State and Local*
1949	$ 2,841	$ 2,923	$ 2,700
1960	4,759	4,912	4,550
1965	5,708	6,087	5,403
1970	7,471	8,413	7,818
1975	10,737	11,712	10,900
Percentage increase, 1949–75	278%	300%	304%
Percentage increase, 1965–75	88%	92%	102%

* These earnings do not include military retirement income received by former military personnel who take civilian Federal jobs after retiring from the military. In 1975, an estimated 141,000 Federal civilian employees—5 percent of the Federal civilian work force—benefited from this practice, called "double-dipping." See 123 *Congressional Record* (1977), p. E5226.

Federal government grew roughly 1.4 times. Yet overall government employment increased 2.1 times during that period, due to a 2.8-times increase in state and local government payrolls.

Earnings statistics over this period also dispel the myth of the poorly paid government worker. Throughout the period, average annual earnings of Federal civilian employees always exceeded the private-industry average, and earnings of state and local government employees exceeded the private average by the end of the period, as the previous chart illustrates.

The right to earn enough to provide adequate food and clothing and recreation.

If we leave recreation aside and substitute "income" for "earnings," we find much more encouraging performance since 1945 than in the area of unemployment. Consider the striking changes in the percentage distribution of family income during this period:

Total Money Income (*Expressed in constant 1975 dollars for all years*)	Percentage of Families			
	1947	*1960*	*1970*	*1975*
Under $3,000	15.0%	10.2%	5.3%	4.5%
$3,000 to $4,999	14.3	9.5	6.7	7.5
$5,000 to $6,999	21.8	10.4	7.5	8.3
$7,000 to $9,999	20.2	19.0	13.0	12.8
$10,000 to $14,999		27.2	24.4	22.3
$15,000 to $24,999	28.6	18.6	30.5	30.3
$25,000 and over		5.0	12.6	14.1

The decline in numbers of those below the poverty line is one of the great social achievements of the post-World War II period. The magnitude of decline differs, depending on the measure of poverty. Using Office of Management and Budget poverty guidelines—that is, the level of income required to purchase a minimum of food and other essential goods and services—and interpolating these standards back to the late 1940s, it is estimated that 27 percent of Americans in 1947 were below the poverty level, a percentage that dropped to 22 percent in 1960 and 11.2 percent in 1974. Even though this forward progress was stalled in

1975 and 1976, when 12.3 and 11.8 percent were below the poverty level, the overall improvement has been spectacular.

The increments in income that have enabled an ever-increasing portion of the population to escape a poverty existence have, unfortunately, had to be supplied from sources other than the employment earnings of those affected, the principal source being Social Security and other transfer payments directly or indirectly from the Federal government. It is no coincidence that cash payments of old age, survivors' and disability benefits by the Federal government jumped from $248 million in 1945 to $928 million in 1950, $11 billion in 1960, $31.5 billion in 1970 and $84.2 billion in 1977.

Today the precarious gap between poverty and subsistence is filled with money from an enormous range of benefit programs: Social Security, Aid to Families with Dependent Children (AFDC), veterans' pensions and Supplemental Security Income (SSI) among them. Federal outlays for such cash benefits in fiscal 1977 were $138.2 billion.

A factor that has been increasingly important in relieving poverty—and one that has attracted relatively little public attention despite its immense growth—has been the Federal Food Stamp program. Except for a limited program that operated from 1939 through 1943, food stamps were unknown in 1945. A Democratic Congress in 1959 gave President Eisenhower authority, which he did not use, to implement a food-stamp plan. To Eisenhower, the proposal would have increased "the already disproportionate Federal share of welfare expenses" and required a "complex" administrative mechanism.[5]

President Kennedy, within two weeks after taking office from Eisenhower in 1961, ordered a food-stamp program established on a pilot basis in eight counties. Congressional approval for a full-dress program was given in 1964. Most recently the program was renewed by Congress in 1977 to run four more years.[6]

Basically the Food Stamp program was designed to supplement, if not displace, the principal food relief programs available in the late 1950s—the distribution to the poor of surplus commodity stocks held by the Federal government. Under the earlier food relief procedures, recipients were required to go to government distribution centers to pick up—usually in large quantities—whatever surplus products might be available. Availability was haphazard and bore no necessary relationship to the nutritional needs of recipients.

Food Stamps may be used in regular grocery stores, as opposed to "bread line" centers, to buy virtually any basic food items. (Alcoholic beverages and tobacco are excluded.)* The face value of the stamps a recipient may receive is based on his need, as determined on the basis of a series of deductions from his money income.†

Food Stamps are available to those who meet the income requirements, irrespective of their participation in or eligibility for other public-assistance programs. Aside from some eligibility rules restricting stamp benefits for students and aliens, and limiting the assets that eligible recipients may own (no "welfare Cadillacs," as the result of the 1977 legislation), the only test is whether the recipient, after applicable deductions are made, has an income below the appropriate Federal poverty cutoff then in effect.‡ Other restrictive preconditions, such as old age or the absence of a father from the household, are not relevant.

One of the interesting side effects of the Food Stamp program has been the narrowing of regional differences in effective welfare benefit levels. In states with low public-assistance payments, welfare recipients receive less cash and are thus eligible for a greater face amount of Food Stamps. And as the result of deductions provided for rent and child-care expenses, recipients living in high-cost areas may have higher total deductions, hence a lower income, hence eligibility for a greater Food Stamp allotment.

Food Stamps have been available in all counties of the United States since mid-1974.[7] This universal availability, plus greater public awareness of Food Stamp benefits, greater eligibility as unemployment has increased and upward adjustments in individual allotments to compensate for inflation, have increased the cost of the program to the Federal government from $36 million in 1956 to an estimated $5.3 billion in

* The wonders of the diversity of the United States, or perhaps the wonders of the inventiveness of our Congressmen, were illustrated when the Food Stamp legislation was amended in 1977. Under that legislation, eligible recipients of Food Stamps in Alaska may use Food Stamps to purchase such items of hunting and fishing equipment as "nets, hooks, rods, harpoons, and knives."

† Until 1977, Food Stamps were purchased at a price determined through a complex formula based on income after various inclusions, exclusions and deductions. The difference between the purchase price as so determined and the face value of the stamps—the so-called "bonus value"—represented the actual benefit conferred on the recipient. The purchase requirement was administratively cumbersome and was believed to exclude the poorest eligibles, unable to come up with cash for the purchase price, from participation. At President Carter's request, Congress eliminated the purchase feature in 1977. Recipients now receive a lesser face amount of stamps, since stamps equivalent to the purchase price are no longer provided.

‡ $6,200 for an urban family of four in 1978. For an explanation of the Federal poverty cutoffs—or "Orshansky index"—see the note on page 108.

fiscal 1978. The number of participants has risen in the same period from 500,000 to over 16 million.

The prodigious growth of the Food Stamp program has contributed greatly to the provision of "adequate food" for a significant portion of the population—again not through the exercise of the "right to earn" envisioned by FDR but through a transfer mechanism operating as a supplement to income.

The right of every farmer to raise and sell his products at a return which will give him and his family a decent living.

"From the review of the past 40 years of governmental programs for agriculture," a House Committee on Agriculture report noted in 1977, "it is clear that the capability of American agriculture to produce has generally exceeded demand at prices that assured adequate returns to [farmers'] committed resources and the federal government has been forced to play a major role in American agriculture."[8]

As we shall see in the next subsection, the presumed laws of the free competitive marketplace are less than what they seem in large segments of the American economy. But basic supply-and-demand principles, in the absence of government intervention, continue to operate for the farmer. Poor weather, which reduces the size of a crop, has an immediate upward effect on prices for that crop. So do the perceptions of millions of individual farmers that it is a good year to increase plantings. Such individual decisions collectively lead to overproduction and lower prices.

Few would disagree with the desirability of government intervention to provide the farmer with a "floor" of protection against the vagaries of the marketplace. The debate has been over which techniques, at which level of cost to the Federal government, should be employed.

The basic intervention techniques were introduced in FDR's Agricultural Adjustment Act of 1938*—payments to farmers to keep acreage out of production; loans and purchases of commodities by the Commodity Credit Corporation (CCC) to limit supplies reaching the open market (thus bolstering prices by manipulating the supply side of the supply-and-demand equation); support payments to make up the differ-

---

* The roots actually run deeper. In 1620, the Governor of Virginia, without conspicuous success, issued a regulation forbidding the harvest of more than 12 tobacco leaves per plant. 95th Cong., 1st Sess., House Report 95–348 (1977), p. 52.

ence between the price received by the farmer and an artificial "parity price"* (defined in accordance with a formula as the price which will return to the farmer his costs, includings costs of investment in his farm); and various preconditions to receiving support prices, such as cutting back on production or acreage planted (again as a means of limiting supply).

The emphasis in farm policy has shifted over the years. The 1938 Act went beyond easing the strain of market fluctuations and resulted in a social program designed to remedy the Depression-level economic and social state of the farmer. As continued in World War II and the years immediately following, farm policy, through support payments, served as an incentive to increase production to meet wartime needs.[9] Only after 1948 did Federal programs really embody the concept of providing a floor of protection for the farmer.

The evolution of the use of its intervention techniques has been largely one of learning-by-doing on the part of the government. Efforts have been made, for example, to simplify payment mechanics and the formulas used to determine allotments. Efforts have also been made to avoid the problem of managing huge surplus stocks of commodities owned by the Federal government resulting from operation of loan and purchase programs.

Today, the range of assistance available to the wheat farmer† looks something like this:

---

* "Parity" or "parity price" is basically determined by a two-step formula for each agricultural commodity:

(1) Adjusted Base Price = Most recent 10-year average price   times $\dfrac{\text{Most recent 10-year agricultural price level}}{1910\text{–}1914 \text{ price level}}$

(2) Parity = Adjusted Base Price   times $\dfrac{\text{Most recent calendar month level of prices paid by farmers}}{\text{General price level, } 1910\text{–}1914.}$

See 7 U.S.C.A. § 1301(a).

† It is recognized, of course, that wheat is not the only commodity. However, the assistance mechanism varies for each commodity and it is simpler for purposes of illustration to describe only one. The support arrangements for feed grains (principally corn) and cotton are basically as described for wheat. For others, such as soybeans, only the CCC loan feature is operative. And some commodities are subject to completely different arrangements, such as regional milk-marketing orders guaranteeing minimum payments by processors to producing farmers.

1. Under the Food and Agriculture Act of 1977,[10] the Secretary of Agriculture is empowered to impose a "set-aside" limitation, whereby the farmer participating in Federal support programs must agree to keep a designated percentage of his cropland out of use during the crop year. This authority was not used at all by the Secretary—meaning there was no limit on the acreage a wheat farmer could plant—from 1973 through 1977. For the 1978–79 crop year, Secretary of Agriculture Bob Bergland invoked the "set-aside" authority to require participating farmers to "set aside" 20 percent of their wheat acreage from production.

2. The 1977 Act provides that the CCC may make loans on wheat at the rate of $2.35 per bushel in 1978–79. This rate is one of the floors protecting the farmer (assuming that he has agreed to participate in the "set-aside" requirement). If the market price for wheat goes below $2.35 (as it did for at least 10 years prior to 1973), he can obtain a loan at the $2.35 rate secured by his wheat as collateral. If market prices subsequently go above $2.35, he can repay his loan, reclaim his wheat, and sell it at the market. Since his loan is without recourse, i.e., the CCC can only look to the wheat collateral for repayment, he can allow the CCC to take title to the wheat in lieu of payment if market prices continue to be below the loan level.* The loan level, which by the terms of the 1977 Act may not exceed either 100 percent of parity or an amount which would not maintain the "competitive relationship [of wheat] to other grains in domestic and export markets" will be set by the Secretary for years after 1978 (until expiration of the 1977 Act in 1981). The $2.35 level in 1978 was below the world price for wheat, taking away the incentive to resort to the loan procedure instead of selling wheat in either the domestic or the export market.

3. The 1977 Act also prescribes a "target price" for wheat, which is deemed to be the price required to return cost to the wheat farmer. In 1978, the target price was raised by the Secretary, using his discretionary authority, from the $3 minimum set by the act to $3.40. If the market price exceeds $3.40, the government pays the farmer nothing. If it is below $3.40, he receives the difference between $3.40 and the higher of the actual market price or the loan level.

* A refinement introduced in 1977 in the loan procedure modifies this description somewhat. Under the 1977 Act, the Secretary is authorized to build up a wheat reserve of a minimum of 300 million bushels. This reserve, designed to provide for emergencies and seasons when harvests are low, is stored by the farmer at his farm, for which he receives an annual storage fee (25 cents in 1978). If a farmer participates in the reserve program, he cannot repay his loan and sell his wheat until the market price is not less than 140 percent of the loan level.

Thus, if wheat sold above $3.40 a bushel (as it did in 1973, 1974 and 1975) the farmer would receive no target-price payment. If wheat sold for $2.50, he would receive 90 cents ($3.40 minus $2.50), and if it sold for $1.24 (as it did in 1968), he would receive $1.15, or the difference between $3.40 and the loan level of $2.25. (As to the remaining $1.01 deficiency, the farmer would make this up by taking out a loan at the $2.25 loan rate on wheat with a market value of $1.24.)

Whether current farm policy gives the farmer a "decent living" is questionable. Farm agitation in 1978 for upward changes in loan rates and target prices was based on the vociferous proposition that it did not. Yet proposals in the Senate to raise loan rates and target prices—from $2.25 per bushel to $2.85 for the wheat loan rate and from $3 per bushel to $3.55 for the wheat target price—were not successful, largely because of a commitment by the Secretary of Agriculture to use his discretionary authority to raise the wheat target price to $3.40.[11]

While it may not provide a "decent living," the current structure of government price support for agriculture, coupled with such programs as Food for Peace and Food Stamps, does maintain a multi-leveled floor protecting the farmer from market declines. And, if the market fails adequately to compensate the farmer, the government does so principally through the loan and target-price devices, not through an excessive stabilizing of market prices at the expense of the consumer.

Since the amount of government support depends on market variations, the cost to the government of its programs may vary widely from year to year. At a time of high market prices in 1973–75, costs were modest. With lower prices, they may increase to over $7 billion in 1978 and subsequent depressed-price years. But whatever the cost, it is likely that future adjustments in benefit levels will reflect, as the House Committee on Agriculture suggested in 1977, "an attempt to strike a deliberate balance between these conflicting forces—to provide additional income to assist our hard pressed . . . farmers and at the same time achieve legislation which is fiscally responsible [and] does not unreasonably increase the agricultural function of the budget."[12]

This balance reflects at least in part the declining influence of the farmer in Washington, which in turn reflects the decline in farm population. While agricultural productivity rose some 65 percent between 1945 and 1975, the number of workers in agriculture declined by more than half in the same period.

In 1948, in choosing between an appeal to farmers and an appeal to the unemployed, Truman had a potential audience of 7.6 million farmers (living on some 5.5 million farms), and 2.3 million unemployed. By the time of the 1976 election, the number of farmers was down to 3.4 million (on 2.8 million farms), the unemployed up to 7.6 million.*

Even assuming that existing programs adequately protect and support farm income, there remain other "farm problems" to which the socially responsible politician should not be indifferent—the failure of social-welfare programs to reach or deliver adequate services to the rural poor (e.g., the scarcity of proper medical services in many rural areas) and the problems of undertrained workers emigrating from the farms to the cities.

The right of every businessman, large and small, to trade in an atmosphere of freedom from unfair competition and domination by monopolies at home or abroad.†

A firm stand against "unfair competition" and "monopoly" is about as risky as a firm stand in favor of the American flag.

Economic practices that interfere with the operation of the free-enterprise system must be rooted out; those who subvert the law of supply and demand must be punished. Otherwise the omnipotent wisdom of the marketplace will be thwarted and prices will no longer be set through free and open interplay among vigorously competing buyers and sellers.

So runs the mythology. Consider the realities that may have confronted a hypothetical entrepreneur starting his own business after World War II (depending on the actual time when he did so):

Our entrepreneurial Candide may start by hiring construction

---

* Reviewing the Nixon and McGovern campaign speeches in 1972, it is hard to find the candidates going much beyond the usual pieties about the farmer being the salt of the earth and the backbone of the nation; Senator McGovern, though from the quintessentially agricultural state of South Dakota, did not include a single speech on farm policy in his collection of 1972 campaign speeches. *An American Journey* (New York: Random House, 1974). And the Ford Administration, after encouraging farmers to maximize grain production in early 1975, apparently felt no hesitation in imposing a three-month embargo on grain sales to the Soviet Union later in the year. See "Ford Grain Policy Angers Farmers," *New York Times* (December 26, 1975), p. 1.

† Roosevelt's Economic Bill of Rights was derived from a series of recommendations for postwar planning made by the National Resources Planning Board in a 1942 report. The policy statement from which FDR's "right" is derived would seem more suited to 1978 circumstances: "The right to live in a system of free enterprise, free from compulsory labor, irresponsible private power, arbitrary public authority and unregulated monopolies." *The Public Papers and Addresses of Franklin D. Roosevelt 1942*, p. 54 fn.

workers to build his plant. The wages he pays them will have been predetermined by the Federal minimum-wage law and an industrywide union contract to which he was not a party. If his plant is made of cement, his chances of obtaining competing price bids will depend on the number of cement suppliers in the immediate area, since, given the cost of transporting cement, competition from distant suppliers will prove nonexistent. If steel is used, our man may be able to get some price break by shopping around, but "trigger price" and other restraints on imports may have contributed to raising the price he pays.

When the plant is built, the rates charged for his electricity and fuel (if natural gas or electricity), his telephone and his telex, if he needs one, will have been set by a Federal or state regulatory body.

Assuming that he buys large quantities of products from others to use in his manufacturing process, the Robinson-Patman Act of 1936 may prohibit his sellers from giving him quantity discounts. The freight rates he pays, whether he uses air, land or sea, will have been set by government regulation. And the rates at which he pays taxes will not be a subject of free-enterprise negotiation with the various taxing authorities.

If he prospers and buys a company airplane, he must have it serviced at the monopoly service agency at his airport required under the Federal Aviation Act (unless he services it himself). Or if he puts his profits into a savings account, the maximum rate of interest he can earn will have been set by the Federal Reserve Board. Or if he chooses to buy listed stocks and bonds, he will pay brokers' commissions set by the stock exchange.

Or he may buy a present for his wife, and if it is a well-known trade-marked product, it may be subject to "fair trade" under the Miller-Tydings Act of 1937, which prohibits his retail dealer from selling to him at a discount price. Or he may take her on a vacation via a carrier charging government-set rates or to a baseball game to watch players who are selected and paid on the basis of mutual arrangements among the owners.

Perhaps he will celebrate with a bottle of whiskey bought in a state monopoly store, or in a private store where prices are regulated by a state liquor authority. More prudently, he may buy milk for his children at prices based on the agreed minimums charged by producers under milk-marketing agreements sanctioned by the Secretary of Agriculture.

When our businessman dies, his widow can collect the insurance he paid for during his life at rates approved by his state insurance commission. Being highly successful at the time of his death, he may well have died vigorously defending the free market and the free-enterprise system.

Our hypothetical businessman led a happy life; not once did he encounter illegal price fixing among competitors (a violation of Section 1 of the Sherman Act of 1890) or prices resulting from an illegal monopolization of a market (a violation of Section 2 of the Sherman Act) or even "oligopoly pricing" resulting from a limited number of sellers following the price leadership of one of their group.

Not all the hypothetical misfortunes of our businessman would have befallen him at all times after 1945, and indeed, his situation today would not be as helpless as pictured. With the recent emphasis on consumerism, and the desire to blunt inflation by encouraging competitive pricing, many economic old wives' tales justifying noncompetitive pricing have been rejected. In 1975, for example, the Congress repealed the Miller-Tydings "fair trade" exemption to the Sherman Act, a depression-born measure allowing manufacturers to fix the prices of their products to protect the "mom and pop" retailer from discount houses. The Congress likewise, amid bloody screams from the securities industry, outlawed fixed brokerage commissions on most stock trading. And, while no action was taken, a task force organized by President Ford recommended in 1977 the repeal of antitrust exemptions shielding otherwise noncompetitive activities in insurance, ocean shipping and milk marketing.

The focus on prices may ultimately bring some sense out of the antitrust laws, which J. K. Galbraith has called "the most marvelous sinkpit of liberal emotion in this country there ever was."[13]

There is general agreement that price fixing is bad and concern about the consumer's interest and the rate of inflation has served to focus on this fact. While the consumer may not be sovereign and, contrary to economic romanticism, may have very little to say about the prices he pays for goods and services, there is seldom if ever any economic justification for collusive price fixing.

The Sherman Act of 1890 explicitly makes conspiracies to fix prices illegal. The problem has been one of enforcement and punishment.

"Some in the business community view price fixing sort of like jaywalking," Thomas Kauper, Assistant Attorney General in charge of the Antitrust Division, told an interviewer when he left office in 1976.

"You look around and you see if there's a policeman standing on the street corner. If he isn't there you jaywalk, even though you know it's illegal."[14]

Under the Antitrust Amendments of 1974, price-fixing offenses by individuals were upgraded from misdemeanors to felonies subject to three-year prison sentences. The maximum fine for corporate violators was also raised from $50,000 to $1,000,000.

In 1976, the Hart-Scott-Rodino Antitrust Improvements Act added another weapon of uncertain efficacy to the antitrust arsenal. Private actions to recover damages for antitrust violations have been available since adoption of the Clayton Act in 1914, that Act specifying that an aggrieved plaintiff may recover three times the amount of damages suffered. The prospect of trebled damages and the ability of private plaintiffs to supplement the necessarily limited enforcement efforts of government are generally conceded to have been powerful deterrents to anticompetitive activity.

Viewing private actions from a consumer point of view, the 1976 reformers perceived a deficiency in situations where the collective effect of price fixing might be great, but where the injury to a single consumer might be negligible. The result was a Title in the Act permitting the attorney general of a state to bring a treble-damage action as *parens patriae* on behalf of "natural persons residing in such State." States were also allowed to enact laws permitting private attorneys to bring such actions on behalf of the state.

Business interests have predicted a flood of troublesome litigation as the result of this law, raising complex problems of proof and even more complex problems of measuring damages and allocating them among the affected "natural persons."

It is too soon to tell whether the flood will take place, but *parens patriae* should certainly be a deterrent to collusive price fixing.

As with price fixing, there is general agreement that "unfair competition" is improper. Such predatory practices as selling below cost (until competition is driven out of business, when prices are raised once again), hidden rebates and the like were undoubtedly what FDR had in mind when he referred to "unfair competition." Again under the influence of the consumer movement, the focus of the Federal Trade Commission in enforcing the provision of the FTC Act of 1914 forbidding "unfair methods of competition" has shifted to conduct directly affecting consumers, such as the mislabeling of goods, the sale of unsafe products and deceptive advertising. While there are many arguments over the FTC's priorities and procedures, there is something approaching general agreement that the Commission has a legitimate interest in enforcing standards of fair play on those dealing with the public.

Here general agreement ends and politicians and economists alike battle over what government should condemn under the rubric of "monopoly." What of "monopoly" that has come about because of the clear superiority of the monopolist's product? What of "shared monopoly," or "oligopoly," where the price behavior of a small group of sellers tends to be uniform, even though there is no "conspiracy to fix prices"? What of a merger of two firms between which competition is potential rather than actual? What of "conglomerate" mergers, resulting in huge corporate enterprises but not directly affecting competition because of the disparate nature of the businesses agglomerated?

These are troublesome questions in theory, and nearly impossible questions when litigated in the courts—witness the government's monopolization case against IBM, the complaint in which was filed in 1969 and the trial of which is still in progress.*

Galbraith has noted that "one must think of industrial production in the United States as divided more or less evenly between a couple of thousand great corporations that are infinitely large and a mass of small firms that are infinitely numerous." But this does not mean that the breaking-up of the economic power of the two thousand great corporations is called for. "If half of the whole economy is illegal, [and] must be broken up, this remedy comes to look foolish. Among economists, if not yet among lawyers, mention of the antitrust laws is coming to be regarded as the last eruption of the exhausted mind."

"The relevant discussion," Galbraith argues, "is concerned with how to live with this power—how a democracy distinguishes between its social and its antisocial use and excludes the latter."[15]

Increased concern over prices may be pointing to the proper direction for antitrust policy. With a focus on pricing, the Antitrust Division would concentrate its resources on price-fixing cases and would somehow resolve, through litigation or a change in the law, the dilemma of "administered pricing," whereby prices are "fixed" (or at least remain uniform) without any clandestine price-fixing conspiracy in the traditional sense.[16] Monopoly as such, and mergers as such, would be

---

* Having had some passing professional involvement with *U.S. v. IBM*, the author refrains from further comment.

ignored until such time as firms fixed prices (in the possibly broader sense suggested) or, in the case of the single monopolist, engaged in predatory conduct, such as selling below cost, designed to force out or forestall the formation of competing firms—what in antitrust jargon would be called *per se* violations of the Sherman Act.

This is not a solution that has appealed to those who believe that "small is beautiful" and that bigness is inherently bad. Those who have taken this position would appear to be satisfied only with a so-called "no fault" antitrust statute under which all firms would be broken up if they achieved a specified share of the market for their products, regardless of what means, fair or foul, they had used to attain that share.

It is unclear whether FDR had the "curse of bigness" in mind when he spoke of "monopoly" in 1944. It remains unclear today whether an appropriate function of antitrust enforcement is to crusade against "bigness" as such.

By way of analogy, big-city police departments have come more and more in recent years to concentrating their limited enforcement resources on major offenses such as murder, rape and theft, devoting very little attention to "victimless" crimes such as prostitution or the peddling of obscene books, even though such crimes are technically illegal and often antisocial. It has been suggested that the Antitrust Division should likewise concentrate on the fundamental anticompetitive offenses: rigged and monopoly pricing and practices generally recognized as being predatory, rather than wrestle with the more elusive problems of bigness.

The right of every family to a decent home.

National housing policy over the years has had two goals: decent housing, whether owned or rented, and a fair chance for every family to own a home. Neither goal has been achieved.

In the most rudimentary sense, great progress has been made in reducing the physical deprivation of inadequate housing. From a government standpoint, these efforts began with the United States Housing Act of 1937, which envisioned a program of slum clearance designed to remedy "the unsafe and insanitary housing conditions and the acute shortage of decent, safe, and sanitary dwellings for families of low income."

The social engineering involved in slum clearance has hardly been a success; so-called public housing has acquired a "vile image," as one housing expert has put it,[17] and social delinquency by inhabitants of public housing projects, notorious construction scandals and aesthetic bleakness have all contributed to the vile image and led to general abandonment of the low-income-project idea.

Yet these projects, together with rent subsidies and other incentive programs, have contributed to an improved standard of physical decency.

The Joint M.I.T.-Harvard Center for Urban Studies has monitored "housing deprivation" over the years on the basis of three factors—physical inadequacy, overcrowding* and excessive cost.†

In 1960, 15.3 million households were found to suffer from housing deprivation as measured by the Center, the deprivation in 71 percent of the cases being due to physical inadequacy (24 percent due to high rents, 5 percent due to overcrowding). By 1973, the total of deprived households had been reduced to 12.8 million, with physical inadequacy as the cause falling to 49 percent, and the high rent burden rising to 47 percent (overcrowding dropping from 5 to 4 percent).[18]

These findings, and the addition in 1973 of an inadequate neighborhood environment as a measure of housing deprivation,‡ lead to the conclusion that rent subsidies and broadly based neighborhood improvement programs are the best means of insuring decent housing for the poor.

In some respects government programs have been more effective in meeting the second goal of housing policy—a fair chance for every family to own a home. The most significant developments with respect to this aspect of housing policy date to the 1930s. With the creation of the Federal Housing Agency in 1934, and related programs for guaranteeing home mortgages, the possibility of home ownership became a reality for millions who could not have hoped to finance homes under then prevailing private lending policies. In the 1920s, banks, insurance companies and savings and loan associations all required substantial down payments—often above 50 percent—and repayments were made

---

* Meaning a household of at least three persons with more than 1.5 persons per room.

† A category consisting only of those renters who, in general, spend more than 25 percent of annual income (in the case of families) or 35 percent of annual income (in the case of individuals) for rent.

‡ "Inadequate Neighborhood Environment" is designed to take account of the situation where physically sound housing is located in neighborhoods afflicted with heavy industrial pollution, high crime rates, and the like. It was estimated on this basis that in 1973 four million households were "deprived." Bernard J. Frieden and Arthur P. Solomon, *The Nation's Housing: 1975 to 1985* (Cambridge: Joint Center for Urban Studies, 1977), pp. 91, 133.

under mortgages with relatively short maturities, often as low as five years. Loan and guaranty programs covering mortgages with longer terms and lower down payments, and the creation of a secondary mortgage market in which lenders could preserve their liquidity by selling "Fannie Mae," "Ginnie Mae" and other government-guaranteed mortgages, made the financing of a house, and hence ownership, accessible to ever greater numbers.[19]

The Housing Act of 1949 expressly adopted Roosevelt's goal of "a decent home and a suitable living environment for every American family." Years later, in 1968, the Housing and Urban Development Act called for the construction or rehabilitation of 26 million housing units by 1978, such goal to include totally public units, totally private units and other units subsidized in one way or another by such devices as tax-shelter benefits to the sponsors and rent subsidies to the tenants.

Even by including mobile homes* in the definition of "housing units," it is clear that the grand objective of the 1968 act simply was not met. Virtually all recent deficiencies of the national economy have conspired against its achievement: recessionary pressures, which have reduced consumer income available for spending on housing; inflationary pressures, which have sent housing costs soaring; Federal monetary policy, which has at times shrunk the supply of money and raised interest rates, increasing the cost of home mortgages and attracting savings—a major source of funds for lending under new mortgages— away from savings banks and savings and loan associations into Federal treasury obligations and other high-interest short-term investments.

In 1946 the housing situation was so tight in the United States that the Veterans of Foreign Wars, at their convention that year, asked Congress to ban all immigration to the United States for ten years.[20]

Thirty-two years later in 1975, housing was unavailable not because of a shortage of units, but because of an inability to afford them. Between 1970 and 1976, median family income rose 47 percent, almost exactly even with the increase during the same period in the overall Consumer Price Index. But the monthly cost of owning a new median-priced home had risen 102.3 percent in the same period.

In 1970, almost half of all United States families could afford a new

---

* Mobile homes should probably not be scoffed at. Mobile homes—what used to be called house trailers—have a substantial share of the new home market, reaching a peak of 22 percent in 1973. One prediction is that replacements for existing mobile homes alone will require the construction of 1,390,000 units between 1975 and 1985. Frieden and Solomon, op. cit., pp. 56–58.

home at the median price of $23,400 (compared with a median family income of $9,900); by 1976, that percentage had dropped to 27, as the median price of a new home rose to $44,200 (compared with a median family income of $14,500).

In 1965–66, 31 percent of all new housing was purchased by those with incomes in the top quarter of incomes. By 1975–76, 58 percent of all new housing was bought by those in the top quarter.[21] It is ironic that the only goal of Roosevelt's Economic Bill of Rights specifically to be recognized in legislation—the right of every family to a decent home—should be so far from vindication a third of a century later.

The right to adequate medical care and the opportunity to achieve and enjoy good health. The right to adequate protection from the economic fears of . . . sickness [and] accident . . .

A national health-care program was a central element of Harry Truman's Fair Deal, yet no Fair Deal program came less close to achievement. Indeed, not until the Medicare bill was enacted in July 1965 was there anything approaching substantial Federal involvement in health care, aside from the activities of Veterans' Hospitals and the Public Health Service.

Through Medicare, which provides Federal assistance in meeting medical costs to those over sixty-five and some under sixty-five who are disabled or have chronic kidney ailments, and Medicaid, which provides Federal and state assistance to those on welfare and some other poor persons, the Federal government has made a massive commitment to helping with the financial burdens of medical care.

All persons over sixty-five entitled to Social Security are eligible for the hospitalization-insurance feature (Part A) of Medicare, which covers all hospital costs for up to ninety days in each "benefit period,"* except the first $160 and a charge of $40 a day for the sixty-first through ninetieth days. There is an additional "lifetime reserve" of sixty days of hospital care not tied to any benefits period, for which costs in excess of $80 a day are covered. As long as the patient is not "custodial" (i.e., in a state where improvement cannot be expected), the cost of a stay in a "skilled nursing facility" after discharge from a hospital is also covered for up to one hundred days, with a deductible of $20 a day

---

* Basically, the period beginning with a "spell of illness" and ending sixty days after discharge from a hospital or skilled nursing facility.

after twenty days, as are the costs of up to one hundred "home health visits" by therapists and nurses following discharge from a hospital or skilled nursing facility.

All participants in Part A of Medicare are automatically enrolled in Part B, which normally pays 80 percent of the costs of physicians' services in each year, over a deductible of $60. Each recipient is charged a premium of $8.20 a month for Part B coverage.* A recipient may opt out of Part B coverage, although only an insignificant percentage do so.

In fiscal 1977, 25 million people had Medicare coverage. More than 139 million claims were received, and total Medicare expenditures were $20.7 billion.

Under Medicaid, the Federal government makes payments to the states based upon state income levels to provide medical care to those on welfare and to the "medically needy" who might be forced on welfare if required to pay their own medical costs. In fiscal 1977, Federal and state payments under the program totaled $16.25 billion.

While not meeting the health-care problems of the entire population, or even of all the nation's poor, Medicare and Medicaid have brought the dual goal of good health and protection from the economic fears of sickness closer for many. In 1964, before the adoption of Medicare and Medicaid, annual doctors' visits per person averaged 4.3 for the poor and 4.6 for the nonpoor. By 1976, average visits per person had increased to 5.6 for the poor and 4.8 for the nonpoor. The average number of days Americans are hospitalized also grew by 6 percent from 1965 to 1975, or from 1,180 to 1,255 days per 1,000 population.[22]

While a comprehensive national health-care program now seems some distance away, the Federal government has become deeply enmeshed in the affairs of the health-care industry. Overall Federal spending on health programs for fiscal 1978 was projected at $58.7 billion, or 12.7 percent of the Federal budget. The Federal government now pays almost one

---

* "In its haste to counter the American Medical Association's objections to the inclusion of doctors' fees under the same system as hospital charges, Congress in 1965 divided Medicare into Parts A and B. Contributions to Part A were added to the joint [Social Security] payroll taxes, but the financing of Part B was sanctified in some mysterious way by placing one half the burden on the government and one half upon old-age beneficiaries when they could least afford to pay." J. Douglas Brown, quoted, 123 *Congressional Record* (1977), p. H 12856.

third of the nation's health expenditures—60 percent of medical research costs, 45 percent of facilities costs, 40 percent of medical education expenses and 30 percent of the bill for individual health care.

In addition, a revenue loss of $2.655 billion is expected in fiscal 1979 because of the deduction of medical expenses by individuals in computing their Federal income tax, and $7.225 billion because of the exclusion from employees' taxable income of employer payments to private health-insurance plans. The nonrecognition of such employer payments as income and the deductibility of such payments by the employer as a business expense have encouraged the growth of private insurance plans. These plans, which range from barely adequate to very comprehensive, covered 79 percent of the population under sixty-five as of December 31, 1975, again creating a substantial barrier against the fear of overburdening medical expenses.[23]

The right to adequate protection from the economic fears of old age . . .

Probably no social-welfare program in American history has achieved the popular acceptance of Social Security. Enacted in 1935, the concept of the act was based on funding retirement benefits through a tax shared equally by each employee and his employer. Called "inept," "conservative" and "regressive,"[24] because of the fixed percentage rate of the supporting taxes, the system has, ironically, probably withstood major attack precisely because of its tax feature.

"I guess you're right on the economics," FDR replied to a critic of the regressive tax, "but those taxes were never a problem of economics. They are politics all the way through. We put those payroll contributions there so as to give the contributors a legal, moral, and political right to collect their pensions. . . . With those taxes in there, no damn politician can ever scrap my social security program."[25]

Having made contributions during a working career toward Social Security, recipients tend to feel that "social security benefits are a right, and so they cash those checks without guilt." The popularity of Social Security has led to regular increases in both coverage and benefits by the Congress over the years, some at a time "when higher taxes for anything else would have produced a new Boston tea party."[26]

In 1972, the Congress took significant steps to ensure that benefits to Social Security recipients would keep pace with inflation. The Social

Security Act amendments of that year provided for an automatic readjustment of benefits each June if there has been at least a 3 percent rise in the cost of living, as measured by the Consumer Price Index, in the previous year. Benefits were raised by 5.9 percent in June 1977 and by 6.5 percent in 1978.

The rate of tax currently payable by employed workers under Social Security is 6.13 percent (in 1979) on a maximum base wage of $22,900; the employer pays a like amount on the base wage. The maximum retirement benefit for a man retiring at age sixty-five in 1979 will be $695.40 a month.

Given the entrenched nature of Social Security, public attitudes toward it, and Congressional willingness to adjust benefits to meet inflation, Social Security has become a formidable protection against the "economic fears of old age." It is estimated that Social Security payments have cut in half the number of elderly below the poverty line.[27]

Another recent legislative innovation, the Employee Retirement Income Security Act of 1974, highly complex legislation designed to protect individual rights and benefits under private retirement plans, remains to be tested, but gives promise of bringing about significant reform in the private pension area.

The right to a good education.

"Education is the American substitute for religion," the late Robert M. Hutchins once commented.[28] If his observation is correct, the educational church was in deep trouble in 1946. Public expenditures for education actually declined during World War II, leaving neglected and deteriorating facilities to meet the needs of returning GI's in the colleges and an expanding secondary-school population.

Teachers, too, were in short supply in 1946. Compelled by the draft or lured away by civilian war work, more than 725,000 elementary- and secondary-school teachers left the profession between 1941 and 1946 at a turnover rate of 20 percent, compared to a normal rate of 10 percent. By 1946, one of seven teachers was teaching under a substandard or temporary certificate. And only 7 percent of college students were enrolled in teachers' colleges, as against 22 percent in 1920.

The exodus from teaching was not hard to understand. In 1947, the average pay of a schoolteacher was $37 a week, with some 200,000 receiving less than $25 a week.[29] In Colorado, 300 schools failed to open in the fall of 1945 because of lack of teachers; the average pay in Colorado for teachers was $110 a month, compared with sheepherders' wages of $140 a month.

"Teaching is the steadiest job in the world," a New Jersey teacher remarked in 1945. "It never gets you anywhere."[30]

A major postwar objective of the National Education Association was to make $2,500 a year the "absolute minimum" salary.[31]

The war had exposed great deficiencies in the nation's educational system. Up to 22 percent of potential draftees in some states had been rejected for educational shortcomings[32]—a condition that is hardly surprising in view of the discrepancies in educational expenditures, ranging in the 1944–45 school year from $44.80 per pupil per year in Mississippi to $198.33 in New Jersey.[33]

"Our national wellbeing demands that the Federal Government, through wise and comprehensive policies, assist the States in financing the education of our young people," Senator Lister Hill (Democrat, Alabama) declared in 1946.[34]

The GI Bill, which made educational benefits available to some 7.8 million World War II veterans, represented the Federal government's first major educational commitment after the war, followed by comparable programs for later veterans.

In the guise of promoting education as a national-defense resource after the Russian launching of Sputnik, the National Defense Education Act of 1958 authorized appropriations of more than a billion dollars for various grants, principally to strengthen training in science, mathematics and languages.

But the greatest impetus to Federal educational assistance was a gradual awakening in the 1960s to the link between lack of education and poverty and unemployment. With jobs becoming more complicated and requiring greater education, and with the need for unskilled nonagricultural labor dropping to less than 5 percent of the labor force, unemployment was then highest for those with only an eighth grade education. It was also found that children doing poorly in school more often than not came from families where the parents had little education; the impoverishment of ignorance was carrying over from generation to generation.[35]

This perception resulted in enactment of the Elementary and Secondary Education Act of 1965, which sought to provide government assistance for disadvantaged children, and a host of other New Frontier and Great Society legislation—the Head Start program for disadvantaged preschool children; the Job Corps to reach and train unemployable teen-agers; the Higher Education Facilities Act of 1963; a work-study program under the Economic Opportunity Act of 1964; various grant, scholarship and loan programs to encourage college participation by minority and low-income students; and the Manpower Development and Training Act of 1962, which provided for vocational training and for the retraining of unemployable and obsolescent workers.

In 1950, governments at all levels spent $9.37 billion on education (including $5.6 billion for elementary and secondary education), rising to $18 billion ($15.1 billion) in 1960 and $91.7 billion ($62.4 billion) in 1975.

The tangible benefits of financially upgrading the nation's educational institutions have been obvious. In 1946, an estimated 47.3 percent of the country's young people completed high school at the traditional ages of seventeen and eighteen; the percentage is now an estimated 75 percent (down from 76.2 percent in 1967, the high point of the period). Almost two thirds of the population over twenty have completed high school today, compared with approximately one third in 1950.

In 1950, 10 percent of those between eighteen and twenty-four were enrolled as college undergraduates; 25 percent are undergraduates today. Of those over twenty-five, 6 percent were college graduates in 1950; 12 percent are today.

These percentage changes represent a tremendous achievement, made all the more impressive if one considers the increase in the number of young people to be educated as the result of the post-World War II "baby boom"* and the larger numbers desiring both to graduate from high school and to attend college.

* The dimensions of the oft-cited "baby-boom" were as follows:

	Births [Thousands]	Fertility Rate[x]	
1945	2,873	2,491.2	
1946	3,426	2,942.7	
1947	3,834	3,273.5	
1948	3,655	3,108.5	
1949	3,667	3,110.1	
1950	3,645	3,090.5	
1951	3,845	3,269.3	(cont.)

Measured statistically, progress toward establishing FDR's Economic Bill of Rights since 1945 has been great. Ironically, the biggest failure has occurred in conquering unemployment, the most central concern of the New Deal. But in other fields, such as health, income security for the aged, and education, the people of the United States are far better off today than at the end of World War II. One can think that Roosevelt would have been pleased. We know Harry Truman was. As he said at the signing by President Johnson of the Medicare bill in Independence, Missouri, on July 30, 1965:

> ... you have made me a very, very happy man. ... Mr. President, I am glad to have lived this long and to witness today the signing of the Medicare bill which puts this Nation right where it needs to be, to be right.[36]

	Births [Thousands]	Fertility Rate[x]
1952	3,933	3,358.4
1953	3,989	3,424.1
1954	4,102	3,542.6
1955	4,128	3,579.7
1956	4,244	3,689.0
1957	4,332	3,767.0
1958	4,279	3,700.5
1959	4,313	3,712.4
1960	4,307	3,653.6
1961	4,317	3,629.0
1962	4,213	3,473.5
1963	4,142	3,333.2
1964	4,070	3,207.5
1965	3,801	2,928.0
1966	3,642	2,736.1
1967	3,555	2,572.6
1968	3,535	2,476.8
1969	3,630	2,465.0
1970	3,739	2,480.0
1971	3,556	2,274.6
1972	3,258	2,021.9
1973	3,137	1,895.6
1974	3,166	1,856.6

x = Number of births per 1,000 women. The approximate "replacement level" of fertility (i.e., a sufficient birth rate only to offset the death rate—"zero population growth") is approximately 2,100.

Three · Report Card: Behind the Statistics

In 5 years we enlarged that real economic pie by $180 billion—after allowing for price increases. That $180 billion has no inflation in it. . . .
Consider what has happened to the people's income since late 1963:

—Total personal income increased by almost half or $220 billion.
—Total wages and salaries are up by $150 billion, nearly one-and-a-half times the Nation's 1967 food bill.
—Corporate profits are up by nearly half, both before and after taxes, and dividends grew by more than half—reaching all time highs.

But the most significant fact of all may be this: All major groups have shared in the growth of the pie. Measure the gains in profits, dividends, wages and salaries, and you discover that the gain has been about 50 percent for each. And these gains have generated a spectacular rise in the living standards of Americans; a bonus of over $2,000 a year for an average family of four.
Consider what has happened to the people's jobs:

—In these 5 years, employment has increased by 7¾ million persons—enough to absorb an increase in the labor force of 6½ million, while reducing unemployment by 1¼ million.
—The unemployment rate, which equaled 5.5 percent in November 1963, averaged 3.8 percent in 1966 and 1967, and was 3.6 in October.
—This gain in jobs has been the single most effective counterstroke against poverty in America. . . .

Federal expenditures for health, education, and welfare—including those from self-financed trust funds—have risen from $28.5 billion in 1964 to $55 billion this fiscal year.
This approximate doubling reflects dramatic innovations such as Medicare and dramatic increases in social security benefits. . . .

• Eight and a half million Americans rose from poverty between 1963 and 1967. In the past 2 years alone, more Negroes and nonwhites have escaped the poverty trap than in the previous 6 years

- *The education gap between young whites and nonwhites has been cut to less than half a year—as measured by years of school experience.*
- *In 1963, only about two-fifths of young nonwhite adults were graduating from high school. Today the proportion is three-fifths.*
- *Our investment in the ability of the poor and the deprived to lift themselves up has already paid rich dividends.*
- *Between 1963 and 1967, the proportion of nonwhite families earning at least $8,000 rose by almost two-thirds—from 15 to 24 percent.*
- *The jobless rate for nonwhite men dropped from 9 percent late in 1963 to 3.8 percent in the third quarter of 1968.*

Now I did not come here to say that these statistics, and what they represent, have solved America's problems. But the facts cannot be begged. The record is clear: Economic growth has been the most powerful social weapon in our hands.

—LYNDON B. JOHNSON (1968)[1]

A review of America's social statistics over the past third of a century, as attempted in the previous chapter, is a rewarding experience for believers in those particularly American talismans, progress and uplift. Viewed on an overall statistical basis, the nation and its people have made social advances, by some measures to an extraordinary degree, since World War II.

Politicians, as the quintessential preachers of progress and uplift, are enamored of statistics, since (assuming that their thrust is in the right direction) they so cogently document and verify an officeholder's achievements.

The recital of Lyndon Johnson quoted above, describing the first five years of his Presidency, is typically American and most businesslike —relying on hard, tangible data to support his conclusions. Unfortunately, despite the masses of data churned out of computers by government agencies, private industry and the universities, the relative well-being of the country cannot be gauged by statistics. Statistics simply cannot measure—or at least have not measured—psychological or emotional reactions and, even when viewed as being of the "hardest" variety, on analysis really prove very often to be based on assumptions and estimates which affect the statistical results.

Consider, for example, the Consumer Price Index, the most popular index of patterns of inflation. The levels of Social Security and Food Stamp benefits—let alone the levels of payments under many labor contracts, divorce settlements, long-term leases and other private agreements—are geared to this Index; the Bureau of Labor Statistics estimates that half the population is affected by arrangements providing for "escalation" on the basis of the CPI.

Many economists would use the Wholesale Price Index or the so-called gross national product deflator* as more current or more meaningful indices of price behavior. But the CPI remains the best-known, and most commonly utilized, measure.

The CPI attempts to measure a "market basket" of goods and services purchased by urban workers. Through periodic revision, the Bureau of Labor Statistics tries to keep the Index "current" by relating its components to changed consumer attitudes. Men's pajamas, for example, were dropped from the "market basket" in 1961—perhaps to reflect changing sexual attitudes in the 1960s.

That the Index is imprecise was acknowledged by the Bureau of Labor Statistics in 1978 when it began publishing two indexes—two "market baskets"—a revised Consumer Price Index for Urban Wage Earners and Clerical Workers (CPI-W) and a Consumer Price Index for All Urban Consumers (CPI-U).[2] The Congress also enacted legislation in 1977 calling for a study of whether still a third index was necessary to reflect the spending habits of retired people, for use in indexing Social Security payments.

However diligent the efforts of government statisticians to keep the CPI current may be, the fact is that important decisions within the economy are made on the basis of a periodic statistic that is less than precise.

Likewise, the stated rate of unemployment is used as a fundamental tool of analysis by both private industry and government. The Public Works Employment Acts of 1976 and 1977, for instance, both provide for automatic "countercyclical" assistance to state and local governments when national unemployment reaches 6 percent. The countercyclical mechanism of these acts is both enlightened and intelligent,

* The "implicit price deflator for gross national product" is generally defined as the measure of changes in market prices of *all* goods and services included in the national income and product accounts, such changes being measured from a base period.

but the fact remains that the published unemployment statistics of the Bureau of Labor Statistics are approximations. The published rates may include college students casually seeking part-time employment, yet so-called "discouraged workers" who have given up the search for employment may not be counted at all. By legislation in 1976, the Congress provided for the establishment of a National Commission on Employment and Unemployment Statistics to consider the deficiencies in existing reporting in these vital areas.

As statistics become subject to more complex variables, both their accuracy and their currency become doubtful. Thus, the count of "children from low-income families"—an absolutely essential measurement for allocating the greatest part of Federal assistance to secondary schools—is less than satisfactory, with such "children" in certain years being counted long after they have left school.*

Once one leaves the area of "hard" statistics, all bets are off. Whatever America's genius for putting the computer to work, its mathematicians and social scientists do not have an enviable record in producing meaningful projections of future behavior. Part of this is due to the foibles of human nature—in the midst of a baby boom, who can foresee that social attitudes toward numbers of children will change, that birth-control techniques will become both more sophisticated and more accepted, and that the legal status of abortion will change, leaving schools, carefully planned for the baby boom, deserted?

Or who could foresee the extraordinary attraction of the GI Bill to World War II veterans?

"How many veterans are expected to enroll?" *New Republic* asked rhetorically in a 1946 survey of educational problems. The answer:

> From surveys of servicemen's intentions, the best estimate of the number of veterans who would go to college on a full-time basis has been six percent—about 660,000. But it appears from the number of veterans now applying for and obtaining certificates of eligibility from the colleges that as many as 1.2 million veterans may go to college. This figure seems exaggerated, and experts believe that a total number of 800,000 will not be exceeded in the next four years, with 600,000 enrolled in 1946–47.[3]

Well, the "experts" were wrong and some 7.8 million World War II veterans enrolled under the GI Bill, including 2.2 million in the col-

* See Chapter Five.

leges, changing the physiognomy and character of American campuses and the national level of educational attainment in the process.

An aspect of information-gathering that has become increasingly sophisticated—the "science" of public-opinion polling—has been used only selectively by our political leaders. Given the various approaches to our energy problems since the Arab embargo of 1973, for example, the rhetoric in Congress about the inalienable right to drive hardly recognizes poll results which show a comfortable majority of Americans willing to submit to gasoline rationing rather than face increased gasoline taxes.[4] Nor could one guess from Congressional behavior that 69 percent of American voters favor stricter regulation of handguns.[5]

Most politicians seem more concerned with what polling tells them about public receptivity of their image—e.g., whether the voters prefer a "clean-cut" candidate or one with sideburns. (Not that politicians should become slaves to polls; the path of leadership in any given instance may well be to consider poll results as a challenge to their ability to lead and to educate.)

The late Senator William Benton (Democrat, Connecticut) once said a great deal about our information-gathering resources when he observed that the "United States has much more adequate information about Dutch elm disease, wheat crops, fish runs, bank balances, horse racing, baseball, and dogs, than it has about education."[6]

Even when social statistics are available they do not always, and perhaps never, tell the full story. The aggregate numbers do not tell us of wide disparities in the impact of social programs on particular groups within the society or of failures and shortcomings in the conception or execution of such programs.

Going behind the statistics to review aspects of the operation and effect of Federal social programs will not justify the conclusion of President Nixon (speaking in large part of the same period reviewed by President Johnson in the quotation above), who said in 1969:

> In the United States, revenues of the Federal government have increased ninety-fold in thirty-six years. The areas of our national life where the Federal government has become a dominant force have multiplied. . . .
>
> The great social demands made upon the Federal government by millions of citizens, guaranteed the continued rapid growth and expansion of Federal power.
>
> Today, however, a majority of Americans no longer supports the

continued extension of federal services. The momentum for federal expansion has passed its peak; a process of deceleration is setting in.

The cause can be found in the record of the last half decade. In the last five years the Federal government enacted scores of new Federal programs; it added tens of thousands of new employees to the Federal payrolls; it spent tens of billions of dollars in new funds to heal the grave social ills of rural and urban America. No previous half decade had witnessed domestic Federal spending on such a scale. Yet, despite the enormous Federal commitment in new men, new ideas and new dollars from Washington, it was during this very period in our history that the problems of the cities deepened rapidly into crises.

The problems of the cities and the countryside stubbornly resisted the solutions of Washington; and the stature of the Federal government as America's great instrument of social progress has suffered accordingly—all the more so because the Federal government promised so much and delivered so little. This loss of faith in the power and efficacy of the Federal government has had at least one positive impact upon the American people. More and more, they are turning away from the central government to their local and State governments to deal with their local and State problems.[7]

While a review of the record would not compel or even enable one to agree with Nixon, the record nevertheless contains lessons for those in public life dealing with social questions.

Disparity: Unemployment

The national average rate of unemployment does not begin to suggest the impact of unemployment within the economy. Each percentage point of unemployment in the civilian labor force means that 1,000,000 people are unemployed, which in turn means an effect on the households and families of those unemployed.

"Fortunately," as economist Arthur Okun has pointed out,

few people stay jobless all year long, even in a slumping economy; but the converse of that proposition is that an extra 1 percentage point of unemployment means as much as 5 percent of the labor force feels some stretch of extra unemployment during the course of a year. And millions more lose pay for overtime work that has become a vital margin to supply the amenities of life to many American families. Others find their full-time jobs converted into part-time employment. Statistical evidence from past periods of economic fluctuations suggests that an extra 1 percentage point of unemployment blocked as many as 1 million people from crossing the line of poverty income. In an opinion survey taken in August 1970, 21 percent of all American families reported that they had felt some impact of the curtailment of job opportunities during the preceding year. Their subjective response looks reasonably consistent with the facts.[8]

The national average unemployment rate also does not reflect the dire situation of some groups within the population, the depressed condition of some geographic areas or the truly explosive and revolutionary potential which these disparities signal.

Looking behind the overall rate, one finds that the burden of unemployment is not evenly distributed by geography, sex, age, race or occupation. Unemployment among some groups in the society is at Depression levels, while other groups are close to or below the "full employment" floor of 4 percent unemployment.

In May 1978, the unemployment rate for women (7.5 percent) was significantly higher than that for men (5.1 percent). And whites (4.7 percent) fared better than blacks and other nonwhites (11.4 percent).* The rate for males of ages fifty-five to sixty-four was 2.6 percent, but for male teen-agers sixteen to nineteen it was 13 percent. And the rates for white and black male teen-agers were 10.3 percent and 37.1 percent, respectively.

Those born in the years prior to the post–World War II baby boom fare better than their more numerous and younger baby-boom colleagues. Unemployment among males aged twenty-five to fifty-four was 3.3 percent, but the rate for baby-boom-era male workers aged twenty to twenty-four was 7.6 percent.

White-collar workers (3.4 percent unemployed) were more fortunate than blue-collar workers (6.1 percent unemployed).

As of the second quarter of 1978, those living in metropolitan areas were more likely to be unemployed than those living outside, the respective rates being 6 percent and 5.5 percent. Within metropolitan areas, those in the central cities had a higher unemployment rate (5.5 percent) than those in the suburbs (5.1 percent). And for those un-

---

* For narrative convenience blacks and other nonwhites are designated as "blacks" in the discussion that follows.

lucky enough to be black, in their teens and living in a poverty area, the unemployment rate was 44.2 percent.

Unemployment rates also vary widely by location. In May 1978, the unemployment rate was 2 percent in Lincoln, Nebraska; 2.3 percent in Raleigh, North Carolina; 11.6 percent in Jersey City; and 14.3 percent in Modesto, California. Within a given state the differences were also wide—3.1 percent in Amarillo, Texas, and 8.3 percent in El Paso; 5.4 percent in Poughkeepsie, New York, and 8.2 percent in New York City.[9]

Disparity: Blacks

The unevenness of postwar social progress can be seen by a brief review of the status of blacks.

Not even the most militant black can deny that major social advances have been made by blacks since 1945. Progress may not have been as swift as desired, but there has been real progress nonetheless.

In 1945, desegregation had not yet come to the armed forces or the schools or public transportation; a fair-employment-practices board set up to tamp down labor unrest during World War II seemed about to go out of business. And there was one lynching in 1945, six in 1946.[10]

President Truman, in strongly espousing civil rights, made strides that at the time seemed radical to many. His intentions were clearly the most honorable, but he obviously felt subject to historical constraints that today seem quaint. For example, in addressing the members of the President's Committee on Civil Rights, which he appointed in late 1946 and which produced two years later a landmark review of the civil-rights situation,[11] Truman said:

> We are making progress, but we are not making progress fast enough. This country could very easily be faced with a situation similar to the one with which it was faced in 1922. That date was impressed on my mind because in 1922 I was running for my first elective office—county judge of Jackson County—and there was an organization in that county that met on hills and worked behind sheets. There is a tendency in this country for that situation to develop again, unless we do something to prevent it.
>
> I don't want to see any race discrimination. I don't want to see any religious bigotry break out in this country as it did then. . . .

I have been very much alarmed at certain happenings around this country that go to show there is a latent spirit in some of us that isn't what it ought to be. It has been difficult in some places to enforce even local laws. I want the Attorney General to know just exactly how far he can go legally from the Federal Government's standpoint. I am a believer in the sovereignty of the individual and of the local governments. I don't think the Federal Government ought to be in a position to exercise dictatorial powers locally; but there are certain rights under the Constitution of the United States which I think the Federal Government has a right to protect.

It's a big job. Go to it![12]

Truman was not able to translate his concern for civil rights into legislation, but was confined to theretofore unheard-of exercises of executive power to achieve some semblance of progress: his appointment of the Commission on Civil Rights; the filing of *amicus* briefs in the early civil-rights cases dealing with discrimination in graduate-school education and racially restrictive real-estate covenants; and, in 1948, executive orders that ended racial discrimination in the armed forces.

President Eisenhower, with limited notions of Presidential power, did not continue the Truman initiatives into the 1950s. With both the Congress and the Presidency in abdication, the civil-rights battle shifted to the courts. The case of *Brown v. Board of Education* in 1954, outlawing school segregation, was both the culmination of earlier, more cautious decisions advancing the cause of equality and the point of departure for later judicial initiatives striking down segregation and promoting integration that continue amid great controversy today.

The Congress and the Executive rejoined the battle in the 1960s. Seizing the legislative initiative in the traumatized climate following President Kennedy's assassination, Lyndon Johnson coerced and cajoled from the Congress the Civil Rights Act of 1964, which prohibited discrimination in employment, and followed it with the Civil Rights Act of 1965, which prohibited voting discrimination, and the Civil Rights Act of 1968, which prohibited housing discrimination.

These initiatives without question improved the social lot of blacks. The segregated drinking fountain and lunch counter seem as distantly anachronistic today as a Stephen Foster lyric. What Adam Clayton Powell called the "Southern phase" of the civil-rights battle—achieving points of middle-class status and dignity, such as the right to sit up front in a bus—has for all intents and purposes been accomplished. But as Powell noted, the "Northern phase"—the "gut issue of who gets the money"—has been "rough," and progress here has been uneven.[13]

Aside from the "Southern phase" gains, blacks' progress since 1945 has been greatest in terms of education. In 1950, 2.7 percent of blacks aged twenty-five to twenty-nine had completed four years of college (as compared with 8.1 percent of whites of the same age); the comparable percentage was 11.6 percent in 1972 (19.9 percent for whites). Similarly, in 1950 24.9 percent of blacks aged twenty to twenty-four had completed high school (as compared with 56 percent of whites); the comparable percentage was 67.9 percent in 1972 (84.9 percent for whites).[14]

In one rare instance where black achievement surpassed white, a higher percentage of black children were enrolled in prekindergarten programs in 1972 and 1973[15] than white, presumably because of the availability of Head Start and similar programs in black inner-city areas.

Indications in 1974 were that blacks constituted 12.3 percent of entering college freshmen, slightly higher than the percentage of blacks (11.4 percent) in the population at large in 1974.[16]

Andrew Brimmer, the black Harvard economist, has concluded that advances in educational attainment have made a "substantial difference" in the economic progress of blacks in the applicable age groups.

But black economic progress is a perilous thing. The shockingly high unemployment rate among black teen-agers compares unfavorably not only to the white experience but also to that of older blacks. Brimmer concludes that the inability of the economy to meet the job needs of black youths was one of the "main shortfalls in national economic policy" during the 1960s—a "shortfall" that unhappily continues.[17]

Black gains are especially vulnerable to downturns in the economy. The 1969–70 recession had a "disproportionately adverse impact" on blacks and, even long after the recession had ended, blacks ended up with a smaller proportion of total jobs than they had had at the time the recession began.

In August 1977, for example, nearly all worker groups had shared in a nearly one-point improvement in unemployment over the previous year, except blacks and Vietnam-era veterans. A 0.2 percent increase in unemployment that month over July 1977 was accounted for almost completely by blacks. Unemployment among blacks was at 14.5 percent—a rate that matched the record post-World War II high of September 1975. The ratio of black to white unemployment was 2.4 to 1—also a postwar record except for one month in 1962.

A more poignant example of the impact of economic downturn on blacks is shown in a recent survey of college expectations. In 1972, the percentage of black high-school seniors planning to attend college was almost equivalent to that of whites and, if those who "may attend" were added, the aggregate percentage was actually higher. By 1974, in a depressed economy, the percentage of black seniors planning to attend, or who may attend, college had declined sharply compared with whites.*

No matter what the statistical measure, the almost invariable rule has been and continues to be that black gains, no matter how substantial, do not bring blacks to a parity with whites. For example, the life expectancy of both white men and black men aged thirty increased by two years from 1945 to 1973; but the black man's life expectancy was still shorter than a white's by six years. And median family income for blacks has never exceeded more than 75 percent of white median family income.

And even when such parity occurs, it is often tenuous and subject to offsetting factors. Thus, while the percentage of black college freshmen approximates the percentage of blacks in the population, as indicated, the college dropout rate among blacks by the senior year (based on freshman enrollment in 1971) was 59 percent, compared with the white rate of 43 percent.[18]

In many respects, blacks have not progressed at all, absolutely or relatively, in recent years. During the period 1970–77, for example, the number of white families headed by a woman increased by 31 percent; the number of black families headed by a woman increased at

---

* The figures are:

COLLEGE PLANS OF HIGH SCHOOL SENIORS (IN PERCENTAGES)

		Plan to Attend College	May Attend College	Plan to Attend Vocational School	Do Not Plan to Attend
1972	Black	44.6	33.4	11.4	10.9
	White	46.4	26.4	12.0	15.2
1974	Black	36.0	31.8	14.5	17.8
	White	44.6	26.2	9.7	19.6

Source: U.S. Department of Commerce, Bureau of the Census, *Current Population Reports—Population Characteristics*, Series P-20, No. 284 (September 1975).

almost double that rate, or 60 percent.[19] In 1960, the proportion of black families living in "deprived" housing conditions was twice as high as for whites; by 1973, when the absolute number of deprived households had declined, the same proportion between blacks and whites was still maintained.[20]

Crime statistics and surveys also show that a black residence is more likely to be burglarized than a white one, that a black woman in America is four times more likely to be raped than her white counterpart, and that murder has become the chief cause of death of black men between the ages of twenty-five and thirty-four living in urban areas.[21]

Disparity: Women

Evaluation of the economic status of women is difficult because of the "discouraged worker" phenomenon already referred to—that is, the retirement from the labor force of those who would like to work but feel that jobs are not available. Women are presumed to have the more ready option of dropping out and staying at home than men. Thus, even if on the face of the statistics unemployment rates for women are comparable to those of men, as they are from time to time in certain categories, such a statistic may mask the discouraged-worker factor.

As indicated in the discussion of unemployment rates above, the statistics for May 1978 show that the rate of unemployment for women (7.5 percent) was higher than for men (5.1 percent). In 1974, median annual earnings of women with four or more years of college were 69.6 percent of comparable male earnings in the 25–34 year group, 58.9 percent in the 35–44 group and 55.7 percent in the 45–54 group.[22] This may indicate a trend toward equal opportunity between the sexes for those entering the job market, as opposed to jobs in senior capacities, where past bias against women may still be reflected in the statistics. Then, again, the trend may not be so favorable. In 1963, the Congress adopted an Equal Pay Act, requiring employers to pay women the same wages as men for the same work. Yet the requirement that employers under Federal government contracts not discriminate against women was not effective until 1970, and the Equal Employment Opportunity Commission was empowered only in 1972 to bring sex-discrimination actions in court.

Whatever the effect of these enforcement efforts may have been, it is becoming clear that poor economic conditions and a weak job market seriously impede the progress of women. In 1975, the median income of working women was 57 percent of median income for working men —a decrease from approximately 64 percent in 1955.[23]

Participation by women in the labor force has risen dramatically, at least among younger women, in the last decade. In May 1978, participation in the labor force by women over sixteen exceeded 50 percent for the first time since World War II. The comparable figures for 1964, 1974 and 1978 (May) are as follows:

	Percentage of Age Group in Labor Force		
Age	*1964*	*1974*	*1978*
16–19 years	37.0	49.2	51.6
20–24 years	49.4	63.0	66.5
25–34 years	37.2	52.4	61.8
35–44 years	45.0	54.7	62.2
45–54 years	51.4	54.6	55.8
55–64 years	40.2	40.7	41.1
All ages over 16	38.7	45.7	50.1

During the 1950s participation by women aged 45–54 grew the most, from 38 percent in 1950 to 50 percent in 1960, influenced in large part by increased job opportunities in "women's work" sectors of the economy, such as education, medical care and personal services generally. Since the middle 1960s, the greatest increases have been among women under 45, with nearly all the rise in the 1950–74 period for women 25 to 34 coming after 1960. The rate for this group went from 34 percent in 1950 to 36 percent in 1960 to 52 percent in 1974. A Bureau of Labor Statistics economist has observed:

> Many women of these ages, constrained by marriage and child responsibilities, did not make the decision to enter the labor force until changing attitudes toward women's role in society became prominent in the 1960's and early 1970's.[24]

Women are also making progress in fields previously closed or partly closed to them. In 1974, 7 percent of lawyers and judges were women, compared to 2.8 percent in 1962. Of doctors, 9.8 percent were women in 1974, 5.5 percent in 1962; of college and university teachers, 30.9 percent were women in 1974, 19.2 percent in 1962. And, for whatever it may say about us, 32.6 percent of the nation's bartenders were women in 1974, practically triple the 1962 figure of 11.5 percent.[25]

Certainly, times have changed since 1953, when President Eisenhower, in his first year in office, had seven dinners for 115 "leaders of America"—all stag.[26] And women may take heart from the new style in bill drafting in the Congress, *viz.*:

> In his or her economic report to the Congress pursuant to the Employment Act of 1946 . . . the President shall . . .*

Despite recent setbacks for the proposed Equal Rights Amendment to the Constitution, which would ban sex discrimination, there appears to be a substantial majority favoring the advancement of women's rights in America. A Gallup Poll in early 1976 showed 57 percent in favor of the amendment with, curiously, more men (59 percent) than women (55 percent) favoring the amendment.†

Failures and Shortcomings

The perfect social program has yet to be devised by the mind of the politician (or, to be fair, the mind of the economist, the social scientist, the philosopher, or even the Chamber of Commerce executive). If such an unlikely and miraculous event should occur, such a program would be formulated on the basis of complete knowledge of the problem to be solved, and after weighing alternative approaches in the light of complete information and precise cost estimates. The program would constitute the most effective attack on the problem at the lowest possible cost, and it would be properly funded by the legislators enacting

* Section 3(a) of the Humphrey-Hawkins full-employment bill (H.R. 50, as introduced in 1975). This is as good a place as any for what has become an obligatory disclaimer: use in the text of masculine pronouns is for convenience only and is not intended to reflect a sexist bias on the part of the author. The author is fully aware that this practice may be dangerous to his health.

† *Gallup Opinion Index,* No. 128, March 1976, p. 18. An earlier poll in 1974, taken before organized opposition to the Equal Rights Amendment began, showed 78 percent in favor (83 percent among men, 73 percent among women). It is unclear whether this change reflects the effectiveness of Amendment opponents or the stridency of its advocates, or both. *Gallup Opinion Index,* No. 113, November 1974, p. 17.

it, and properly and efficiently carried out by its administrators. Its benefits and burdens would fall equitably on the public, and it would not have distorting side effects on other social policies and programs.

Unfortunately, the brain children of social reformers do not behave in this approved fashion; problems may occur in their rearing from conception onward. Such problems may be endlessly categorized and subdivided, but four broad areas of difficulties have all too often been characteristic of postwar Federal social programs:

1. The inequitable distribution of program benefits and burdens.

2. Failure of the program to achieve its ostensible purpose, either because of overselling of that purpose, underfunding by the Congress, or failure to perceive the dimensions of the problem at which the original program was directed.

3. The tendency to view a program as having solved a problem when it in fact has not, and the tendency for a focus on the solution of one problem to distract attention from the need for the solution of others.

4. Failure to administer the program efficiently and economically.

Social Security

Social Security, as noted in the last chapter, is probably the social program that comes closest to the unlikely and miraculous ideal. Leaving aside Senator Barry Goldwater's attacks on Social Security in his odd campaign for the Presidency in 1964, there is probably no Federal program to which there has been less opposition. It is directed toward a goal that almost everyone would support—the self-sufficiency of the aged. Involving the maintenance of millions of individual accounts and the prompt disbursement of millions of monthly checks, Social Security is generally efficiently administered at relatively low cost. Yet even here there are shortcomings.

Social Security coverage has been greatly broadened over the years, and now includes over 90 percent of all workers. Payments to those retired or disabled and their dependents and survivors exceeded $82 billion in 1977 to over 31 million recipients, or 15 percent of the total population.[27]

Benefits to the elderly are computed on a formula based on the recipient's average monthly wages prior to retirement. Not only is this formula exceedingly complex,* but it also perpetuates into retirement discrepancies that existed in preretirement wages. Thus, in 1973, when the maximum-wage base for computing Social Security benefits was $10,800, such maximum was reached by 25 percent of covered white workers, but only 10 percent of blacks. Since benefits are computed on the basis of a nineteen-year earning history—rising gradually to thirty-

---

* A standard guide to Social Security benefits described (as of 1978) the computation of the average monthly wage, on which benefits are based, this way:

Step 1. *Figure your elapsed years.* If you were 21 or over in 1950, count up the number of years beginning with 1951 and ending with the year before the one in which you will be age 62 (a special rule, discussed below, applies in the case of men reaching age 62 in 1973 or 1974). *Men who reached age 62 before 1973 must count the years before attainment of age 65, regardless of when they actually apply for benefits.*

If you reached 21 after 1950, start counting with the year after the one in which you became 21.

Under the special rule for men reaching age 62 in 1973 or 1974, the number of elapsed years is set at 24.

If a person dies before reaching the required age, only the years after 1950 (or after the year in which he reached 21, if later) and ending with the year before his death are counted.

For disability benefits, count the years after 1950 (or after you reach age 21, if later) and before the year in which the waiting period begins, or, if there is no waiting period, up to the year in which entitlement begins. (Special rules apply if entitlement begins at age 62 or later.) Do not count any year that was wholly or partly within a period of disability.

Step 2. *Deduct 5 years.* Deduct from the number of years arrived at in Step 1, above, but do not reduce the number below 2. This leaves the number of years to be used in figuring your average monthly wage.

Step 3. *Figure your earnings.* Write down your earnings covered by social security for each year beginning with 1951 and ending with the year before the one in which you became entitled to benefits. If you do not apply for benefits when you become eligible and continue to work, include earnings for years before you do apply. In case a person dies before he can get benefits, count his earnings through the year in which he died.

Do not include more than:
$ 3,600 a year from 1951–1954
  4,200 a year from 1955–1958
  4,800 a year from 1959–1965
  6,600 a year for 1966 and 1967
  7,800 a year from 1968–1971
  9,000 for 1972
  10,800 for 1973
  13,200 for 1974
  14,100 for 1975
  15,300 for 1976
  16,500 for 1977
  17,700 for 1978.

Earnings for the year in which a worker qualifies for benefits, or for later years, are used later in an automatic recomputation.

Step 4. *Figure your average monthly wage.* From your list of earnings (Step 3,

five years by 1995—present wage differentials stand to affect the eventual retirement income of young people working today, prolonging present-day discrepancies into the distant future.[28]

Those chronically unemployed, or receiving low wages, will most likely retire with an earnings history too low to provide subsistence income in the retirement years. Basic minimum payments not related to past earnings will continue to be required, along with other public-assistance programs. There is nothing fundamentally wrong with a combined system of earned and unearned benefits; indeed, to the extent that payments to the needy can be denominated part of "Social Security," the dignity and pride of the aged poor are less likely to be offended than if such payments had the aura of welfare or the county old folks' home.

But on the other side of this coin is the popular view of Social Security as an insurance or savings program, with the worker entitled to benefits at the end of the line as a reward for his prior thrift. In fact, all benefits of whatever kind are paid out of current revenues of the Federal government (but for payments from the Social Security reserve funds, which have normally been kept funded at a level roughly equal to a year's projected benefit payments). Past contributions by today's retired worker have long since been paid out, and such worker is wholly dependent on taxes raised from his colleagues currently in the active work force.*

That the public should be confused is not surprising. Social Security taxes are levied under the Federal Insurance Contributions Act—a complete misnomer, since payments thereunder are taxes rather than

---

above), select the years in which your earnings were highest. *The number of years selected must be the same as the number arrived at in Step 2.* Add up your earnings in the years selected and divide the total by the number of months in those years. Round your answer to an even dollar amount by dropping anything less than $1. This is your average monthly wage.

Commerce Clearing House, *1978 Social Security Benefits* (1977), pp. 14–15. Perhaps the object is to give the elderly something with which to occupy themselves in retirement.

* One analyst has estimated that if Social Security were fully funded—that is, had sufficient funds in hand today to meet all future obligations—a fund of between $2.7 trillion and $4.1 trillion would be required. Leaving aside the question of how to raise such a fund, there would remain the question of how to invest it. The fund could perhaps buy *all* the outstanding bonds of the Federal government or could buy all the stock of all the companies listed on the New York Stock Exchange. See Lindley H. Clark, Jr., "Speaking of Business—Social Security?" *Wall Street Journal*, January 18, 1977, p. 24.

contributions. Yet the "insurance idea" has a "strong hold on the thinking of the Social Security Administration and the Congressional tax committees, as well as the public."[29]

It is understandable why there should be no attempt to deemphasize the "security," "savings" and "insurance" aspects of Social Security, since they all presumably contribute to popular acceptance of the program itself and, what is perhaps more important, to acceptance of a steadily increasing Social Security tax burden.

But to the extent that for active workers the cost of funding benefits for retired workers increases substantially, there may be a greater tendency to view Social Security "contributions" as taxes, and heavily regressive taxes at that, rather than as thrifty and prudent payments to insure minimal comfort in retirement. The older generation may regard benefits as "a bargain in retrospect," but the younger generation may consider them "a rip-off in prospect."[30]

As the baby-boom generation reaches retirement, the burden of paying for their old-age benefits will fall on a smaller work force behind them. Today there are an estimated 30 Social Security beneficiaries for each 100 active workers. This ratio will narrow in the future and, by the year 2030, it is projected that there will be 45 beneficiaries for each 100 workers.[31] The actual ratio will, of course, depend on a number of factors, but the trends most evident today point to a higher proportion of beneficiaries to workers—a declining birth rate, later entry of young people into the labor force and greater longevity of those retiring.

Just on the basis of these trends, the potential for future dissatisfaction with the Social Security system is very great.

The burden of supporting Social Security has also become more onerous as the result of Congressional sensitivity to increasing benefit levels to adjust for inflation. If anything, Congress has been too sensitive on this point. A worker retiring at age sixty-five in 1960 at the maximum benefit level, for example, had had his benefits increased 120 percent by June 1975, as against an 87 percent increase in the Consumer Price Index during the same period. A worker retiring in 1970 would have received a 58 percent increase in benefits by June 1975, as against a 45 percent increase in the CPI.[32]

Under the Social Security Act amendments of 1972, the Congress attempted to build into Social Security benefits an automatic "escalator" for inflation, obviating the need for periodic and specific adjustments by legislative action. Under the amendments, increases are now made each June to increase Social Security benefits on the basis of increases in the Consumer Price Index. Corresponding increases were also mandated in the wage base against which Social Security taxes are levied, so that in theory increased tax revenues would fund increased benefits.

By 1977, there was every indication that the theory would not work in the years immediately ahead. Price inflation (which has a direct impact on the Consumer Price Index) was pushing up Social Security adjustments at the same time as increased unemployment was reducing Social Security tax revenues. In May 1977, the trustees of the Social Security Trust Funds projected that the disability insurance fund would be exhausted in 1979 and the old age and survivors insurance trust fund in 1983.[33]

This projection left the President and the Congress with three alternatives: reducing benefits to the retired (which was undoubtedly politically impossible, if not close to being morally wrong); funding benefits in part out of general (i.e., income tax) revenues; or raising Social Security taxes (by increasing either the rate of tax or the wage base against which the tax is levied).

The 1977 dilemma required both the President and Congress to confront the regressive features of the Social Security tax, that is, the fact that it is assessed at a constant rate regardless of the level of income (up to the amount of wages subject to the tax) and regardless of the family situation of the taxpayer. There are no deductions, exemptions or variations in rate, as there are in the Federal income tax.

FDR's lack of concern for the fact that the Social Security tax was regressive is perhaps understandable, since the original tax rate in 1937 was 2 percent (1 percent for the employee, 1 percent for the employer) on a maximum wage base of $3,000. As of 1979 (including the tax covering Medicare) the rate was 12.26 percent (6.13 percent employee, 6.13 percent employer) on a maximum wage base of $22,900.

At this level of taxation, and assuming the employer portion of the Social Security tax would be passed on to the worker as increased wages if not paid to the Federal government, the combined social-security tax is, for more than half of all wage earners, larger than their income tax.[34]

In 1977, a family of four (with one parent working) with an income of $10,000 paid $446 in Federal income taxes and $585 in Social Security taxes (without regard to the employer tax). The Social Security tax bill increased to $605 in 1978 and, after the Social Security amendments enacted in December 1977, will go progressively upward to $613 in 1979, to $665 in 1981 (after the 1980 Congressional and Presidential elections) and to $765 in 1990.

Increases in the wage base against which Social Security taxes are levied were also made in 1977, to $22,900 in 1979 to $25,900 in 1980 and to $29,700 in 1981, with annual increases after 1981 being based on increases in the cost of living.

Although the Social Security amendments of 1977 differed radically from the proposals made by President Carter for improving the funding of Social Security, the President, in signing the amendments, acknowledged only that they differed "in some respects" from his proposals and hailed the amendments as "wise."[35]

The 1977 amendments seem anything but wise. The increased Social Security tax rates served to shift even further the burden of providing for the nation's retired to those least able to bear it. And at a time when consumer spending to bolster the economy was in order, a tax increase reducing take-home pay seemed an odd way to foster such spending.

The mischievous effects will not be likely to stop there. Employers will also have to pay the increased tax rates—on the increased wage base—and can be expected either to pass these increases on to customers through price increases, thus adding to inflation, or to cut back on existing payrolls or new hiring, thus increasing unemployment.

By its devotion to the insurance concept of Social Security, Congress adopted solutions to Social Security funding likely to increase the system's two basic problems—unemployment (which reduces payroll-tax receipts) and inflation (which increases benefits that must be paid).

Dean J. Douglas Brown of Princeton, one of the architects of Social Security in the 1930s, has written that it was never contemplated that a mature system would continue to be funded exclusively through employer-employee payroll taxes. He points out that government contributions from general revenues were not required in the early years, because of the relatively low cost of benefits, but that as the system matured it was expected that government contributions would be necessary, with funding of Social Security coming roughly one third each from employers, employees and the Federal treasury.[36]

Using general revenues to prevent further increases in the payroll tax would have several important effects: resentment by the young of increasing Social Security taxes to support the old would be mitigated;

those most able to pay for the necessary funding increases would do so through the progressive income tax; the take-home pay of those most likely to buoy consumer spending would not be reduced; and the direct impact on employers—a direct impact expected to lead to higher prices and less expansionary hiring practices—would be eliminated or at least reduced.

President Carter, in his May 1977 message to Congress on Social Security, had maintained a clever balance between the insurance concept and the idea of using general revenues. He proposed that Congress help fund the Social Security reserve funds from general revenues with a contribution equal to what the system would have received if unemployment since 1975 had remained at 6 percent. He would not have made the contribution permanent or pegged it at one third of annual contributions, but his proposal at least would have compensated for the shortfall in payroll-tax revenues resulting from high unemployment.[37]

The Congress would have none of the President's proposal. The high-tax insurance concept prevailed, despite what would seem to be the entirely predictable consequences already discussed.

What appears to be a growing public outcry against the 1977 increases may yet persuade Congress to revise Social Security funding still another time.*

One alternative is, of course, to make appropriations from general revenues for one third of the system's funding needs. A second would be the Carter proposal of 1977, geared to "counter-cyclical" general funding in periods of high unemployment.

And still a third would be to fund disability† (as opposed to retirement) benefits and Medicare "Part A" benefits from general revenues.

That Congress should not have acted perceptively in its approach to Social Security funding is not altogether surprising, since another problem that it confronted in 1977 was a mistake of its own making, dating to its amendment of the Social Security Act in 1972.

---

* On March 1, 1978, a proposal in the House Ways and Means Committee to reduce Social Security taxes and make an offsetting reduction in President Carter's proposed income-tax cut was defeated by a single vote, 19–18.

† In 1956, pensions for disabled workers, starting at age fifty, were added to Social Security. Liberalization of the disability requirements over the years—including elimination of the age-fifty requirement—has vastly increased the scope of this aspect of Social Security. By September 1977, 4.8 million disabled workers or their dependents received benefits as compared with 26 million receiving old-age benefits; in September 1977 disability benefits were being paid at a rate of $889 million per month, or 12.5 percent of the combined total of old-age and disability benefits.

In addition to the annual adjustments in benefits based on the Consumer Price Index already described, the 1972 amendments made provision for adjusting the so-called primary insurance amount (PIA) for inflation, again on the basis of the Consumer Price Index. The PIA is the formula used in computing benefits, with a recipient's average monthly wage multiplied by the PIA or a fraction thereof to determine the amount of his monthly retirement payment.

As the result of the 1972 "escalator" in the PIA, workers retiring thereafter could look forward to the advantage of two escalator rides at once, for both components used in determining their benefits would be adjusted upward: the average monthly wage (either through increases in real wages bringing them up to the wage ceiling counted for Social Security purposes, or through increases in that ceiling made each time benefits were increased) and the PIA.

One does not have to be a mathematician to realize that if a high rate of inflation continued—resulting in ever-higher double adjustments in calculating benefits—the Social Security system might ultimately require all the money in the world to fund its obligations. Even on more rational projections, the anomalous and unintended result would be reached in some cases that the retirement benefits of a beneficiary would exceed his income while working.*

Perhaps Congress, before it attempts to "escalate" for inflation, should take lessons from the less-developed Third World countries that have acquired experience in indexing and adjusting for inflation. The double-benefit effect adopted in 1972 was unquestionably a mistake and, since it was a mistake that would affect only the benefits of those retiring in the future, was presumably subject to correction without a great deal of political conflict. Yet Congress ignored the problem for five years—during which time the double-escalator adjustments were in fact being made—despite warnings by, among others, President Ford, the trustees of the Social Security funds and Senator Lloyd Bentsen (Democrat, Texas).

In 1977, Congress halted the double escalator by providing a new formula for future adjustments in determining an individual's level of benefits at the time of retirement that "index" only one factor—his earnings history—for inflation.

Other problems remain with our most fundamental social program,

* This is true today, but only to the extent that a higher retirement benefit is paid to those with very low wages at the time of retirement.

including the question of whether coverage of employees of Federal, state and local governments should be made mandatory,* and the elimination of inequitable conditions for qualifying for benefits based on sex or marital status. Both are the subject of studies commissioned by the Congress in 1977, but when and whether they will be addressed by the Congress or the President remains to be seen.†

National Health Policy—Medicaid and Medicare

Conservatives argue that the United States has a national health policy that serves the public adequately.

"With the existence of Medicare, Medicaid, Veterans' Hospitals, public-health services and various kinds of private charity services provided by the United Fund and other groups," a *Wall Street Journal* editor wrote recently,

the equity problem [of equal access to health care] is far less serious than it sometimes is painted by national health [insurance] advocates. When it is considered that some 90% of the population has some form of health insurance, it is not so easy to identify those remaining who still have a problem of access to medical care.[38]

In fact, the $162 *billion* in expenditures now being made annually for medical care, public and private, are not being made pursuant to a

---

* Federal employees are now covered under an entirely separate retirement system, and participation by state and local government units is optional. This can create a variation on "double-dipping" referred to in the note at page 28, whereby a government employee elects early retirement under a non-Social Security program and then works in a private job covered by Social Security for the minimum period (six calendar quarters), after which he would be entitled to the minimum monthly Social Security benefits of $121.

† Also slated for reappraisal is the Supplemental Security Income (SSI) program adopted by Congress in 1972 to assist the elderly poor (as well as the needy blind and disabled). SSI, which became effective January 1, 1974, was designed to combine assistance for the needy aged, disabled and blind in a Federally administered program with uniform minimum benefits nationwide. It is more comprehensive than the old-age assistance, aid to the blind and aid to the permanently disabled programs formerly operated by states with funding shared by the states and the Federal government. A total of $6.2 billion was paid under the SSI program in 1977, $4.7 billion by the Federal government and the remainder as supplements by certain of the states.

Under SSI, a basic monthly payment is made to an eligible individual of $157 or $236 for an eligible couple. Social Security payments over $20 are deducted, as are 50 percent of earnings over $65 and 100 percent of unearned income, such as interest, rents and dividends.

coherent and rationalized public policy, if by a "policy" one means a rational plan for "(1) ensuring that all persons have access to medical care, (2) eliminating the financial hardship of medical bills, and (3) limiting the rise in health care costs."[39]

As described in Chapter Two, the elderly and disabled enrolled in Social Security are entitled to benefits under the Federal Medicare program, while welfare recipients and various other poor people, depending on state eligibility requirements, receive benefits under Medicaid. Veterans, regardless of their income, are also entitled to care at Veterans' Hospitals. These programs, plus reimbursement under private insurance plans, such as Blue Cross, Blue Shield and so-called major medical policies (which provide an insurance "override" for a portion of the costs not covered by Blue Cross or Blue Shield), constitute the infrastructure easing the burden of paying Americans' medical bills.

An estimated ten million people below the poverty line do not receive Medicaid benefits.[40] Similarly, the hard-core elderly poor who have never come under Social Security (or comparable public retirement plans, such as the Railroad Retirement system) can participate in Medicare only by paying a prohibitive $63-a-month premium.

And the "some form" of insurance coverage referred to by the *Wall Street Journal* editor may be pretty close to formless, covering a substantial portion of hospital care but a much smaller portion of other costs. In 1975, for example, health insurance covered 80 percent of private expenditures (i.e., expenditures not paid by any government program) for hospitals, but only 48.4 percent of expenditures for physicians' services, 6.8 percent of the cost of prescription drugs and 14 percent of expenditures for dental care.[41] It was estimated that twenty-four million Americans did not have any form of health insurance (private or public) in 1978, eighteen million more had insurance inadequate to meet basic charges and a total of eighty-eight million lacked protection against the costs of catastrophic illness.[42]

For those not qualifying for Medicare or Medicaid, private insurance is generally the only protection available for medical costs. Such insurance is normally so-called group insurance provided by an employer; individual or family policies, while available, are usually prohibitively expensive. The unemployed often do not have coverage; less than 30 percent of those who lose their jobs remain covered. Because of pre-existing health conditions, many people are deemed uninsurable, and others, as the result of previous expensive illnesses, have reached the lifetime ceiling of benefits under their insurance coverage. Karen Davis has observed:

> While only 20 percent of the population under sixty-five has no private hospital insurance, a disproportionate number of the working poor, of blacks, and of people living in the South are among those uninsured. So are people regarded by insurance companies as health risks. Forty percent of all black people under sixty-five and 75 percent of poor children do not have hospital coverage. . . . Of people under the age of sixty-five, 82 percent have insurance coverage in the Northeast compared with only 72 percent in the South. . . . Insurance coverage among farm residents is also low, with 40 percent uninsured for hospital expenses.[43]

Even among those covered by Medicare and Medicaid, benefit experience varies widely. The individual states, within certain limits, set eligibility requirements. Accordingly, the accident of geography can drastically alter an individual's access to Medicaid assistance. A detailed analysis of Medicaid payments to adults aged twenty-one to sixty-four in 1970 showed an average payment nationwide of $308; individual state average payments ranged from $179 and $183 in Arkansas and West Virginia to $738 and $848 in Texas and Wisconsin. In fiscal 1972, Medicaid payments averaged $292 in the Southern states, $511 in the Northeast. The South, with 46 percent of the nation's population below the poverty line, had only 20 percent of Medicaid recipients and 17 percent of Medicaid payments in 1972.

Davis' study concludes that rural residents have not made any gains relative to urban areas in the use of medical services since the introduction of Medicaid. This reflects in part the fact that poor rural families are more likely to have a father (although perhaps an unemployed one) present, thus making the family ineligible for welfare and usually for Medicaid, and the relative scarcity of medical resources in rural areas. Medicaid expenditures per poor child in rural areas average about $5 annually; the comparable average for children in the inner cities is $76.[44]

Another factor that cuts use by lower-income recipients is the existence of a $60 deductible on physicians' fees and a 20 percent coinsurance feature. For the very poor, Medicaid normally picks up the Medicare deductible and any coinsurance amount. The deductible and coinsurance features are thus of no concern to the very poor or to the relatively affluent, who can afford them; but those with incomes between poverty and affluence are seriously affected by them.

One of the consequences of Medicare and Medicaid—and a consequence largely unforeseen at the time of their enactment—has been a truly dramatic increase in medical costs. One observer has noted:

> The social conscience and political pressures that prompted the nation to adopt these measures [Medicare and Medicaid] were unaccompanied by a comparable effort to encourage the large-scale introduction of more efficient systems for providing medical services or to increase the supply of health manpower. Accordingly, close to half of the increase in spending for health services in the past decade was accounted for by higher prices for medical care and not by increased services.[45]

Between 1950 and 1974, medical-care expenditures rose by 750 percent. Since the enactment of Medicare and Medicaid in 1965, the average annual increase in health expenditures has been more than 11 percent per year.[46]*

The original Medicare-Medicaid legislation concentrated on reimbursing costs, but did not attempt to enter the politically sensitive area of regulating hospital and doctor charges, imposing cost controls or incentives to cut costs. These programs continued the bias of Blue Cross and Blue Shield in favor of hospital treatment. Complete coverage of short hospital stays tends to promote more costly hospital treatment at the expense of treatment in outpatient clinics and doctors' offices, which are often not covered by either public or private insurance.

Under Medicare and Medicaid a hospital is paid a daily rate based on its cost of operation. As a result, the "hospital administrator can no longer deny requests for higher wages or more supplies on the ground that money is lacking; to get money, he need only spend more."

> From general experience [H. E. Klarman has written] it is known that cost-plus contracts are not likely to promote efficient operation. However, in 1965 the Social Security Administration faced a record of experience in the hospital field that could not be gainsaid. First espoused as a desirable method for paying hospitals in the early 1950's, cost reimbursement was established by 1965 as the vehicle for financing the care of two-thirds of all Blue Cross subscribers. The expressed intention

---

* For other statistics on health-care costs, see pp. 253–55.

of Congress not to interfere with existing arrangements and the aim of the Social Security Administration's representatives not to antagonize anybody needlessly should also be considered. It was therefore determined to reimburse participating hospitals in relation to their own cost. . . .

What was not anticipated in 1965 was the possible change in a hospital administrator's behavior associated with a shift in the proportion of total patient days paid for at cost from 20 to 30 percent to 75 to 90 percent. This change was described by administrators from the outset and received confirmation from the high rate of increase in non-payroll expenses.[47]

Increased fees and increased hospital charges reimbursed by the Federal and state governments ultimately affect the taxpayers' burden. But they also affect the uncovered user of medical services, who must pay from his own pocket at the higher rates that Medicare and Medicaid have encouraged, as well as the user or employer paying for private insurance, the carriers of which must charge higher premiums to meet higher health-costs.

Many states, in the face of increased Medicaid costs, have legislated or are considering legislating reductions in benefits. The result is to make many poor people, who were able to receive a modicum of medical care from free clinics and voluntary medical programs before Medicaid, worse off. Losing their Medicaid eligibility, and with the former charity and free services no longer available, they are faced with paying for medical services at the inflated prices induced by the very program originally conceived to help them.

The Medicare-Medicaid legislation, so scrupulous in its noninterference in matters of medical policy, nonetheless created a number of distortions because of its bias in favor of institutional care. One consequence has been the growth of the nursing-home industry, including such stock market high fliers as the now-defunct Four Seasons Nursing Homes, Inc., and the slimy nursing-home entrepreneurs recently uncovered under their rocks in New York State.

Nursing-home care is covered by Medicaid; services to the elderly in their own homes generally are not. Although most doctors would argue that old people should be kept at home wherever possible, the bias of Medicaid in favor of institutional care has completely distorted this medical principle, since principle for most must give way to the inexorable lure of Medicaid's financial benefits.

The reluctance of government to monitor costs or standards of care has often been accompanied by inertia, even in seeing that institutions meet minimal standards for their occupants or that doctors are not operating "Medicaid mills" that proliferate referral fees and encourage perfunctory office visits. In 1975 then Congressman Edward I. Koch (Democrat, New York) discovered that the Department of Health, Education and Welfare assigned *only one* auditor to spend *only part* of his time checking Medicaid reimbursements—hardly the way to administer what was then an $8.7 billion program.[48]

Such laxity is an open invitation to fraud, and the recent nursing-home scandals in New York State indicate that there are many only too willing to take advantage of the license to steal granted by government. Spurred into action by public airing of nursing-home abuses in New York, New York State Department of Health auditors in 1975 examined the books of 104 nursing homes and disallowed more than $10 million of alleged overpayments.[49]

The good that has been done by Medicare and Medicaid in the past thirteen years is undeniable. At the same time, operation of the program has resulted in inequities in the delivery of health care, the unfortunate side effect of drastically increasing the cost of health care, and a complacent atmosphere that has deterred movement toward a comprehensive national health policy. And lax and indifferent administration has also brought discredit on health-care programs in general, leading to blanket condemnations by such otherwise responsible citizens as former Governor John Gilligan of Ohio, who said:

> In the decade since Medicare and Medicaid have appeared, we have poured billions into the health care delivery system of this country, without, so far as I can see, improving materially either the level of health care or its availability for most American families.[50]

Four · Congress at Work: Aid to Education, 1945–1965

Compulsory school attendance laws and the great expenditures for education both demonstrate our recognition of the importance of education to our democratic society. It is required in the performance of our most basic public responsibilities, even service in the armed forces. It is the very foundation of good citizenship. Today it is a principal instrument in awakening the child to cultural values, in preparing him for later professional training, and in helping him to adjust normally to his environment. In these days, it is doubtful that any child may reasonably be expected to succeed in life if he is denied the opportunity of an education. Such an opportunity, where the state has undertaken to provide it, is a right which must be made available to all on equal terms.

—CHIEF JUSTICE EARL WARREN in
Brown v. Board of Education,
347 U.S. 483 (1954)

The history of education since the industrial revolution shows a continual struggle between two forces: the desire by members of society to have educational opportunity for all children, and the desire of each family to provide the best education it can afford for its own children.

—JAMES S. COLEMAN[1]

If one were to instruct a school child in the civic virtue and wisdom of the United States Congress, it would be just as well to steer him away from questions about the Congress' role in providing his school, his books and his teachers. For an analysis of that role is disillusioning —an unpretty story of a willful minority of Congressmen exploiting divisive social currents and of parliamentary maneuvers, first to delay

Federal participation in education and then to inhibit the logical and efficient development of that participation.

Looking only at Federal assistance for elementary and secondary education—government aid to higher education is a whole separate story—the need for assistance at the end of World War II has been briefly sketched in Chapter Two.* Despite the obvious need, Federal aid was not forthcoming until enactment of the Elementary and Secondary Education Act of 1965 (ESEA). This chapter will attempt to analyze the parliamentary and political maneuvering that caused the delay of almost a generation in facing up to a major national problem.

Even in the best of circumstances, committing the Federal government to a major role in elementary and secondary education would have been difficult. Unlike many countries of Europe, the United States has never been committed to a cohesive, unified school system run by the national government; the autonomous local school district has instead been the norm. And the pluralization of American society has produced sincere and deeply felt—but diametrically antithetical—views on the basic role of the school, on its relationship to organized religion and on its use as a vehicle to combat racial discrimination.

Reconciling these differences would never have been easy. Reconciling them through the complex national legislative process proved for many years almost impossible.

An extended look at the Congressional treatment of aid to education up through the enactment of ESEA is justified. Such an examination dramatically illustrates the problems in a functioning democracy—in a functioning and heterogeneous democracy—of achieving a consensus on how to implement a basic right, the right to a good education, on which there is virtually universal agreement. If achieving consensus in the context of education requires twenty years, it is perhaps easier to see why enactment of social legislation in areas where there is less of a basic commitment will take considerably longer.

Reviewing the history of Federal aid to education, one is tempted to liken its Congressional opponents to Reinhold Niebuhr's "children of darkness"—the "moral cynics who know no law beyond their will and

---

* See pp. 47–50. Also excluded from discussion is the "impact areas" program, first enacted after World War II to assist school districts affected by the presence of large numbers of Federal workers. Every President since has tried to get rid of impact aid without success. It is a "temporary" measure which has grown into a permanent Congressional boondoggle, costing $765 million in fiscal 1978.

interest."[2] The appellation is perhaps too strong, though the hard core of opponents of Federal aid have certainly over the years been cynical in their manipulation of questions of race and religion and single-minded in their willful determination to defeat or hamper Federal assistance.

The hard nucleus of opposition to Federal aid has by no means been confined to the Rankins, Eastlands, Stennises and Thurmonds. That folk hero of Watergate, Sam Ervin, Jr., was certainly a member, and such would-be Republican "progressives" as Charles Goodell, Donald Rumsfeld, Thruston Morton and John Anderson of Illinois were often allies, as were future Presidents Richard Nixon and Gerald Ford. The basic coalition of conservative Republicans and Southern Democrats was also often able to distort the framing of the issues under debate so that vigorous supporters of Federal aid—John F. Kennedy, Abraham Ribicoff and Lister Hill come to mind—sided with the conservatives on crucial votes.

It is difficult to assess the true motives of the conservative nucleus of Federal-aid opponents. One of the recurring themes of their argument has been that Federal assistance would diminish the sacrosanct principle of "local control" of education. Yet deference to "local control" has never stopped the conservatives from attempting to mandate conduct from Washington—no voluntary desegregation involving the busing of children, for example.

Senator Eastland and other Southerners argued for years that parents had a nearly inalienable right to select the schools their children would attend and that such schools, even if segregated and lily-white, were entitled to Federal support. But parents exercising that right by sending their children to religious schools were not so entitled.

Federal money earmarked for education must not be wasted, but on the other hand local school districts must not be held accountable for how such money is spent.

It is easy to say that the conservative nucleus based its opposition on an ideological antipathy to spending the taxpayers' money, as evidenced by the likes of reactionary Congressman John Taber (Republican, New York), who called a bill to provide for a moderate school-lunch program in 1946 "one of the most dangerous bills that has ever been brought to the floor of the House."[3]

But this is an oversimplified generalization that does not hold up when one looks at the voting records of these same conservatives on spending for defense, highway construction, or Army Corps of Engineers projects.

The more likely basis of opposition is a shrewd realization that Federal spending for education will inevitably have disrupting social consequences. Such aid has been tied, though not terribly effectively, to the principle of desegregation and to the principle of wider educational opportunity.

The struggle that Professor Coleman noted between a societal urge for greater opportunity for all and a selfish urge to maximize the educational advantages of one's own children is very real.

If one's perception is that the best education that can be provided is in an all-white school adequately funded by local property taxes, why risk changing this comfortable status quo by expanding an overall commitment to educational opportunity generally? Why challenge the restrictive "country club" mentality with a commitment to having racially and economically heterogeneous populations within a school? Why run the competitive risk of lengthening the lines of qualified applicants at the doors of college admissions officers and employers? The quality of education is just fine in the white, property-rich enclaves of America. Why undo the whites' perceived comfort by integration, by financially compensating the less fortunate school districts, by reallocating tax resources in the name of equality?

This attitude is profoundly undemocratic and contrary to the commitment, which we are presumed to share, to providing educational opportunity for all. It is an attitude that can never be respectably expressed in political debate in direct and explicit terms. "Local control" must be seen as a benign exercise in town-meeting democracy, not a mean instrument for favoring the affluent and neglecting the poor in the dividing up of resources. "Busing" must be viewed not as a traditional common-sense means of getting children from home (or farm) to school but as a disruptive tool of social engineering. "Integration" must be analyzed in terms of comparative reading scores and never considered as perhaps the only effective means of improving race relations among succeeding generations of Americans.

Aid to Education: 1945–1964

The idea of Federal aid was not a new one in 1945. As early as 1884, Senator Henry Blair, a New Hampshire Republican, raised the question of whether the national government should "apply the public money" to local education "when made necessary by local neglect or inability."[4]

By 1945, an informal bipartisan Committee for the Support of Federal Aid for Public Schools had been formed in the House. In 1946, Senators Elbert Thomas and Lister Hill, Democrats of Utah and Alabama, and Robert A. Taft, Republican of Ohio, sponsored an aid bill that gave recognition to the fact that "the children are where the money ain't,"[5] with state differences in per pupil expenditures ranging as high as 60 to 1.

Under the bill, each state would have been eligible for aid only if it dedicated 2.2 percent of its income to education and if state funds were inadequate to provide $40 a child a year; the Federal government would provide up to the difference between 2.2 percent of state income and the amount required to provide $40 for each child a year. The annual cost to the Federal government was estimated at $225 million.[6]

The bill was reported to the floor of the Senate by the Committee on Education and Labor in June 1946, but was never acted on before adjournment.

In the first session of the Eightieth Congress in 1947, a slightly revised education bill was reported, but again not acted on. To attract broader support, the proposed distribution formula was altered, so that each state would have received some funds, expressed in the debates (incorrectly) as being $5 per school-age child.*

In 1948, this bill was passed by the Senate, 58 to 22, but was then blocked in a parliamentary maneuver in the House Committee on

* The formula provided for aid equal to the difference between (a) $45 times the number of school-age children and (b) 1 percent of the state's average income over the previous five years. If state funding was sufficient to reach the $45 level (as it was in twenty-five states), a flat grant of $5 per pupil would be made. However, in each case the amount so determined would be multiplied by an "effort percentage" derived from the ratio of the actual percentage of state income devoted to education to a theoretical maximum percentage of 2.5. Under this formula, Mississippi, which devoted 1.8 percent of state income to education, would have received 72 percent of the amount needed to reach the $45 per pupil level and New York, which devoted 1.7 percent of its income to education, would have received only 68 percent of the $5 per pupil flat grant. 94 *Congressional Record* (1948), pp. 3391–93.

Education and Labor. Reactionary Republican Chairman Fred Hartley, Jr., and his colleagues, including freshman Congressman Richard Nixon, voted to kill the bill.

Most Southerners, representing states that stood to benefit the most from Federal assistance dollars, favored the 1948 bill. Even such conservatives as Senator James Eastland of Mississippi and John McClellan of Arkansas supported it. But Senator Tom Connolly, representing oil-rich Texas, which would have received relatively less under the bill's formula, introduced an amendment which would have prohibited anti-segregation conditions to aid in subsequent appropriations. His amendment was defeated. Left standing was a provision that required a minimum $45 per pupil expenditure for all children regardless of race, but which was silent on "separate but equal" segregated education.

The public discussion of aid to education in these early postwar years foreshadowed the nature of the opposition that was to coalesce in various ways to defeat later proposals. Raising the specter of "socialism," "Federal control" and the potential "bankruptcy of the Federal government," the conservatives were able to enlist such supporters as the United States Chamber of Commerce against aid generally, and against programs that would give aid to the wealthier states in particular—even though inclusion of the wealthy states on some basis was politically a necessary precondition for support, given the sizable Congressional delegations from those states.

In 1949, the conservatives brought General Eisenhower under their banner. Eisenhower expressed qualified support for aid to the neediest states but warned, in terms of a broader program, that "unless we are careful, even the great and necessary educational processes in our country will become yet another vehicle by which the believers in paternalism, if not outright socialism, will gain still additional power for the central government."*

* General Eisenhower was then President of Columbia University and was careful to point out that "in no way should my position be interpreted to mean that I am opposed to Federal contractual arrangements with schools for scientific research which is essential to the public interest. Federal Government support of such ventures, and even certain types of fellowships and scholarships to meet unusual Federal requirements, would not weaken local government or sap community enterprise." The higher-education ox was not to be gored. 95 *Congressional Record* (1949), p. A3690.

Senator Robert Kerr (Democrat, Oklahoma) observed of Eisenhower's statement: "Without Federal aid our roads would be of little use to the military, and the same principle applies to human resources." Quoted, "Eisenhower on Education," *New Republic,* June 27, 1949, p. 8.

Friends and enemies of aid to parochial schools had also begun to be heard from. The 1948 bill, like its predecessors, ducked the question of aid to parochial schools by throwing it back to the states. If the states wished to apply Federal aid money to parochial schools or students, they would be free to do so. At the time, about 10 percent of elementary-school pupils and one sixteenth of high-school students were enrolled in private (principally Catholic) schools.[7] The issue had been complicated by Supreme Court decisions in 1947 and 1948 casting doubt on the Constitutionality of government aid to parochial schools.[8]

Taking a dog-in-the-manger attitude, the National Catholic Welfare Conference opposed the bill before the Senate in 1948 as an "unwarranted Federal interference with the Nation's schools."[9] On the Senate floor, amendments both to prohibit parochial-school aid and to increase it were decisively defeated.

The conservative opponents of aid were not able to recruit the Senate Republican leader, Robert A. Taft, who had "almost single-handedly" defeated an aid bill in the Senate in 1943,[10] but who now had become a cautious convert to the education-aid cause.

In remarks on the Senate floor in 1946, Taft noted his earlier opposition but said that subsequent "study" had convinced him that the states "are unable to provide an adequate basic minimum education for their children, due to the great difference in income as between the States."[11] Two years later he told the Senate:

> ...I think we have a tremendous obligation to provide equality of opportunity to the children of the United States. When the Declaration of Independence said that all men are created equal, it perhaps made an extreme statement; but I have always felt that what was meant was that all men in the United States are entitled to equality of opportunity. No child can have equality of opportunity, in my opinion, unless to start with he has a basic minimum education. ... The ordinary child who receives no education is, in effect, condemned to a life of poverty, a life on the basis of a low standard of living, a life of little interest, and a life which is of little value to the people of the United States.[12]

The prospects for a bill providing for Federal aid looked brighter in 1949. Both the Republicans and the Democrats had endorsed Federal aid in their 1948 platforms and President Truman made it a part of his "Fair Deal" program, outlined in his 1949 State of the Union Message:

It is . . . shocking that millions of our children are not receiving a good education. Millions of them are in overcrowded, obsolete buildings. We are short of teachers, because teachers' salaries are too low to attract new teachers, or to hold the ones we have. All these school problems will become much more acute as a result of the tremendous increase in the enrollment in our elementary schools in the next few years. I cannot repeat too strongly my desire for prompt Federal financial aid to the States to help them operate and maintain their school systems.[13]

Once again a Senate bill, providing for up to $300 million in Federal aid on basically the same terms as those proposed in 1948, passed the Senate handily, 58–15. Proponents of aid to parochial schools had refrained from opposing the bill, in exchange for support of a bill to provide health benefits to parochial children.

But fatal trouble soon developed in the House. Representative Graham A. Barden, a conservative North Carolina Democrat, shepherded through a subcommittee of the Committee on Education and Labor a bill providing for aid to public schools only, as well as omitting any provision prohibiting discrimination against racial minorities.

Congressman John Lesinski, a Michigan Democrat, a Catholic and chairman of the committee, accused Barden of writing a bill which was "anti-Negro" and "anti-Catholic," and which "dripped with bigotry and racial prejudice."[14]

Cardinal Spellman of New York joined the controversy by calling the Barden bill "a craven crusade of religious prejudice against Catholic children" and calling Barden and his supporters "new apostles of bigotry."[15] The issue soon became even more heated when the Cardinal attacked Eleanor Roosevelt, widow of the late President, for her public stand against aid to parochial schools.

The upshot of the controversy was to make school aid too hot a subject for House debate; the Committee on Education and Labor failed to report a bill.

The religious controversy continued to simmer into 1950. Commenting on the situation that year, the New Republic noted that education conditions had not improved since World War II, that three fourths of state school boards had less purchasing power per pupil than they did in 1940 and that "shamefully low" teachers' salaries had placed teachers even farther below other groups in average earnings.

"These hard truths are so generally deplored that no politician today could safely oppose a program to remedy the situation if a clear-cut vote were taken on this issue alone," the magazine observed.

But such a "clear-cut vote" was not to be. The opponents of a general Federal-aid program knew that they would be beaten on a straight up-or-down vote. Therefore "their strategy has been to kill the program behind committee doors. The passions roused by religious debate made their jobs easy."

In debate in the House Committee on Education and Labor, a "compromise" version was drafted that would again have allowed states the option of giving aid to parochial schools. On a 13–12 vote, the committee killed the bill for the Eighty-First Congress, the majority consisting of seven conservative Republicans (including Nixon), a conservative Texas Democrat opposed to any aid, two Protestant Democrats (including Barden) opposed to any parochial aid, and three liberal Catholic Democrats who did not favor the bill because it did not specifically provide for parochial aid (including Lesinski and John F. Kennedy).[16]

The impasse over parochial aid killed aid to education not only in 1950, but for the balance of the Fair Deal years and the first year of the Eisenhower administration. Attempts were made in those years to earmark tidelands oil revenues for education, but the "oil for education" proposals of Senator Lister Hill and others achieved no more success than the bipartisan Hill-Thomas-Taft proposals of the late 1940s.[17]

Conditions, meanwhile, had not gotten any better in the classrooms. A 1951 survey of male teachers in St. Louis showed that only 8 percent lived on their salaries as teachers. Moonlighting, family inheritances and working wives were required to make ends meet.[18] As Harold L. Ickes had noted in 1947, too many children were being taught by "what might be called academic gigolos—men and women who want to teach but who . . . must be subsidized from private sources."[19] And a 1950 survey of fifteen large cities showed in all cases teachers receiving lower salaries than policemen, firemen and garbage collectors.[20]

The postwar baby boom, deferral of maintenance of existing plant and the lack of funds for building new schools and paying teachers adequately were impairing the education of an estimated three million pupils in 1950.[21] By 1950, the nation's schools needed a projected 600,000 new classrooms over the ensuing seven years. Senator

Hill warned in 1952 that "a veritable tidal wave of 6-year-olds will hit the schools over the next 5 or 6 years. . . . Heaven knows how we are going to educate these children."[22]

A new weapon had also been added to the arsenal of right-wing critics of school aid—"subversion in the schools," although the more sensible dismissed charges of "communism" and "subversion" as "dishonest" and as a "cloak" for general opposition to school expenditures.[23]

With construction becoming a more serious problem, a bipartisan group of Senators attempted in 1954 to focus aid efforts on construction in the hope that, as in the case of the Hill-Burton program for Federal assistance for hospital construction, first approved in 1946, sectarian issues might be less strong than in the case of outright general aid. The Labor and Public Welfare Committee of the Senate reported a bill authorizing "emergency" grants for construction over a two-year period.

The measure did not receive White House support. President Eisenhower, in his 1954 budget message, had rejected general aid grants and had called for a national conference to study education and various other advisory and survey proposals. In classic on-the-one-hand-this fashion, Eisenhower said:

> I do not underestimate the difficulties facing the States and communities in attempting to solve the problems created by the great increase in the number of children of school age, the shortage of qualified teachers, and the overcrowding of classrooms. . . . At the same time, I do not accept the simple remedy of Federal intervention.[24]

Congress authorized a White House Conference on Education for 1955, and Mrs. Oveta Culp Hobby, Secretary of Health, Education and Welfare, urged in 1954 that school-aid legislation be postponed until after the Conference. Despite heated criticism of the President's meager program, Mrs. Hobby's counsels of delay prevailed, and no further action was taken on a school bill in 1954.

President Eisenhower muddied the waters the next year by proposing still another method of school aid. He advocated a confusing combination of direct grants to very poor school districts, the formation of state authorities to build classrooms for districts which could not raise money through school bond issues, and a Federal program for purchasing the securities of districts which could not sell their bonds at competitive interest rates.[25]

While his former Education Commissioner was declaring that educational problems were "national problems [that] will be solved only by national efforts,"[26] the fine print of Eisenhower's proposal made clear that the $7 billion he saw as necessary for construction over a three-year period were to be provided largely by state and local governments.

Adlai Stevenson, in a major address to the National Education Association, noted that Eisenhower had outlined the need for new schools, but "to help get them, he recommended that Congress pass not a law but a miracle. For meeting this $7 billion need, the President proposed grants of $66 million a year for three years. This is 33 cents a year to meet every $35 of admitted present, crying need."

Stevenson continued:

> It is, I think, interesting if disheartening to reflect that while proposing an effective grant of only $66 million a year for 3 years for school-construction aid, the President at the same time proposed a Federal grant for highway-construction aid—mostly on [a] matching basis—of $3 billion every year for the next 10 years. This is $45 of Federal funds for highways to every $1 for schools.[27]

Dismissing the President's proposal as "government by gimmick,"[28] the House Education and Labor Committee reported its own aid bill in 1955—the first such bill reported by the Committee after World War II—providing for $1 billion over four years in matching grants for construction, $750 million for the purchase of local school construction bonds and $150 million to assist in debt service on an additional $6 billion of local bonds.

But the conservative majority on the House Rules Committee refused to grant a "rule" allowing floor debate. The Rules Committee was, however, under severe pressure to bring the bill to the floor, and it did so a year later, in 1956. For the first time since 1945, the opponents of school aid in the House had to fight in the open in floor debate. That fight turned out to be an easy one. At the time the South's rearguard action against the Supreme Court desegregation decision of 1954 was in full swing. Senator Eastland summed up the conservative Southern position nicely:

> It is the law of nature, it is the law of God, that every race has both the right and the duty to perpetuate itself. . . . Free men have the right to send their children to schools of their own choosing, free from govern-

mental interference, and to build up their own culture, free from governmental interference.[29]

Concerned that court litigation on a district-by-district basis would be too time-consuming in bringing about school desegregation, Representative Adam Clayton Powell (Democrat, New York) introduced an amendment to the House aid bill barring funds to any district not in compliance with the Supreme Court's decision.

The Powell proposal troubled and divided liberals committed to equal opportunity and integration. Failure to support the amendment might be viewed as capitulation before the strident Southern onslaught. But if the amendment passed, a coalition of Republican conservatives and Southerners would surely defeat the aid bill, wiping out the first postwar opportunity to pass such a bill in the House.

Most liberals ended up by following the lead of Adlai Stevenson, then a candidate for President, who told a black audience in Los Angeles in February 1956 that he opposed the Powell amendment because it would defeat the education bill.

Supporting Stevenson's stand, Senator Richard Neuberger (Democrat, Oregon) cited his own long support for civil-rights measures and the Supreme Court decision, but reluctantly refused to back the Powell amendment: "I favor civil-rights legislation on its own, and I favor Federal aid to education on its own."[30]

President Eisenhower, prodded both by the pro-Federal-aid position of his 1955 White House Conference and reelection pressures, favored the aid bill before the House and opposed the Powell amendment. But he failed to guide the House Republicans.

"With his own party divided and wavering on what to do," James Reston wrote, "he did not send a single word to the Congress during the week's debate, though he had repeatedly and publicly urged the Congress to adopt his views on foreign-aid legislation the week before."[31]

Without White House direction, the Republicans in the House played a cynical game. With their help, the Powell amendment passed 225–192, and the final bill, with the Powell antisegregation amendment tacked to it, lost, 194–224. Ninety-six Congressmen voted to pass the Powell amendment and then turned around and voted against the basic bill. All 96 were Republicans, and included Charles Halleck, the Minority Leader, and Congressman Gerald Ford.

Commenting on the House action, Senator Hubert Humphrey (Democrat, Minnesota) said that civil-rights supporters "must recognize that cynical opponents of school aid have been at work to use us, to split and divide us, and to kill the school construction bill."[32]

The irresistible politics followed by the Republicans were described by the St. Louis *Post-Dispatch:*

> There is more than a suspicion that some of the backers of [the Powell amendment] are moved by cold cynicism which is quite willing to defeat Federal aid to schools, court the northern Negro vote, and expose the Democratic Party split over segregation, all in one fell swoop.[33]

Lack of Presidential leadership enabled the conservative coalition to kill an education bill on the House floor in 1958. Eisenhower in 1957 renewed his cautious 1956 proposals for temporary construction assistance, Federal purchases of local bonds and the use of the Federal government's credit to back local school bonds.

The House Education and Labor Committee and the Rules Committee sent to the floor a compromise proposal that rejected the Eisenhower approach and provided for general school aid to be allocated one half on the basis of local school population, one half on the basis of need.

Once again an antisegregation amendment was tacked on to the bill, this time offered by Stuyvesant Wainright, a New York Republican and an avowed opponent of Federal aid.

Then a parliamentary maneuver was engineered that justified the observation of Drew Pearson that "things move fast in the House of Representatives. They move so fast that experts can hardly keep up with them."

The Democratic managers of the bill, within striking distance of achieving House passage for the first time, sought to gain the margin for passage by agreeing to Eisenhower's original bill. Representative Samuel K. McConnell, a pro-education Republican from Pennsylvania, was "jubilant" and went to call the White House, "confident he could get an immediate message from Eisenhower supporting the [Eisenhower] bill."

But Charles Halleck, the Republican Minority Leader, and Howard Smith, the reactionary Virginia Democrat, with the knowledge that "the tide was going against them; a school bill might be passed," conspired to introduce a motion to "strike the enacting clause of the bill" (i.e., kill the bill). The House passed Smith's motion, 208–203, before the bipartisan compromise could be put into place.[34]

Eisenhower's commitment to his own proposal appears somewhat dubious. Had he been closer to the situation in the House and more willing to assume an active role, it is inconceivable that he could not have changed the three votes necessary to defeat the Smith motion. Asked at a press conference about his failure to act, he said only that "I don't get up and make statements every twenty minutes."[35]

And two days before the President delivered his education message in January 1957, Vice President Nixon had warned that the proposal "of the Federal Government to build local schools" would open a "pandora [sic] box" of spending that would, in a singularly un-Republican metaphor, "begin as a mouse and quickly become an elephant."[36]

"It is often asserted that all the subsidies and grants which appear in the Federal budget are there because of the special interests of pressure groups," Walter Lippmann wrote of education politics in 1957. "But as a general rule it is untrue and grossly unfair. In the case of Federal aid for schools, it is truer and fairer to say that the opposition comes from pressure groups, whereas the support is truly national and public spirited."[37]

The Russian launching of Sputnik in October 1957—demonstrating, as the Russians put it, how "the freed and conscious labor of the people of the new socialist society turns even the most daring of man's dreams into reality"—created the climate for passage of the National Defense Education Act of 1958 (NDEA).

Despite cries of the Old Guard that the national education problem was not lack of funds but a "debasement of the curriculum," whereby "date behavior, beauty care, consumer buying, stagecraft, square dancing, pep club, marriage and family relationships, junior homemaking for boys, etc." were the preferred subjects of instruction,[38] the bill passed the Congress with ease.

Questions of race, parochial aid and regional favoritism were subordinated to larger concerns over national security and education's role in maintaining that security. As the Act itself said

The present emergency demands that additional and more adequate educational opportunities be made available. The defense of this Nation depends upon the mastery of modern techniques developed from complex scientific principles.*

Suddenly there was realization that scientific preeminence was not going to be achieved by a nation producing only 125 new teachers of high-school physics per year.[39]

The Eisenhower program was in no sense a general aid program, and funds for construction—the most pressing issue to the President a year earlier—were not even mentioned. At the subcollege level, the act called for four-year expenditures of $70 million per year to enable elementary and secondary schools to acquire equipment and materials to improve science, mathematics and modern foreign-language instruction, plus funds to encourage college graduates to become teachers and to improve vocational-guidance counseling.

The act also established the principle of "by-passing" state agencies prohibited by law or state constitutions from aiding parochial schools. In such situations, the Federal government was authorized to make low-interest, long-term loans to sectarian schools to carry out the purposes of the act.

With the passage of NDEA, President Eisenhower proposed only a modest school bill in 1959. Declaring himself against outright grants, he called for assistance to local school districts over a 30–35-year period to pay interest and principal on local district construction bonds. The cost was estimated at $85 million per year, or $2 billion over the 30–35-year amortization period.

Liberal Democrats again ignored the Eisenhower proposal, and the House Education and Labor Committee reported a bill to provide $1.1 billion for construction and teachers' salaries over four years. But the House Rules Committee, still dominated by conservatives, refused to bring the bill to the floor. The Senate Labor and Public Welfare Committee reported a similar bill, calling for $1 billion in grants for construction only over two years, such grants to be matched by the states and with an equalization formula granting three times as much to the

* Public Law 85–864, Section 101. The NDEA was not the first legislation benefiting education passed for reasons other than the merits of education as such. The GI Bill and support to secondary schools impacted by defense installations, both of which began in 1946, are good examples. Fred and Grace Hechinger have pointed out that the tradition is even more venerable: the ostensible reason for passing an education-aid bill in Massachusetts in 1647 was to thwart "that old deluder, Satan" who keeps "men from the knowledge of the Scriptures." *Growing Up in America* (New York: McGraw-Hill, 1975), p. 17.

poorest states as to the wealthiest. No action was taken on this bill on the Senate floor in 1959.

In 1960 the Senate passed the bill reported in 1959, 51–34, with amendments that broadened the grants to cover teachers' salaries and the formula changed to provide $20 per school-age child for two years. An amendment to include the Eisenhower debt-service scheme in the bill was defeated.

In the House, the Education and Labor Committee reported, and the Rules Committee sent to the floor, a straight construction bill providing for $1.3 billion in grants without any equalization formula. Again, the antisegregation amendment tactic was attempted, with liberals opposing such an amendment and Republicans voting overwhelmingly for it. But this time there were enough votes to pass the bill as amended, despite Southern and Republican opposition. The final vote was 206–189.

The conservatives nonetheless had the last parliamentary laugh. Since the House construction bill differed from the Senate construction and teachers' salary bill, a conference was necessary. The Rules Committee, consisting of eight Democrats and four Republicans, voted 7–5 against authorizing a conference. All four Republicans, plus Chairman Howard Smith and his conservative Democratic colleagues William M. Colmer of Mississippi and James W. Trimble of Arkansas, blocked the final steps to ironing out the differences between the bills passed by clear majorities in the House and Senate.

Advocates of Federal aid were confident that parliamentary tricks would not stop an aid bill in 1961. There was encouragement from the narrow defeat in 1960, plus new promises of full support from the Kennedy administration. The autocratic power of Chairman Smith's Republican-Southern coalition in the Rules Committee had been diluted by changing the composition of the committee from 8 Democrats and 4 Republicans to 10 Democrats and 5 Republicans; the change, narrowly approved in a House vote, gave liberal Democrats an 8–7 margin over the Republicans and Southerners. Congressman Adam Clayton Powell, now chairman of the House Education and Labor Committee, promised not to push for his antisegregation amendment. And Abraham Ribicoff, Kennedy's Secretary of Health, Education and Welfare, mollified Southerners by promising that he would not withhold aid from segregated districts unless directed to do so by Congress.

In his first State of the Union Message in 1961, Kennedy noted that "our classrooms contain 2 million more children than they can properly have room for, taught by 90,000 teachers not properly qualified to teach."[40] A month later he sent to Congress a message on education, calling for passage of an omnibus bill that would provide a three-year program of aid for construction and teachers' salaries at the elementary and secondary levels, an extension of NDEA and funds for loans for college construction and scholarships. At the secondary level, aid would not be provided for church schools, "in accordance with the clear prohibition of the Constitution," and church-school pupils would not be counted in determining allocations among the states.[41]

A bill providing for $2.5 billion in grants for construction and teachers' salaries was passed in the Senate, 49–34. Senator Wayne Morse of Oregon, the floor manager, staved off fifteen amendments designed to raise civil rights and religious issues or otherwise to cripple the bill.

Conservative Republicans and Southern Democrats then began courting Catholic members of the House. In reaction to these maneuvers, a counterstrategy was devised whereby a bill would be reported renewing NDEA, extending its "loan" provisions for private schools to cover English and physical fitness as well as science, mathematics and foreign languages, and providing also for loans for construction of classrooms in which such subjects would be taught. Parochial schools thus would be aided in areas deemed crucial to "national defense."

The House Education and Labor Committee, under Powell, reported a construction and salary bill similar to the one passed in the Senate, but a majority of the Rules Committee—the conservative diehards plus two Catholic Democrats, James Delaney of New York and future Speaker Thomas P. O'Neill of Massachusetts—voted to hold the bill up until the Education and Labor Committee had reported out the NDEA extension bill with the private-school loan features. The theory was that both measures should be considered together, or the public-aid bill might be passed alone without the NDEA sweeteners.

The Education and Labor Committee did report a bill extending NDEA and providing for $275 million in long-term, low-interest loans to private schools for classrooms where "defense" subjects could be taught. The Rules Committee nonetheless tabled both bills, the five Republicans, the reactionary Democrats Smith and Colmer, and Delaney, dissatisfied with the "loan" provisions of the NDEA extension, voting to table.

A month later, Congressman Powell attempted to bring a one-year bill for construction grants to the floor under the "calendar Wednesday" procedure, which would have avoided Rules Committee action. The bill lost 242–170, with many normally liberal Congressmen, disgusted with the whole wrangle, voting against it.

Thus, the near-miss of 1960 had become a debacle in 1961, a resounding defeat for Kennedy and a mockery of the supposed reform of the Rules Committee. One observer predicted that the defeat meant that general Federal aid "was to be dead not just for the Eighty-seventh Congress, but probably for the decade of the 1960s."[42]

The Elementary and Secondary Education Act of 1965

An attempt to pass a general aid bill—or more precisely a substitute for a general aid bill—was not made until 1965, when President Johnson pushed the Elementary and Secondary Education Act through the Congress as part of his Great Society program. The accomplishment was an enormous one; despite the pessimism after 1961, Johnson succeeded in persuading the Congress to pass the most comprehensive educational aid measure in the nation's history.

Many factors account for the victory, ranging from the new spirit of religious ecumenism after Pope John XXIII and Vatican II to the "message" of the Johnson electoral landslide in 1964. This message was not lost, for example, on the freshman Congressmen who had defeated Republicans in the wake of Johnson's election; every one of them voted for ESEA.

The civil-rights issues had also been defused a year earlier with passage of the Civil Rights Act of 1964. With the Congress at long last on record against racial discrimination, there was no longer pressure inextricably to bind antisegregation provisions into an education bill.

But the two principal factors leading to the passage of ESEA would appear to be the changes that took place in the public perception of education and the exercise of firm Presidential leadership.

As noted, complacency about the status quo in education had shored up conservative opposition to Federal aid before 1965. The Johnson administration challenged this unspoken complacency by emphasizing the link between educational deprivation and poverty, a link that cost the taxpayers money.

"We now spend about $450 a year per child in our public schools," President Johnson said in a Special Message to Congress in January 1965. "But we spend $1,800 a year to keep a delinquent youth in a detention home, $2,500 a year for a family on relief, $3,500 a year for a criminal in state prison."

Lack of education was the "tap root" of poverty and, "just as ignorance breeds poverty, poverty all too often breeds ignorance in the next generation."

Unemployment of young people with an eighth-grade education or less was four times the national average; jobs for high-school graduates rose by 40 percent between 1955 and 1965, but declined by nearly 10 percent for those with less than a high-school education.[43]

Educational deprivation was not only an abstract failure of the American dream but an economic phenomenon expensive in dollars and cents. Education was at last seen as an essential means of breaking the shackles of poverty and the vicious cycle in which the undereducated, at the bottom of the economic ladder, bred and raised undereducated children to take their places on the welfare rolls.*

Secretary of Health, Education and Welfare Anthony J. Celebrezze estimated in 1965 that, of 48 million school-age children, 5 million came from families with annual incomes less than $2,000 and 10 million from families with annual incomes less than $3,000.[44]

In 1963, an influential private group, the Committee for the Support of the Public Schools, headed by Mrs. Agnes E. Meyer, had issued a comprehensive report on the state of education that supported the education-poverty link. The Committee concluded:

> The evidence is compelling that lack of schooling and poor schooling are associated with such social problems as low earning capacity, unemployment, rejection from military service, and dependence upon public relief in its various forms. . . . One of the priorities that must be included in a realistic program to eliminate, or at least sharply reduce, the mounting numbers on relief rolls is adequate educational opportunity for every child in the United States. . . .
>
> Educational action to these ends is fully justified solely on the basis

* As Congressman Andrew Jacobs (Democrat, Indiana) said in the House debate on ESEA: "I recall that Abraham Lincoln once said: 'All that I am or ever hope to be, I owe to my Angel Mother.' But what if, in a cultural sense, one's mother were not an angel? What would he be or ever hope to be?" 111 *Congressional Record* (1965), p. 5742.

of our commitment to equality of opportunity. There is the additional fiscal consideration that it will probably cost less to provide adequate schooling for all than to pay for the rising relief expenditures, which are at least in part due to lack of such schooling.[45]

A year later Henry Ford II echoed the Meyer Committee's conclusions. He called for a "fresh approach" to educational problems, noting that "low income and lack of education tend to feed upon each other and to perpetuate themselves." He called the role of schools "crucial," and he observed:

Today, it is clear that the schools in our poorest communities and neighborhoods are not able to do their jobs as well as they must. Part of the reason is that many of the schools that have the biggest educational problems also have the most limited educational resources. The result is that youngsters who get the least stimulation and encouragement from their homes and families and friends often get the least from their schools, when they need the most.[46]

The Johnson linkage of poverty and education thus built on substantial learning that had gone before, going back, indeed, to Senator Taft's justification for Federal aid in 1948.* But, more important, it gave a new focus to the legislative effort, cutting through the trite and overworked arguments that had been made for aid ever since World War II and appealing to American "selfish and altruistic" sensibilities as well.

But Johnson was not content with merely simple appeals. If President Eisenhower did not get up and make statements every twenty minutes, President Johnson did precisely that, at least in private, as he cajoled the Congressional barons.

And, as important as anything, he insisted that his subordinates do their homework. Secretary Celebrezze and Education Commissioner Francis Keppel were instructed to hammer out an acceptable compromise on the church-school issue well before ESEA was sent to Congress. Celebrezze and Keppel succeeded, getting the National Catholic Welfare Conference representatives and the National Education Association to agree on a formula whereby children attending parochial schools would be permitted access to facilities and services provided under the bill (on nonparochial-school premises) and bringing parochial edu-

---

* See p. 85, *supra.*

cators into the local decision-making process on programs for deprived children.

Regional jealousies were also ameliorated by gearing payments in each state to the per pupil expenditure in that state.

Despite warnings by the likes of Congressman Howard Smith that ESEA was a "crown of thorns placed upon the heads of the mothers and local people"[47] of America, ESEA passed the House 263–153 and the Senate 73–18.

The Johnson negotiations had worked. ESEA was, as then Congressman Hugh Carey (Democrat, New York) observed, "the result of the evolution of Federal-aid proposals going back nearly 20 years in search of a workable approach."[48]

In addition to the commitment to deprived children in Title I, ESEA had four other titles: Title II, which provided support for the purchase of textbooks and instructional materials (including materials for students in parochial and private schools); Title III, which provided for supplementary centers and services to draw on community resources other than the schools in improving education; Title IV, under which regional educational laboratories to foster basic educational research were to be established; and Title V, which was to provide assistance to state educational departments to upgrade their administrative performance.

Much of the ESEA program has atrophied since enactment. Eighteen Federally funded research centers established under Title IV, envisioned as being crash facilities like the wartime atomic-energy laboratories, have suffered from lack of continuity in funding and have not had funds available to apply research results.

A total of $1.4 billion has been spent on community innovations under Title III, "yet a decade . . . later we know little more than we did [in 1965] about what 'innovation' really is, how to bring it about and how to catalyze it on a grand scale."[49] And funds for textbooks and instructional materials under Title II have been inconsistently appropriated.

The enduring part of ESEA has been Title I, which was originally funded at $959 million for fiscal 1966, with appropriations growing over the years to $2.28 billion for fiscal 1978. But more about Title I funding in the next chapter.

Five · Congress at Work: Aid to Education, 1965 and After

Let's get started . . . and get a bill through here, and begin to get some money into our school systems where we now know it is badly needed, and then we can take another good look and get closer to the goal that both you and I want; and we make no bones about it, that we want a general education bill.

—ANDREW BIEMILLER, chief
Congressional lobbyist of
the AFL-CIO (1965)[1]

In the drive to pass the Elementary and Secondary Education Act in 1965, many problems were swept under the rug. President Johnson had to hold his coalition together; there would be time later to address subsidiary questions and refine the Congress' answers:

1. How should Title I funds be allocated?
2. What should the level and timing of Title I appropriations be?
3. What should the accountability standards for state and local use of Title I funds be?
4. How does Federal funding relate to school desegregation?
5. What is the Federal government's role in promoting uniformity of school expenditures?

Questions such as these were left to future action by the Congress. As long as they were unanswered, and as long as annual appropriations to fund Title I were required—as they inevitably were—the battles of 1965 and before could be refought.

The role of Congress before ESEA was to reach agreement on the basic parameters of Federal assistance. The role since 1965 has been that of financier and overseer—determining the funding levels for Title I and who gets the money and under what conditions.

A detailed analysis of this latter role shows Congress to have behaved in cumbersome fashion in dealing with questions of funding and allocation. It also shows the Congress either unable or unwilling to tackle the difficult questions of school desegregation and inequality of expenditure among school districts or states. Given the legislative vacuum on these vital issues, it is necessary to complete the picture by analyzing the attempt of the courts—Federal and state—to come to terms with these difficult aspects of the basic problem.

FORMULA POLITICS

By its specific terms, Title I of ESEA is designed "to provide financial assistance . . . to local educational agencies serving areas with concentrations of children from low-income families to expand and improve their educational programs by various means . . . which contribute particularly to meeting the special educational needs of educationally deprived children."[2]

To build a coalition to get ESEA passed in 1965, it was necessary to devise an allocation formula that disbursed the funds appropriated for Title I over a wider area than would have been the case if the formula had more efficiently targeted aid to districts "with concentrations of children from low-income families." Fortunately, the largest share of the funds appropriated reached those districts most in need.[3] But the leakage was not inconsiderable and, indeed, it is estimated that almost 95 percent of the nation's school districts have received at least some Title I assistance. Coupled with chronic underfunding, the result has hardly represented a maximum concentration of resources on the deprivation problem, which Title I was supposed to attack.

An examination of the 1965 Title I formula and its subsequent evolution is instructive, as it illustrates the pressures and the political trading involved in working out a formula under which large amounts of Federal funds are allocated. "Targeting"—the provision of program funds to the areas where they are most needed—is a fashionable word in Washington at the moment, as proposals fly about to "target" aid to areas of chronic unemployment and decaying urban centers, for example. The experience with Title I indicates that efficient "targeting" of specific programs may not be easy.

Governor Hugh Carey of New York once remarked that Federal grant-in-aid formulas are devised in Congress with "a Chinese abacus locked away in a vault in the Southern Caucus."[4]

The formula for allocating Title I funds among the states (and among local school districts within a state) is, however, far from being a random calculation worked out on an abacus. It is a distilled manifestation of political power.

The allocation formula in use since 1965 looks basically simple:

State Allocation = Federal Percentage times
Per Pupil Expenditure
times Counted Children*

But the original definition of the elements of the formula, and subsequent adjustments since 1965, have had profound effects on how Title I dollars have been spread among the nation's schools.

The key element to understanding the formula is that it is a means of allocating a fixed sum of dollars—the amount appropriated by Congress each year for Title I—and not a means of distributing aid without any limitation.

For example, assume that the Federal percentage is 40 (which it is today), that the per pupil expenditure in state X is $1,000 and that there are 500,000 counted children (i.e., poor children) in state X. If the Title I formula measured entitlements, the school districts in state X would be entitled to receive an aggregate of $200 million (.40 x $1,000 x 500,000). Assuming for the moment that all states were in exactly the same situation as state X (same per pupil expenditure, same number of counted children), Congress would have to appropriate $10 billion ($200 million x 50) to "fully fund" Title I or to give each state its full entitlement under the formula.

But Congress has not appropriated, and is not about to appropriate,

---

* Although the reader may not believe it, the discussion that follows has been simplified to eliminate features of the allocation process for certain Title I funds, which do not affect the allocation for the largest portion of Title I funds. Even as "simplified," the analysis of the Title I formula remains complex, because the Title I formula itself is exceedingly complex. Accidentally so, as the result of political compromises? Deliberately so, to mask policy decisions inconsistent with the stated objectives of Title I? Probably a little of both. Let the reader decide.

$10 billion for Title I. A figure of $3 billion is more realistic and, on this basis, there would be 30 cents available to distribute for each dollar of allocation ($3 billion of appropriations divided by $10 billion of allocation). State X thus would receive $60 million rather than the $200 million calculated under the formula.

The name of the formula game for state X is thus to maximize its allocation—to have the highest per pupil expenditure and the greatest number of counted children possible—so that its share of the finite Title I pie will likewise be maximized. If the allocations of other states can be reduced in the process, so much the better; this, too, serves to increase state X's share of the pie.

Since the formula is the vehicle for distributing a limited aggregation of resources, every element of it is an expression of political power, and an exercise of power that may or may not accord with the Title I policy objective of aiding "local educational agencies serving areas with concentrations of children from low-income families."

One should note before getting to the intricacies of the formula that the presumed beneficiaries of assistance—educationally deprived children—are not necessarily the recipients of the assistance, for aid is targeted to local districts "with concentrations of children from low-income families." The number of "children from low-income families" measures the amount of assistance received, but once received by the local district it may be used for "educationally deprived children" without reference to family income.

This discrepancy results from the basic assumption that "educationally deprived children" are more likely to be found among "children from low-income families." By making this assumption, Congress avoided the necessity of requiring a means test for each child admitted to a local Title I program, and a requirement that both educational deprivation *and* poverty be demonstrated in the case of each child. Better to measure poverty on an aggregate statistical basis—number of children from low-income families—than on an individual basis.* The

* The equation between educational deprivation and poverty is obviously an inexact one; there are plenty of children with learning problems who do not come from poor families. In 1974, Congressman James G. O'Hara, representing a blue-collar suburban district in Michigan, noted that an Office of Education study had found that two thirds of pupils with persistent reading problems came from families with incomes in excess of $3,000 per year. He unsuccessfully proposed an amendment to ESEA under which funds would be distributed two thirds on the basis of low income, one third on the basis of school population. The end result, of course, would have been to disfavor poorer areas. 120 *Congressional Record* (1974), pp. 8244 ff.

cry of "Federal interference" would surely be raised if inquiries were made into each school child's family income. And rightly so.

"Per Pupil Expenditure"

If all "areas with concentrations of children from low-income families" had similar expenditure and taxing patterns, the per-pupil-expenditure concept in the formula would not be necessary. A flat grant could be made for each child from a low-income family, without regard to location. But expenses in an urban school district are likely to be greater than in a one-room school on an Indian reservation. And some states spend more on education than others, because the state has more wealth to spend or because its citizens desire to spend more. Thus, in 1965 a flat grant of $100 per poor child would have equaled almost 50 percent of the amount spent on each child in Mississippi, 33 percent of such amount in Texas and 20 percent of such amount in New York.[5]

The compromise reached in 1965 was to base each state's allocation on its own per pupil expenditure. As a result no state could really complain that it was being shortchanged. The "wealthy" states were not seen as subsidizing the poorer states.

Congresswoman Edith Green (Democrat, Oregon) criticized this concept, declaring that the poorer states, which spent less on education because of their lesser incomes, should receive relatively more assistance. But the House leaders were unsympathetic to an amendment she proposed to tilt the formula in favor of the poorer states. Many supporters of the amendment hoped by such support to defeat ESEA, Congressman James G. O'Hara (Democrat, Michigan) warned, adding that this might "not be a vain hope." Noting that the Green amendment would substantially reduce allocations to New York and California, he said that "these States have large delegations and their interest in this amendment is obvious." His warning was blunt:

> This is a good bill. This is the best formula that could be obtained for the South and for everyone else. If we want this bill we had better protect this formula.[6]

After passage of ESEA, the formula was in fact changed by Congress in 1966 to provide that a state's allocation would be based on the *higher* of the state's own per pupil expenditure and the national average per pupil expenditure. The "poorer" half of the states were thus able to raise their allocations.

A major revision of the formula in 1974 placed an upper limit on the amount of a state's per pupil expenditure taken into account in the formula. Before 1974, as a state raised its expenditures for education, its allocation increased. Thus New York, with an average per pupil expenditure 150 percent above the national average, was able to increase its share of the Title I pie. The 1974 amendments to ESEA limited a state's per pupil expenditure for purposes of the formula to the lesser of its actual per pupil expenditure and 120 percent of the national per pupil expenditure. At the same time, the lower limit was set at the higher of a state's actual per pupil expenditure and 80 percent of the national average per pupil expenditure.*

The per-pupil-expenditure part of the formula, based as it is on statewide averages, makes no allowance for the "overburden" dilemma of most urban areas in the United States. Municipal "overburden" has come to be recognized as one of the most difficult of contemporary urban problems. Most local governments, urban or rural, raise revenues to provide local services, including education, from the real-property tax. In nonurban jurisdictions, a higher percentage of property tax revenues can be devoted to education because other services—police and fire protection and sanitation, for example—are less costly. Cities, on the other hand, must provide relatively more expensive services with property-tax revenues, leaving less of such revenues for spending on education; urban property-tax revenues are thus said to be "overburdened."[7] Neither this inability to spend more for education nor the probable fact that education for the disadvantaged is more costly is reflected in the basic Title I allocation.

The report of President Nixon's Task Force on Education, a report prepared before Nixon took office in 1969, called "the failure of education in most of our larger cities . . . one of the nation's most serious domestic problems." This report cited a host of reasons for this:

---

* If the new ceiling had been applied fully to a high-spending state like New York, the New York allocation (and resulting share of Title I funds) would have been drastically reduced. However, the 1974 amendments contained a "hold harmless" clause, which provided that no state should receive less in any fiscal year than 85 percent of the amount received in the preceding year. Thus the initial reduction for New York was limited to 15 percent—drastic, but not as drastic as if New York were subjected to the full impact of the new ceiling all in one year.

a general shortage of funds in relation to the special problems faced by urban educational systems, the frequently inequitable distribution of state funds to the cities and, in some cities, unequal allocation of funds between poorer and better-off neighborhoods; the influx to the cities of children with educational deficiencies acquired elsewhere; massive inflexible and anachronistic bureaucracies for the administration of urban education that deny the possibility of a supportive community relationship to the schools; the difficult home conditions of urban children from poverty backgrounds; the irrelevancy of educational programs and curricula; poor teaching; and many others.[8]

Just as Nixon ignored the report of his Task Force,* the Congress has been slow, in revising the Title I formula, to recognize urban realities.†

"Counted Children"

Determining the other inputs to the allocation formula is relatively simple compared with the problem of calculating the number of "children from low-income families." America may be good at figuring out how many citizens watched a particular television sitcom on the preceding evening or calibrating the flying time to the moon in fractions of a second, but it does not seem very good at counting its poor people on anything like a current basis.

As originally enacted, the basic component of "Counted Children" was the number of children of ages five to seventeen coming from families with incomes less than $2,000, as counted in the 1960 census.

Such a base had obvious flaws. A single child from a family with an

* See p. 177 fn.
† In February 1978, President Carter proposed an increase in the Title I appropriation for fiscal 1979 of 15 percent and also proposed earmarking $400 million of Title I assistance for school districts with more than 5,000 poor children or with school populations consisting of more than 20 percent poor children. Such aid would benefit larger urban districts—but not exclusively. The 20 percent test (which is not based on any minimum total of children) would divert 33 percent of the new money to rural and suburban districts. *Elementary and Secondary Education, Message to the Congress,* February 28, 1978. The House, in July 1978, authorized the $400 million additional expenditures to be allocated as the President had suggested, with the additional proviso that at least 1.5 percent of the new "concentration" funds must go to each state. The actual amounts of these "concentration" moneys available will, of course, in any event depend on annual appropriations based on the $400 million authorization.

income of $1,999 would be counted in the formula; nine children from a family with an income of $2,001 would not be. And, even though great population shifts might have occurred since 1960, or local economies might have deteriorated to the point of pushing more families below the $2,000 cutoff, the 1960 yardstick was still used. Indeed, the 1960 figures were still being used in fiscal 1973, even though every child counted in the 1960 census had by then graduated from or left secondary school!

The Congress (and the Executive Branch before it) searched to find a means of updating the 1960 census figures. Poverty determinations were new in 1965, and the closest to a current index available were statistics as to Aid for Dependent Children (AFDC) payments in the states. Despite widely varying AFDC payment levels and eligibility standards in the various states, it was thought that increases in AFDC recipients would identify increased "concentrations of children from low-income families" and provide a correcting and continuing adjustment to the 1960 census figures. Accordingly, children from families receiving AFDC payments in excess of $2,000 were also included in the formula. The assumption was that children from families receiving AFDC payments of less than $2,000 were already included in the figures based on the census—a perfectly valid assumption in 1960, but an increasingly less valid one as the census figures became more stale.[9]

Twice before 1974, the Congress had raised the income cutoff for Title I, first to $3,000 and then to $4,000. Congressmen pointed with pride to these "expansions" of ESEA to cover more poor children. But the new cutoffs in fact never applied, because the amending legislation in each case provided that the states must get their full allocations using the $2,000 cutoff before funds were distributed on the new basis. The amounts appropriated for Title I never came close to "fully funding" the states' allocations on the basis of the $2,000 formula, so the trumpeted "increased coverage" the Congress enacted was a fiction.

The sleeper in the Title I formula was the AFDC factor. In fiscal 1966, only 10 percent of "Counted Children" were included on the basis of AFDC payments, the totals being 4.9 million counted from the 1960 census and 0.6 million counted on the basis of AFDC payments in excess of $2,000. In fiscal 1973, the 1960 census count of 4.9 million children was still being used, but the number of AFDC children counted had risen to 3.2 million. Then, in fiscal 1974, when 1970 census data were available for the first time, the number of children from families with incomes less than $2,000 had declined to 2.6 million and the number of AFDC children had risen to 3.6 million.

Increases in the number of AFDC children dramatically inflated the allocations of those states making high AFDC payments.

To see how this worked, Mississippi had no "Counted Children" included on the basis of AFDC in fiscal 1966 because it did not make any AFDC payments to families in excess of $2,000. In fiscal 1973, it still had not added to its count, because its AFDC payments (averaging $52.94 per month) still did not exceed $2,000. New York, by contrast, made AFDC payments at the generous average rate of $284.76 per month, and added 466,000 children to its count on the basis of AFDC payments between 1966 and 1973.[10]

With New York receiving 18 percent of all Title I money in fiscal 1974, and five states receiving almost 40 percent, "adjustment" of the formula was inevitable when the Congress extended ESEA in 1974.

In 1974 the Congress adopted a new income cutoff based on a variable dollar amount derived from the Orshansky index of poverty.* For good measure, the Congress provided that only two thirds of AFDC children were to be counted for purposes of the formula.

This revision penalized the states with the most generous welfare programs—the "wealthiest" states, as they were consistently referred to in the Congressional debates. Since the Orshansky index takes into account such factors as family size, the inflexibility of the fixed $2,000 cutoff was eliminated. But the higher cutoff, averaging $5,038 in 1974, meant that more children from the 1970 Census were included as "Counted Children." It also meant that fewer children would be added on the basis of AFDC payments, since even the wealthiest states had many fewer children from families receiving AFDC payments at the rate above the new cutoff.†

* The Orshansky index was developed by Mollie Orshansky of the Social Security Administration in 1964 and, as subsequently refined, was adopted by the Office of Management and Budget as the official index of poverty in 1969. The index is really a series of 124 indices (or cutoffs) based on family size, number of children, age and sex of the head of household, and farm or nonfarm residence. The indices are based on food expenditures and are revised annually on the basis of changes in the Consumer Price Index. The Orshansky index has been studied and restudied and accused of many shortcomings, such as not taking into account differentials in housing costs in rural and urban areas, but as yet has not been supplanted by an index generally agreed to be superior. The weighted average cutoff for a nonfarm family of four was $6,200 in 1978.

† The House, in voting on an extension of ESEA in July 1978, restored the inclusion of 100 percent of AFDC children in the formula count. With ever-higher

FUNDING

The battles over ESEA were concerned with the *authorization* of Federal funds for educational assistance. But the passage of ESEA and its periodic extensions would not have put one dime in the hands of local school districts without *appropriations* of funds pursuant to ESEA's authorizations.

The appropriations process has provided another battleground for the foes of Title I. Battles lost in the authorization process can be refought each year as appropriations are considered. This has in fact taken place. Antibusing riders that have been defeated in deliberations over ESEA have been successfully attached to appropriations bills; indeed, the severest Congressional legislation on busing was a rider to the fiscal 1978 Health, Education and Welfare appropriation bill.* And priorities acknowledged by Congress—such as the education of deprived children under Title I—can be rearranged in the annual struggle to allocate Federal funds among the demands of competing programs.

Starting with fiscal 1966, appropriations for Title I have been as follows:

Fiscal year	(in millions)
1966	$ 959
1967	1,053
1968	1,191
1969	1,123
1970	1,339
1971	1,500
1972	1,598
1973	1,810
1974	1,719
1975	1,876
1976	1,900
1977	2,050
1978	2,285

poverty cutoffs, due to inflation, it is uncertain how much the restored count will benefit the "wealthy" states in the future.

The bill passed by the House also provided that future appropriations exceeding the amount appropriated for fiscal 1979 are to use the Bureau of the Census 1976 Survey of Income and Education, rather than the 1970 census, in allocating such excess funds.

* See p. 116, *infra*.

This history shows not only two absolute year-to-year decreases, but, after giving effect to inflation, funding levels in at least three additional years (depending on the measure of inflation) were less, in real dollar terms, than in the previous year.

By failing to increase appropriations and to take inflation into account, local Title I programs, once begun, are often curtailed, and the number of children served by them decreases. In fiscal 1973, for example, an estimated 6.7 million children participated in Title I programs; by fiscal 1976 that number had shrunk to 5.5 million, a contraction which the National School Boards Association declared unjustifiable "in either human or fiscal terms since the program is such an obvious means for reducing the future problems of today's nine million poverty-based children."[11]

It is small wonder that many poor parents, desperate as they are to have their children succeed, are reluctant to have them participate in Title I programs, such as special reading classes, for fear that the programs will be summarily discontinued in subsequent years.[12]

Nor is it a great surprise that variations in funding have thwarted the long-range planning efforts of local school districts, in view of the uncertainty of such local districts as to the future availability of funds and the impact of changes in the allocation formula, as earlier discussed.*

Until the appropriation for fiscal 1976, Title I funds were appropriated for the fiscal year then in progress, meaning that often a school district did not know for certain how much money it would receive for its school year until that year was nearly over. In the September 1974–June 1975 school year, for example, the Office of Education made final adjustments in allotments on May 13, 1975, and notified the various state agencies. With luck, the final figures reached local districts before their deprived children were released for the summer.[13]

Such timing, of course, runs absolutely counter to the workings of a well-managed school district. Either local law or sound management would dictate that plans for a school year beginning in September be made during the *prior* spring. Budgets must be adopted and often approved by voters; programs must be planned and coordinated; teachers

---

* Once appropriations are made, still another hurdle to delivery of funds is "impoundment," or failure to spend funds appropriated, at the executive level. This problem was particularly acute in the Nixon administration.

must be hired; and books must be purchased, often after competitive bids have been let.

School boards are rightly reluctant to hire teachers for Title I programs before they are sure that funding for the full year will be available; indeed, in many states they are prohibited from doing so. It is simple common sense that the most desirable teachers will conclude their negotiations in the spring and will not be waiting around to be hired when the school year opens.

All of these problems have been compounded by a requirement contained in ESEA that ESEA funds may not be used for obligations incurred prior to the issuance of a grant.

From the inception of ESEA, educator after educator pleaded in Congressional hearings for advance funding for Title I so that effective planning to use Title I moneys could be undertaken.[14]

Until the fiscal year 1976 appropriation—which was made a year in advance—the Congressional timing of appropriations was at drastic odds with orderly local planning. By thwarting such planning, and later complaining about poor administration of Title I at the local level, Congress resembled the child who murders his parents and then seeks the mercy of the court because he is an orphan.

ACCOUNTABILITY

Despite the magnitude of Title I, ESEA originally contained no provision for establishing standards of accountability for recipients of Title I funds; it was feared that the teacher groups backing ESEA would desert the coalition if accountability standards were included. Only reluctantly, at the insistence of Senator Robert Kennedy (Democrat, New York), were vague provisions inserted requiring states to adopt "effective procedures, including provision for appropriate objective measurements of educational achievement . . . for evaluating at least annually the effectiveness of the programs in meeting the special educational needs of culturally deprived children."[15]

A decade later, the House Education and Labor Committee decried the total absence of nationally uniform evaluation standards and a nearly total lack of state standards. As a result, "it simply is not possible to come up with one uniform set of national statistics, or with State-wide statistics within most States, to measure the effectiveness" of Title I.

Calling this a "major failing" of the Office of Education, the Committee declared that the Federal administrators should have exercised "decisive leadership" years before in at least standardizing state and local reporting requirements.[16]

In the 1974 extension of ESEA, Congress authorized appropriations of $25 million for program evaluation and called for annual reports to the Congress by HEW on the "effectiveness" of ESEA, the "goals and specific objectives in qualitative and quantitative terms for all programs and projects," the "cost of benefits" of each program, and "plans for implementing corrective action" where that might appear necessary. The Commissioner of Education was further ordered to "develop and publish standards for evaluation of program or project effectiveness"—a requirement that would have been "politically unthinkable" a decade earlier.[17] The Republican minority in Congress predictably opposed this new attempt at accountability.*

OTHER MISCHIEF

Extensions of ESEA since 1965 have been voted by increasingly large margins in both houses of Congress.

"Along with votes for women, night baseball and the 40-hour week," Harold Howe has observed, "the basic desirability of federal money for the schools has joined those formerly controversial issues that once threatened the Republic but that have now gained widespread acceptance."[18]

---

* In so doing, the Congressional Republicans ignored the very sound advice of Herbert Hoover. Asked to comment in 1949 on the limited bill to grant Federal aid to the most backward states, Hoover criticized the bill because "it is based upon involved economic calculations instead of upon certain specific standards of education which should be established." Hoover went on to say, in a statement the wisdom of which puts his ideological descendants to shame:

Such specific standards could be based upon the average educational performance of, say, 30 of the most forward states. These standards should include teachers' fitness and salaries, the hours of attendance, and facilities. An additional standard should be that of nondiscrimination with reference to race or religion. And these standards applied to the backward States will need to include another requirement. Some of the so-called educationally backward States are spending large sums on improvements such as highways, etc., which should be subordinated to the education of their children. These standards should not be difficult to determine through an appropriate independent commission. I use the term "average," as above, as a base, because it represents at any one time the real progress of the Nation in this field.

Quoted, 95 *Congressional Record* (1949), pp. A4054–4055.

This is not to say that rear-guard attempts have not been made to undo ESEA, many of which are highly ironic, given their authors.

As already noted, Title I got away from the general education aid concept, which had not met with success in the Congress, and concentrated on the needs of deprived children. Yet in 1967, many of the same conservatives who had strongly opposed general aid prior to 1965 proposed to amend the ESEA formula so that aid would be distributed on the basis of block grants to the states, with the states determining who should get the money. No longer would aid be based on the needs of children, for there would be no guarantee that the states would distribute aid to localities on the basis of need.

The proposed amendment, offered on the floor by Representative Albert Quie, a Minnesota Republican, would also have wiped out the compromise features of ESEA under which deprived children in parochial schools received assistance and not the parochial schools themselves. By channeling aid through the state governments, the approach threatened to "rekindle the flames of controversy over the church-state issue,"[19] since a substantial number of states were, and are, prohibited by state constitutions from providing any aid to parochial schools.

As the Boston *Globe* noted, the "Republican plan" for amending ESEA "would carry more weight if its principal backers were not men who had voted up, down and across practically every aid-to-education bill which has come up in the past decade."[20]

The Quie amendment was defeated, but attempts to change the focus of ESEA did not cease. Most notable was President Nixon's proposal in 1971 for "special revenue sharing" in education, which would, again, have remitted decision-making as to priorities to the states, enabling "officials to return to past practices of allocating funds on the basis of political power rather than demonstrable need."[21]

The move toward greater accountability would likewise have been thwarted. Local districts would have been required to publish their plans for using Federal funds, but would not have been required to submit such plans to any higher authority for approval.[22]

Nixon's proposal was ignored, as was President Ford's 1976 education-assistance plan. To Ford, the standards and premises of ESEA constituted "narrow and restrictive categorical programs," which "have made it more difficult for the schools to educate."

"We at the Federal level cannot know what is best for every school child in every classroom in the country," Ford declared. Therefore "greater responsibility and freedom" must be given to state and local governments.

Under the Ford plan, 75 percent of a state's allocation would have had to be spent on the educationally deprived and the handicapped, but the proposed legislation did not specify any allocation formula binding on a state.[23] A state would thus have been perfectly free to tilt its allocations to local districts toward the politically powerful suburbs and, once again, away from urban centers.

Other maneuvers have smacked more of P. T. Barnum than of statecraft and, one assumes, were designed for back-home consumption. Republican Congressman J. Arthur Younger's proposed amendment to substitute the word *Commissar* for "Commissioner" (of Education) each time it appeared in ESEA, for example.[24] Or Senator Everett McKinley Dirksen's proposal to solve the school drop-out problem by denying Federal aid to districts not strictly enforcing truancy laws.[25] Or Senator James Buckley's amendment, passed in 1974, giving parents and students access to student records[26]—a mischievous amendment compliance with which has been both costly and troublesome.

BUSING AND DESEGREGATION

In no area has the Congress been more demagogic or less effective than in its dealings with desegregation. As described earlier, cynical use of the race issue helped to delay Federal aid legislation for two decades. And every new extension of ESEA, and virtually every appropriation bill relating to ESEA, has involved a struggle over the emotional issue of desegregation.

The Department of Health, Education and Welfare, in administering ESEA funds, must comply with the mandatory provisions of Title VI of the Civil Rights Act of 1964, which prohibit recipients of Federal funds from discriminating and require the appropriate Federal agency to "effectuate" such prohibition.

Unlike a court, HEW may not order a school district to cease racial discrimination, but it may cut off ESEA funds if a local district does not take remedial action to get rid of discrimination. This in itself is a powerful sanction, and the last decade has seen a struggle to curb HEW's exercise of its powers, particularly with respect to busing.

In 1966 an amendment was adopted explicitly to express the policy that nothing in ESEA was meant to "*require* the assignment or transportation of students or teachers in order to overcome racial imbalance." A year later, the ESEA Amendments of 1967 provided that all rules, regulations and guidelines promulgated under ESEA were to be "uniformly applied and enforced throughout the fifty states."

Congressional conservatives sponsored an improvement on this "even treatment" amendment in 1970, when Senator John Stennis (Democrat, Mississippi) obtained passage in the Senate of an amendment requiring antisegregation standards under ESEA to "be applied uniformly in all regions of the United States without regard to the origin or cause of such segregation."

Stennis' amendment had the plausibility of fairness—what was good for the South should be good for the North. But what it would have done was reduce Federal compliance efforts to the lowest common denominator of the situation prevailing in a Northern inner-city school district that is all black, or nearly so, because of housing patterns (so-called *de facto* segregation). Since desegregation would be virtually impossible in such a district, the amendment's even-handed requirement would have prevented Federal compliance efforts in a district where segregation had been maintained by force of law (so-called *de jure* segregation).

The Stennis amendment was probably unconstitutional, but its potentially divisive and possibly devastating effect was avoided only by a somewhat specious statement in the Conference Report, as adopted by the House and the Senate, that the amendment simply meant that standards dealing with *de facto* segregation were to be consistently applied and standards dealing with *de jure* segregation were to be consistently applied.

In 1976, the constraints on HEW were tightened further. Use of Federal money to pay for transportation "in order to overcome racial imbalance" had earlier been prohibited. A "compromise" amendment to the HEW appropriations bill in 1976 offered by Democratic Majority Leader Robert C. Byrd went further and forbade ESEA funds to be "used to require, directly or indirectly, the transportation of any student to a school other than the school which is nearest the student's home . . . in order to comply with title VI of the Civil Rights Act of 1964."[27]

HEW, and the Department of Justice, split hairs over the interpretation of the Byrd Amendment,* which led to the most restrictive amendment yet adopted, in the fiscal 1978 HEW appropriations bill. Emboldened by Supreme Court decisions that held that movement of pupils between school districts was not constitutionally required to eliminate segregation,† "liberal" Democratic Senators Thomas Eagleton of Missouri and Joseph Biden of Maryland succeeded in pushing the amendment through the Senate Appropriations Committee. Its intent was to make sure that HEW would not go beyond the minimum Constitutional requirements set by the Court by compelling local school districts to meet higher standards in order to obtain ESEA funds. The amendment, which passed the committee 13–9 and later became part of the appropriations bill, added a new clause to the Byrd formulation as adopted in 1974:

> For the purpose of this section, an indirect requirement of transportation of students includes the transportation of students to carry out a plan involving the reorganization of the grade structure of schools, the pairing of schools or the clustering of schools, or any combination of grade restructuring, pairing, or clustering. The prohibition described in this section does not include the establishment of magnet schools.[28]

By limiting and prohibiting busing, the Supreme Court and the Congress together have effectively made integration impossible in most urban centers with inner-city concentrations of minority children, as in New York (67 percent minority enrollment), Chicago (70 percent), Detroit (81 percent), Baltimore (75 percent), the District of Columbia (96 percent), New Orleans (80 percent), St. Louis (72 percent), Memphis (71 percent) and Kansas City (68 percent).[29]

---

* In a 1977 memorandum, Drew S. Days III, Assistant Attorney General in charge of the Civil Rights Division, concluded that the amendment did not prohibit HEW from withholding funds from a school district that had perpetuated discrimination by adopting a neighborhood plan under which children were assigned to the nearest school for their grade. In his view, the amendment only limited what HEW could require in the remedial plans submitted by the local district in efforts to comply with Title VI. HEW could not require transportation beyond the neighborhood school in such remedial proposals, but could nonetheless reject "remedial plans which did not attempt to desegregate through pairing (with appropriate restructuring of grade levels and assignment of students to the closest school serving their grade level following grade restructuring) if such a properly constructed pairing plan would result in the greatest degree of desegregation of any possible remedial plan." The Days Memorandum is set out at 123 *Congressional Record* (1977), pp. S10908–109011.

† See pp. 123–24, *infra*.

Few issues are as specious as "busing." A cool, dispassionate assessment of busing of school children cannot be made without taking into account the following facts:

1. In rural and suburban areas, school children get to school by bus for reasons that have nothing to do with segregation; it is simply the most sensible means for children to get from their homes to school. An estimated 43.5 percent of the nation's school children (19 million) were "bused" in 1972 (not counting those riding public transportation) and had traditionally been so, and of this 43.5 percent, 3 percent were bused for racial reasons. While busing may be inconvenient, school children were bused more than 2 billion miles in 1972 for reasons wholly unrelated to segregation.[30]

2. "Busing" was not considered unsafe or unreasonable when used to *maintain* segregation prior to the *Brown* case. Indeed, integration often reduced the volume of busing, for it was no longer legally permissible to separate the races by means of busing.*

3. The ultimate threat of achieving desegregation by transportation policies is perhaps the most effective way for a Federal district court to persuade local authorities to devise and implement alternative desegregation plans. Without this weapon, compliance methods initiated by local educational authorities would be inhibited.

4. The power of courts to impose busing orders is not unfettered. The Supreme Court in 1974 upheld busing as a permissible remedy for lower courts to use in effecting desegregation but warned that "busing will not be allowed to significantly impinge on the educational process." And, in later decisions, interdistrict busing has not been permitted by the Court.

5. In situations where there has been patient local leadership and adequate preparation, "busing," however reluctantly used, has been a success in achieving peaceful desegregation. Despite the hue and cry raised at the outset, desegregation plans involving busing have proved workable in such cities as Charlotte, North Carolina, and Pontiac, Michigan.[31]

---

* Before integration, there were a black school and a white school in rural New Kent County, Virginia, for 740 black students and 550 white students. Since black and white residents were scattered throughout the county, eleven buses were used to take the black students to the black school and ten buses were used to transport whites along overlapping and crisscrossing routes. See *Green v. County School Board of New Kent County,* 391 U.S. 430 at 432 (1968).

"Busing" is a convenient mask for making opposition to desegregation respectable. But one would never sense this from reading the grave debates in the *Congressional Record*. The straight words of Vice President Mondale were considered electrifying in 1972, when he dared to say on the floor of the Senate that Emperor Busing had no clothes:

> Let us just be candid with ourselves and with the American people for once on this issue of school desegregation.
>
> Busing is the way the overwhelming majority of school children outside our central cities get to school. . . . The issue is not busing or racial balance. The issue is whether we will build on hopeful examples of successful integration to make school desegregation work—or endorse segregation on principle; whether we will help the courts to avoid educational mistakes—or leave them to face the complexities of school desegregation alone.[32]

It can be argued that the Congress properly provides a forum for venting social frustrations. But surely one should expect the legislative branch of the national government to be more than a safety valve for pent-up antisocial feelings. The sad fact is that the Congress has abdicated resolution of one of the great social issues of contemporary America to the courts. Its members have consistently refused to make the solution of the desegregation problem a cooperative effort engaging the resources, energies and collective intelligence of the legislative as well as the judicial branches, remaining content to debate endlessly over the fake problem of "busing." The Congress, often aided and abetted by the President, has brought unhappy fulfillment to Adlai Stevenson's observation in 1956:

> I can think of no greater disservice to our country than to exploit for political ends the tensions that have followed in the wake of the Supreme Court [desegregation] decision.[33]

EDUCATION AND THE COURTS

A discussion of education is an appropriate place to say a word about the courts, for the field of education illustrates most clearly the vital institutional role of the courts in filling the void left by legislative failure.

Any contemporary analysis must start with the United States Supreme Court and *Brown v. Board of Education,* the Court's unanimous decision of 1954 invalidating segregation in American public schools.

The Fourteenth Amendment to the Federal Constitution, adopted in 1868, provides that no state may deny "to any person within its jurisdiction the equal protection of the laws." Section 5 of the Amendment further provides that "the Congress shall have power to enforce, by appropriate legislation, the provisions" of the Amendment.

Section 5 was meaningless in 1954 and remains so today, atrophied as it has been by

> the continuing influence of John C. Calhoun, whose mischievous device of the concurrent veto finds current expression in the Senate filibuster and the seniority rule in the organization of congressional committees, either of which is a sufficient barrier to legislative implementation of the fourteenth amendment. If the fourteenth amendment is to have meaning, the Court must provide it.[34]

In the absence of Congressional action, the "separate but equal" doctrine permitted segregated education under specific racial segregation laws or Constitutional provisions in seventeen states and the District of Columbia, and local option laws in four additional states. Forty percent of the nation's public-school children were subject to the "separate but equal" standard of the 1896 decision in *Plessy v. Ferguson*[35]—a case dealing specifically with segregated transportation but traditionally applied to public schools as well. Children could be separated on the basis of race so long as the education provided to each race was "equal."

The Supreme Court began chipping away at this concept as early as 1938, critically examining the "equality" of facilities offered to black law students and graduate students in a series of cases culminating in *Sweatt v. Painter* in 1950, where the Court unanimously held that the Texas law school established for blacks was inferior in both tangible and intangible respects to the facilities of the University of Texas Law School.[36] The *Sweatt* decision left little doubt that it would be virtually impossible for a state to provide separate professional facilities for blacks that would meet a standard of "equality."

In the 1952 term, the Court heard arguments in *Brown* and three companion cases, but was unable to reach a decision. Then, after reargument a year later, the final blow to "separate but equal" education was delivered on May 17, 1954. Regardless of comparability of facilities, the Court held flatly and unanimously that segregation was a denial of equal protection of the laws under the Fourteenth Amendment.*

Speaking through Chief Justice Earl Warren, the Court held that "in the field of public education the doctrine of 'separate but equal' has no place." It rejected lower court decisions before it, which had ordered local school boards to equalize facilities for white and black children but stopped short of prohibiting segregation, and which had found Negro and white schools "substantially equal" with respect to buildings, transportation, curricula and educational qualifications of teachers.

A year later, in *Brown II,* the Court discussed appropriate remedies. It held that "all provisions of federal, state, or local law requiring or permitting . . . discrimination must yield" to the principle that "racial discrimination in public education is unconstitutional," but recognized that implementation of this principle "may require solution of varied local school problems."

School authorities would have the "primary" responsibility for solving desegregation questions locally. And the local and district courts, with greater "proximity" to actual conditions, would judge whether school authorities were acting in good faith to implement desegregation.

Local authorities were put on notice that they would be held to a standard of good faith, that a "prompt and reasonable start" in desegregation was required, and that efforts must go forward "with all deliberate speed."[37]

Congressional reaction was predictable. The Justices were personally excoriated, and no legislation was passed to implement or support the *Brown* decision, to make the trauma of transition easier for the affected communities and the children of those communities. The only concrete Congressional response was a "Declaration of Constitutional Principles" issued in March 1956 and ultimately signed by 19 Senators and 176 representatives, pledging resistance to the decision by all "lawful means."[38]

Despite the lack of Congressional—and Presidential—support, the Federal courts generally continued to implement the basic principle

* In a related case, the Court held that segregation in the District of Columbia, to which the Fourteenth Amendment does not apply, was a violation of the Due Process Clause of the Fifth Amendment. *Bolling v. Sharpe,* 347 U.S. 497 (1954).

of *Brown*. District courts that took a dilatory attitude were reversed, most notably in the Fifth Circuit Court of Appeals, based in New Orleans, and the District of Columbia Circuit in Washington.[39] "Freedom of choice" plans that in practice maintained the status quo were rejected; the legitimacy of a "plan" to desegregate depended on whether such a plan "promises realistically to work, and promises realistically to work *now*." "Neutrality" was not enough if segregation remained: local school boards had "the affirmative duty to take whatever steps might be necessary to convert to a unitary system in which racial discrimination would be eliminated root and branch."[40] And as the years passed after *Brown,* the Supreme Court began to lose patience with dalliance passing for "deliberate speed." "The obligation of every school district is to terminate dual school systems *at once* and to operate now and hereafter only unitary schools," the Court observed in a 1969 *per curiam* decision.[41]

Two years later, the Burger Court unanimously upheld the use of busing as a tool to achieve desegregation. "Desegregation plans cannot be limited to the walk-in school," the Court declared in *Swann v. Charlotte-Mecklenburg Board of Education*. Other things being equal, it would be desirable to assign students to their neighborhood schools, but "all things are not equal in a system that has been deliberately constructed and maintained to enforce racial segregation."[42]

The Court also affirmed a district court decision declaring the North Carolina Anti-Busing Law, which prohibited "involuntary busing" to create racial balance, unconstitutional because it purported to prohibit absolutely the use of the busing remedy by the courts to implement *Brown*.[43]

The Supreme Court ceased to speak with one voice on desegregation in 1973. A harbinger of the future was a 4-4 decision (Justice Lewis F. Powell not participating) in a case involving a district court decree that had ordered the two county school districts surrounding Richmond, Virginia, combined with the Richmond district to achieve a "viable" racial mixture of students in the three districts.[44] No opinion was written, but the tie vote meant that the opinion of the Fourth Circuit, which had reversed the district court decree, was upheld.

Later in the 1973 term, the first dissenting opinion in a segregation case since 1954 was filed in a case involving the niceties of *de facto,* as opposed to *de jure,* segregation.

Beginning with *Brown,* the Court had held segregation based on specific laws or government action—*de jure* segregation—unconstitutional. But in 1973 it had not—and has not—decided the constitutionality of so-called *de facto* segregation, or segregation arising as the result of housing patterns or other factors not directly traceable to a specific law or pattern of governmental action.

Cases from Northern cities often presented a mixture of segregation, part of which might be called *de jure*, part *de facto*. As long as a majority of the Court was unwilling to condemn all segregation, fine distinctions would be required, and the Justices began quarreling over just such fine distinctions.*

In *Keyes v. Denver School District No. 1*,[45] for example, the Court in 1973 considered patterns of segregation in the City and County of Denver, Colorado, which operated as a single school district. In the racially mixed Park Hill section of Denver, segregation had been maintained not under a segregation law but through the manipulation of attendance zones and school site selection. But in the core city, such actions had not been required to maintain segregation, because of the minority population patterns in the core city. Segregation had thus existed *de jure* in Park Hill and *de facto* in the core city. Maintaining the *de facto/de jure* distinction, Justice William J. Brennan for the majority directed the District Court to determine whether Park Hill could logically be isolated from other areas in Denver. If not, the Court was to find whether segregation practiced in Park Hill made the entire school district a "dual system." If so, affirmative action to eliminate segregation on a citywide and countywide basis would be required. And, even if not, the active desegregation in Park Hill could be used to show the Board's "segregative intent" with respect to the core city schools.

Both Justice William O. Douglas and Justice Powell rejected the "*de facto/de jure*" distinction. Justice Powell called for a uniform standard nationwide, wherever segregation was found.

"Public schools are creatures of the State, and whether the segregation is state-created or state-assisted [*de jure*] or merely state-perpetuated [*de facto*] should be irrelevant to constitutional principle," he wrote.

---

* As one observer has sagely noted, the effect of segregation, be it *de jure* or *de facto,* is the same on the segregated child. Various state courts have had no difficulty in abolishing the distinction. See *Jackson v. Pasadena School District* (Sup. Ct. Calif. 1963), 382 P. 2d 878, and *Jenkins v. Township of Morris School District* (Sup. Ct. N.J. 1971), 279 A. 2d 619.

But Justice Powell had harsh words for advocates of excessive busing. He agreed that the lower courts should be free to utilize busing, but cautioned that there should be "a sound exercise of discretion" as to when busing was ordered and that courts should give more recognition to the "personal interest" in having children attend community schools near home. He did not advocate a prohibition on "court-ordered student transportation in furtherance of desegregation," but he urged that "the legitimate community interests in neighborhood school systems be accorded far greater respect."

Justice William H. Rehnquist, on the other hand, objected to any linking of the Denver School Board's segregation actions in Park Hill with the Denver district taken as a whole—thus providing the first full-blown dissent in a desegregation case in the Supreme Court since *Brown*.*

The consensus finally came completely apart in *Milliken v. Bradley* in 1974. The Federal district court in Detroit had been faced with the fact that desegregation within the confines of inner-city Detroit would not work. Under the most optimistic desegregation proposal, which involved massive busing, the schools of Detroit would still have been 75 to 90 percent black in most cases. And the district court feared that such a plan would encourage more "white flight," further altering the mix of roughly two thirds black students and one third white students in Detroit. The court thus proposed to develop a plan covering the Detroit metropolitan area. Such a plan would substantially reduce the amount of busing required and could be expected to achieve true desegregation, the overall student population in the area being 81 percent white and 19 percent black.[46]

The Circuit Court of Appeals had agreed with the district court, concluding that "any less comprehensive a solution than a metropolitan-area plan would result in an all-black school system immediately surrounded by practically all-white suburban school systems, [despite] an overwhelmingly white majority population in the total metropolitan area."

* Arguably the crack of dissent had come even earlier in *Wright v. Council of City of Emporia*, 407 U.S. 451 (1972), where Rehnquist and the other three Nixon appointees had dissented from a majority decision prohibiting the City of Emporia from establishing a separate school system within Greenville County, Virginia, because it would impede efforts to dismantle the dual school system in Greenville County. The Court of Appeals had held that the primary purpose of the change was "benign" and not a "cover-up" for discrimination.

The four Nixon appointees to the Court—Chief Justice Warren E. Burger and Justices Harry A. Blackmun, Powell and Rehnquist—and Justice Potter Stewart held in a 5–4 decision that, in the absence of a showing of unconstitutional segregation in the outlying districts, a metropolitan-area solution to relieve unconstitutional segregation in the inner-city district was not permissible. The majority supported the position of Nixon Solicitor General Robert H. Bork, and in the process rejected considerable evidence that district-by-district segregation was supported by actions of the State of Michigan (and not just local school boards), and the principles enunciated in *Brown II* that deference should be accorded to the lower courts with "proximity" to local problems and that the "revision of school districts and attendance areas" was a possible desegregation remedy.

The result, Justice Byron R. White argued, was to force the district court "to impose an intracity desegregation plan more expensive to the district, more burdensome for many of Detroit's Negro students, and surely more conducive to white flight than a metropolitan plan would be."

"Today's holding," Justice Thurgood Marshall, who had argued the original *Brown* case, added,

is more a reflection of a perceived public mood that we have gone far enough in enforcing the Constitution's guarantee of equal justice than it is the product of neutral principles of law. In the short run, it may seem to be the easier course to allow our great metropolitan areas to be divided up each into two cities—one white, the other black—but it is a course, I predict, our people will ultimately regret.

Only as subsequent decisions are announced will it be possible to assess the impact of *Milliken*. Unfortunately, the decision may signal a trend toward limiting the scope of remedies to erase segregation, both in terms of the geographic area covered and the means, such as busing, employed.*

Influenced by the Supreme Court's activist concern for education,

---

* In subsequent litigation a desegregation plan confined to the City of Detroit and emphasizing remedial reading and other such programs was upheld by the Supreme Court, *Milliken v. Bradley*, 433 U.S. 267 (1977), and a unanimous court (Justice Marshall not participating) found that the lower courts had fashioned a desegregation plan in Dayton, involving extensive busing, which exceeded the findings of desegregation within Dayton. *Dayton Board of Education v. Brinkman*, 433 U.S. 406 (1977).

state courts turned their attention to school problems other than desegregation, most notably inequities in local school finance.

The California Supreme Court, in the 1971 case of *Serrano v. Priest*,[47] held that education was a "fundamental interest" protected by the Equal Protection Clause of the Fourteenth Amendment and that the taxation scheme for supporting education in California deprived children in the poorer districts of their equal-protection rights. The Court noted that education in California was financed through a combination of local property taxes and state assistance. The property taxes were based on assessed value of district property, which ranged in 1968–69 from $3,706 per child in the Baldwin Park district in Los Angeles, where Serrano went to school, to $50,885 per child in Beverly Hills.

State assistance was designed to ensure that at least $355 would be spent for each child in California irrespective of local tax revenues. This was accomplished by providing for an "equalization" grant equal to the difference between $355 and the amount which could be raised locally on the basis of a $1 tax on each $100 assessed value of property. The state also made a flat grant of $125 per child, which was credited against the "equalization" amount or, if there was no equalization amount, paid outright. A district where assessed valuation was less than $12,500 per pupil could also obtain "supplemental" aid of $125 per pupil if it raised its tax rate in accordance with an incentive scheme. As a result, local school expenditures for elementary students ranged in 1969 from a low of $407 to a high of $2,586, with even the wealthiest districts being paid the $125 flat grant by the state.

The California court found that wealth was a "suspect classification" and that education was a "fundamental interest." These findings were of great importance. Under established Constitutional precedent, a governmental body has great leeway in making distinctions if a purely economic interest is at stake.

In the realm of economic regulation, a distinction drawn by a government is upheld if it bears "some rational relationship" to a "conceivable legitimate state purpose."

But the standard of judgment changes if the distinction that a government attempts to draw creates a "suspect classification" or involves a "fundamental interest." In this area a court will subject a standard to "strict scrutiny," with the government having the burden of showing a "compelling" interest for the distinction, and that the distinction is "necessary" to a legitimate governmental purpose.

The California court noted that the United States Supreme Court had shown a "marked antipathy" toward legislative classifications based on wealth, as in its decisions invalidating the poll tax or requiring the provision of a free transcript to an indigent defendant appealing his conviction. It also quoted from Chief Justice Earl Warren's opinion in *Brown* as to the importance of education and termed education a "fundamental interest" ranking with the right to vote and the rights of criminal defendants—both rights protected by the Supreme Court as "fundamental interests."

Having found that "strict scrutiny" applied to its determination, the court then reached the conclusion that California's pattern of educational finance denied children from poor districts the equal protection of the laws.

But the California court had misread the signals emanating from Washington. Two years later the Supreme Court held in a 6–3 decision in *San Antonio School District v. Rodriguez*[48] that education was not a "fundamental interest" for purposes of the Equal Protection Clause.

Justice Powell noted that Texas "virtually concedes" that the educational finance system at issue in *Rodriguez* could not withstand "the strict judicial scrutiny that this Court has found appropriate in reviewing legislative judgments that interfere with fundamental constitutional rights or that involve suspect classifications."

But the Mexican-American parents who were the plaintiffs in *Rodriguez* did not win. Analogies to the cases of indigent defendants were inapposite. True, the Supreme Court had held that an indigent defendant was to be provided with counsel. But if he were not indigent but merely poor, the Court had not interfered; it was not concerned with "relative differences in the quality of counsel acquired by the less wealthy." Unless the Texas financing system had excluded some children altogether, creating an "absolute deprivation," there was no discrimination based on wealth.

Employing the principles of "strict construction" so dear to the President who appointed him, Justice Powell searched the Constitution in vain for "explicit" or "implicit" references to education as a right entitled to Constitutional protection. He was unable to make the connection, spelled out by Justice Brennan in his dissent, between education and meaningful exercise of such clearly protected rights as free speech or the electoral franchise. *Effective* speech and *informed* voting were worthy goals, but not ones which could be achieved by "judicial intrusion." The Court had an "historic dedication to public education," but its "importance" did not determine whether it was a "fundamental interest."

"Strict scrutiny" was not the proper standard. The proper, and lower, standard was whether the Texas system "rationally furthers a legitimate state interest"—a standard that the Texas system "abundantly" satisfied.

The Supreme Court decision in *Rodriguez* at least temporarily suspended attacks on financing inequities based on the Federal Equal Protection Clause. But it did not end attacks grounded in violations of state laws or constitutions. The most notable example was the tortuous litigation in the New Jersey case of *Robinson v. Cahill*,[49] decided two weeks after *Rodriguez,* where the New Jersey Supreme Court held that the state's school finance scheme, based largely on local property taxation, violated the provisions of the New Jersey constitutional mandate requiring the legislature to maintain and support a "thorough and efficient system of free public education for the instruction of all the children in the State."

The New Jersey court deferred invoking any remedy in 1973 against the unconstitutional funding system until after the state legislature had had an opportunity to act. It again deferred any decision in 1974 but, faced with continued inaction by the legislature, made temporary reallocations of legislative appropriations in 1975 and finally, in May 1976, enjoined all state officers from disbursing funds in accordance with the laws previously held unconstitutional after July 1, 1976.

The public schools of New Jersey in fact closed on July 1, 1976, and did not reopen until July 8, when an income-tax measure to fund a revised educational financing plan was passed and signed by Governor Brendan Byrne.[50]

The California Supreme Court, which had earlier relied on the Federal Equal Protection Clause in *Serrano,* later upheld a lower court decision holding the California education finance system in violation of the equal-protection clause of the California constitution. It found the California clause "possessed of an independent vitality" and in effect reaffirmed its earlier *Serrano* decision despite the Supreme Court's position in *Rodriguez*.[51]

Court prodding to reform educational finance has not been as dramatic in other states as it was in New Jersey, but the trend toward reviewing the existing system of financing has continued, with reforms of one sort or another already undertaken in some twenty states.[52]

Reviewing the period since World War II, we find that three major issues in American secondary education that have become political issues have been the proper role of the Federal government in educational finance, racial desegregation and the proper method of state and local finance.

Title I of ESEA represents Congress' response to the question of Federal assistance. This was a response delayed by parliamentary maneuverings for twenty years and one the effectiveness of which has been significantly hobbled by opponents of Federal aid and legislators unwilling to make a clear-cut, effective commitment to the lofty if limited purposes of ESEA.

The Congress has made only slow and not really very substantial commitments toward meeting the increasingly obvious "overburden" problems of the cities or toward equalizing educational expenditures on a national basis. Discrepancies in expenditure levels among districts in a state have increasingly been perceived as unfair. Logically, similar discrepancies among the states should be considered equally unfair. As Agnes Meyer wrote more than twenty-five years ago:

> We speak constantly and proudly of the high promise of American life. We do not speak of the high promise of life in New York or Illinois or California. When we think of American life, we refuse to admit that its privileges and high hopes are reserved to certain geographical areas.[53]

Congress, which must be the moving body in encouraging the amelioration of these differences, simply has not acted. Thousands of pages of testimony on this issue have been taken, most notably by the Senate Select Committee on Equal Educational Opportunity in 1971, but no meaningful legislation has been passed to give incentives for greater tax efforts in low-spending states or to give assistance to enable the poorer states to catch up. And given the parochial interest of the members of the national legislature, no such national legislation is likely, in the absence of a sustained effort by the President to convince the Congress and the public of the social costs for all Americans of deficient education in any part of America.

As to desegregation, the record of the Congress has been demoralizing indeed. State and community efforts to desegregate have simply not been encouraged or assisted in any meaningful way in Congress. In the face of Congress' craven abdication of legislative responsibility, the courts have been required to become the instruments of vindication for the fundamental Constitutional rights of minority children. It is surprising that with the constraints of the litigation process, the social revolution of desegregation has progressed as well as it has, given the nearly total absence of moral backing or supportive guidance from the legislative branch.

Finally, state and local governments faced with the profound and difficult problem of improving the allocation of educational resources have not been assisted in Washington. With rare exceptions, no thought at all has been given in Congress to encouraging more equitable and efficient financing systems in the states.*

With its power over national revenues, the Congress, through judicious appropriations and financial incentives to local governments, could have an immense and positive effect on American secondary education. But its performance over the last third of a century does not encourage one to expect it.

* As is often the case, Congress has made a token effort to meet the local finance problem, enabling Congressmen to point to their concern with the issue. Section 842 of the Education Amendments of 1974 authorized financial assistance to the states to pay the cost of developing state school-financing plans. Assuming adequate appropriations, each state may receive up to one million dollars for such expenses. Not peanuts— but not really attacking the central problem, either.

Six · Congress at Work: Federal Energy "Policy" (1975)

Obviously President Ford was mistaken when he said Congress has no energy program. The unfortunate truth is, we have 535 programs—one for each Member.

—CONGRESSMAN JIM WRIGHT[1]
(Democrat, Texas) 1975

Our resources of coal, oil, gas and water power provide the energy to turn the wheels of industry, to service our homes, and to aid in national defense [the President wrote]. We now use more energy per capita than any other people, and our scientists tell us there will be progressively increasing demand for energy for all purposes.

Our energy resources are not inexhaustible, yet we are permitting waste in their use and production. In some instances, to achieve apparent economies today, future generations will be forced to carry the burden of unnecessarily high costs and to substitute inferior fuels for particular purposes. National policies concerning these vital resources must recognize the availability of all of them; the location of each with respect to its markets, the costs of transporting them; the technological developments which will increase the efficiency of their production and use, the use of the lower grade coals; and the relationships between the increased use of energy and the general economic development of the country....

The widening interest and responsibility on the part of the Federal Government for the conservation and wise use of the Nation's energy resources raise many perplexing questions of policy determination.[2]

The author of this Presidential statement was not Nixon, nor Ford nor Carter, but Franklin Roosevelt, writing to the Congress in 1939.

130

His statement, transmitting a report on the nation's utilization and conservation of energy, was filed and forgotten.

Failure over the years to formulate a carefully deliberated national energy policy led to a crisis in 1975, when at last our leaders were required by circumstances to confront the issue.

The performances of both President and Congress in the face of this crisis were not especially edifying, the "resolution" of the crisis being neither adequate nor imaginative. But what is perhaps even more discouraging, the ineffectual maneuvering of 1975 turned out to be only a dress rehearsal for continued ineffectuality in 1977 and 1978. Dealing with a complex subject under pressure—the pressure of time and political pressure from powerful interest groups—simply does not seem to fit the Congressional style.

Background

After World War II and up until the Arab embargo of October 1973, energy policy was not an issue that commanded attention. The oil depletion allowance, variously characterized as a tax giveaway and as an essential incentive to domestic oil production, was an occasional campaign issue, but few took seriously energy matters in a period when increasing energy demand was easily met with cheap and increasing supplies.

As far as petroleum was concerned, the National Petroleum Council, consisting largely of industry spokesmen, had traditionally advised the President on energy matters. The Council's policy was consistent and straightforward: let private enterprise assume the task of producing and supplying petroleum without government intervention except, of course, tax incentives and an assist when necessary in keeping out "cheap" foreign imports. The Department of Defense too was involved, insisting that developing oil reserves on federally owned lands be postponed, in the interests of conserving those reserves for national defense needs.

The United States had become a net importer of petroleum for the first time in 1947, but no one seemed to notice. Petroleum consumption grew in the United States at an annual rate of 4 percent in the 1960s, rising to 5.4 percent a year during the five years prior to the embargo.

In 1970, domestic crude-oil production peaked at 3.32 billion barrels. With domestic production declining and demand increasing, imports inevitably rose. By 1973, they represented more than 30 percent of consumption. By the time of the boycott, direct imports of Arabian oil were running at a rate exceeding one million barrels a day—up from less than half that rate in 1971.

To thoughtful observers, the crisis made manifest by the Arab price rises and embargo in October 1973 had been evident before the Arabs acted.

In an important article in *Foreign Affairs* in July 1973, Professor Carroll L. Wilson of MIT foreshadowed the October crisis:

I believe the United States is facing a national energy emergency. It arises from our extravagant and wasteful use of energy and from a shift in the sources of fuels. Per capita consumption is three times that of Western Europe, and we may ask ourselves whether our greater use enriches the quality of life by any such margin. Our cars are twice as heavy and use twice as much fuel as European cars which run about the same mileage each year, and the ratio is getting worse because of the sharp drop in fuel economy on recent models of American cars, owing to emission controls and air conditioners. We keep our houses and buildings too hot and use large amounts of fuel in air-conditioning everything. We have not given a thought to fuel conservation and efficiency since the days of rationing in World War II—an era which only 30 percent (those over 45) of the population can remember. These are some of the reasons why with six percent of the world's population the United States uses 33 percent of the world's energy—and why Europe and Japan are unlikely to be sympathetic to our plight as we ask them to share with us their traditional supply sources in the Middle East.[3]

And in a companion article a month earlier entitled "The Oil Crisis: This Time the Wolf Is Here," James E. Atkins, Director of the State Department's Office of Fuels and Energy (and later Ambassador to Saudi Arabia), had pointed out that virtually every recent projection of petroleum needs, regardless of the expertise and respectability of the sponsorship, had erred on the low side.

The Arab states raised the "posted" price of crude oil from $3 to $5 per barrel on October 18, 1973, and this was followed within the week by an embargo on exports to the United States. The embargo was lifted in March 1974, enabling the United States once again to purchase

Arabian crude oil—but at the price of $11.651 per barrel set by the Organization of Petroleum Exporting Countries (OPEC) in December 1973.

The oil crisis occurred at the height of the Watergate crisis—the "firestorm" over Nixon's firing of Special Prosecutor Archibald Cox occurred two days after the October 18 price increase. The administration finally pulled itself together to make a response on November 7, 1973, when the President called for "Project Independence":

> Let us set as our national goal, in the spirit of Apollo [the space project, not the Grecian deity], with the determination of the Manhattan Project, that by the end of this decade we will have developed the potential to meet our own energy needs without depending on any foreign energy sources.
>
> Let us pledge that by 1980, under Project Independence, we shall be able to meet America's energy needs from America's own energy resources.[4]

Project Independence never got started. With the end of the boycott in March 1974, the nation turned to other concerns, notably Watergate. It was not until 1975 that the new Republican President and the Democratic Congress elected the previous November seriously focused on questions of energy policy. As they did so, the "perplexing questions of policy determination" foreshadowed by FDR dominated the year-long debate which culminated in the enactment of a so-called Energy Policy and Conservation Act in December 1975.

The basic policy goal was clear to all: the need to reduce foreign imports by increasing domestic supply and decreasing domestic demand (or at least slowing the rate of increase in demand). But that was about the extent of the consensus. The "perplexing questions" with which the President and Congress wrestled produced little agreement:

- Was American energy "independence" a realistic or even a desirable goal?
- What incentives were needed to encourage greater domestic oil, natural gas and coal production?
- How could consumption be reduced—through higher prices, through taxes or through rationing?
- Should nuclear energy be encouraged, or were the risks of nuclear accident unacceptably great?

- Could the automobile industry substantially increase fuel efficiency over a period of years?
- Who should take the initiative in developing new sources of energy, the Federal government or private business?

As such questions were debated, the Congress found that powerful constituencies existed on both sides of almost every issue: coal operators and the United Mine Workers, eager to keep out foreign oil and to prevent regulation of strip mining; the auto manufacturers and the automotive unions, opposed to fuel-efficiency standards and excise taxes or penalties to discourage the production of "gas guzzlers"; Eastern fuel consumers, opposed to restrictions and fees on the foreign oil on which they were dependent; Western producers, eager for maximum prices and investment incentives; petrochemical and industrial users of energy, eager to transfer the burdens of conservation to transportation users; the transportation industry and farmers, equally anxious to throw the conservation burden back on industry; urban consumers, perhaps willing to regulate automobile use if mass transit assistance were increased; suburban and rural consumers, prepared to defend the sanctity of unrestricted automobile use; environmentalists, concerned that energy policies not compromise clean-air and safety standards. And, of course, the general public, anxious for uninterrupted and cheap supplies of fuel to power its cars and heat its homes.

"It is extremely difficult to write an energy bill," then Majority Leader "Tip" O'Neill said of the 1975 efforts. "This, perhaps, has been the most parochial issue that could ever hit the floor."[5]

The President and the Congress alike reacted in a conventional and pedestrian fashion. Four lines of approach to energy policy questions emerged in the 1975 debate:

1. *The Coolidge Approach.* President Ford, predictably, offered a program that would have done credit to Calvin Coolidge, relying principally on a combination of laissez-faire economics and protectionism. In January 1975 he announced that he would inhibit imports by imposing a $3 per barrel fee on foreign oil, the fee to be increased in graduated steps over three months.[6] The Congressional outcry was immediate, led by Congressmen from New England and the Northeast, representing the biggest users of imported oil. Congressional feeling

was sufficiently strong to pass a bill suspending the authority of the President to impose the import fee, and canceling the first-stage imposition of $1, which the President had placed in effect. Ford vetoed the bill but, in exchange for Congressional agreement not to override the veto, agreed not to raise the fee from $1 to the second stage of $2.*

The second aspect of Ford's program was to propose deregulation of natural-gas prices and decontrol of domestic crude-oil prices, the theory being that the expected increases in prices would operate, in traditional supply-and-demand fashion, to decrease natural-gas and crude-oil consumption and, at the same time, encourage greater production.

The question of regulation by the Federal Power Commission (now the Federal Energy Regulatory Commission) of prices of natural gas sold in interstate commerce is extraordinarily thorny. In 1945, natural gas was regarded as a by-product of oil production, and it was priced accordingly. But the combination of increased long-distance pipeline-transmission facilities after World War II, the relative cheapness of natural gas, and its "clean" qualities, which made it appealing from an environmental point of view, led to sharply increased demands for natural gas. Indeed, between 1950 and 1970, natural gas provided more than half the total growth of energy in the United States, displacing coal in particular for many industrial uses.

In 1954, the Supreme Court had decided that the Natural Gas Act of 1938, which regulated the prices of gas sold by pipelines, also applied to sales at the "wellhead" of gas that was destined for shipment in interstate commerce.[7] The Federal Power Commission then began its regulation of wellhead prices.

Attracted by the ceiling prices, users demanded greater and greater quantities of natural gas. Producers, on the other hand, attempted to confine sales to intrastate transactions not subject to FPC ceilings or, failing such sales, withheld their supplies from the market. Despite increases in the FPC ceilings (to 51 cents per thousand cubic feet in December 1974), the regulated ceiling price was well below com-

---

* Faced with continuing Congressional inaction on an energy program, Ford did raise the import fee to $2 in June 1975. In August, the governors of the Northeastern states and Congressman Robert Drinan (Democrat, Massachusetts) succeeded in obtaining a court ruling that the President had exceeded his authority. The $2 fee was revoked when the President signed the Energy Policy and Conservation Act in December 1975.

parable prices of up to $2 per thousand cubic feet in the intrastate market. Both increased demand and producer reluctance had contributed to United States imports of foreign oil for, in times of shortages, natural-gas users had turned to foreign oil as a substitute. One analyst estimated that "1.5 to 2 million barrels [of oil] per day had been added to imports by 1973 owing to the shortage of gas."[8] The Senate approved deregulation in the fall of 1975, and the House adopted a different bill in February 1976 deregulating prices for small producers but expanding regulation to cover both interstate and intrastate sales by the major natural-gas producers. The result was a deadlock and failure to adopt a final bill before adjournment of the Ninety-fourth Congress.

As far as crude oil was concerned, the focus prior to the OPEC price increases and the Arab embargo had been on keeping oil prices down, not on whether domestic or foreign sources fed United States consumption. In April 1973 the administration had abolished limits on petroleum imports as a means of increasing supply and putting downward pressure on domestic prices. Similarly, the Cost of Living Council in August 1973 had placed a ceiling on prices for "old" oil (i.e., oil produced from existing wells at 1972 production levels), while "new" oil (and imported oil) prices were not restricted.

The lack of restrictions on "new" oil prices would enable prices to rise to a level where additional production would be encouraged, or so the theory ran; the restriction on "old" oil prices would prevent a "windfall" profit to producers on sources already developed.

The effective domestic price for oil thus became an amalgam of the price for old oil (about 40 percent of supply in January 1975, when the price remained fixed at $5.25 per barrel), imported oil (another 40 percent, priced at $12.50 per barrel) and new domestic oil (the remaining 20 percent, priced at approximately $11.50 per barrel). In January 1975 the domestic price was roughly $9.50 per barrel, up from $4 per barrel when the boycott began in October 1973.[9]

Again there was great outcry at Ford's proposal to decontrol domestic crude prices on old oil. Without controls, old oil prices would inevitably have moved toward the OPEC world price, without regard for the actual costs of domestic production. Prices for oil substitutes, such as coal and natural gas, would also tend to rise as old oil prices rose. Senator Henry M. Jackson (Democrat, Washington) summed up the majority reaction in the Congress:

This administration has conclusively demonstrated its ideological commitment to rationing energy by prohibitive pricing. This unbending commitment to prohibitive energy pricing is a simplistic and dangerous approach for which the American consumer will heavily pay. . . . Consumers will not only pay higher prices at the gas pump, but for all goods and services they purchase. They will also pay the burdensome economic and intolerable social costs imposed by increased unemployment.[10]

The Ford proposals naïvely assumed the existence of a free market—a difficult assumption to make in the face of the price moves of the international OPEC cartel and an assumption that even many oil men would not make. For example, Thornton Bradshaw, the astute President of Atlantic Richfield, wrote in February 1977:

A free market for crude oil does not exist. OPEC controls the price, and we have no assurance that it will exercise that control in the interest of the consumer nations. . . .

In the most basic sense, our national energy goal is obvious: less dependence on foreign oil. And there is no way the "free" market can direct industry to accomplish that goal. What we need is a comprehensive national energy policy—and this means national planning by the only instrument that represents all sectors of society and is capable of developing such a policy.

The federal government must set a clear-cut, explicit goal. . . .[11]

The Ford proposals also assumed that the resulting increased revenues to energy producers would fund new exploration and drilling activities. But there was no provision in the Ford plan to compel this result, despite the increasing trend among oil and natural-gas companies to use their profits to diversify into nonenergy businesses and the undeniable fact that, in the case of petroleum, domestic production had declined since 1970 despite successive price increases after 1970.

Opposition was so fierce that Ford did not even formally present his program until June 1975, when he backed off from his position that decontrol should take effect immediately and proposed instead that decontrol take place over a period of twenty-five months. The final resolution, after months of proposals and counterproposals, was contained in the Energy Policy and Conservation Act, which provided for decontrol over a period of forty months but with a ceiling on the average price for domestic crude oil of $7.66 per barrel. In fact, this meant that Ford had to roll back domestic oil prices in the first instance, since the prevailing average price was $8.75 per barrel at the time of passage of the act.

2. *The Messianic Approach.* In September 1975 President Ford proposed creation of an Energy Independence Authority, an independent corporation to be funded by a $25 billion equity contribution from the Federal government and $75 billion in public borrowing with the backing of the Federal government's credit. The authority, which was to have a ten-year life, would have been empowered to make loans and investments and to guarantee private loans to further such energy projects as shale oil development, the development of technologies for producing geothermal and solar energy, and projects of unusual size and scope that private enterprise could not finance on its own.

According to the President, the object of the authority would be "to work, with private enterprise and labor, to gain energy independence for the United States in ten years or less."*

Despite the President's disclaimer that the authority would "undertake only those projects which private business cannot undertake alone," the concept of the Authority appeared to conflict with Ford's frequent calls for economy, decreased government spending and unfettered free enterprise.

"Resource allocation is one of the government's most important functions. It is almost incredible that President Ford, supposedly a fiscal conservative, would propose that we set up an independent agency, with far less of the usual Executive and Congressional review than other agencies, to allocate $100 billion of our gross national product during the next 10 years," Representative John La Falce (Democrat, New York) observed.[12]

The inconsistency is probably best explained by the fact that the notion of the authority as a political option had been taken up by Vice President Rockefeller and his staff.

The basic idea had in fact originated with MIT Professor Wilson in his *Foreign Affairs* article. Wilson, a former general manager of the Atomic Energy Commission and a former mining executive, had proposed in broad outline a hard-headed and practical authority proj-

---

* Remarks to Annual Convention of AFL–CIO Building and Construction Trades Department, San Francisco, September 22, 1975. Less than three hours later, when speaking before a nonlabor audience, the President omitted any mention of working with labor. Remarks to World Affairs Council, San Francisco, September 22, 1975.

ect, which would emphasize both government and private participation in the development of such new energy sources as the gasification of coal and expanded—and safer—nuclear installations.

With a scientist's optimism, Wilson envisioned technological breakthroughs rivaling the Manhattan Project and the space program that would substantially reduce dependency on foreign oil and make relatively cheap energy available in a short period of time.

The White House, in announcing the authority proposal, noted that "its outlays will not be included in the Budget of the United States," although "losses or gains from its operations will be included."

This approach clearly was more typical of Rockefeller than of Ford, reflecting the financing pattern that Rockefeller had espoused for twenty years as Governor of New York.* With his boundless enthusiasm, Rockefeller coopted Wilson's authority idea and in the process discredited it by proposing to capitalize the Energy Independence Authority on a gargantuan $100-billion scale which could easily have upset

---

* Just as President Nixon was able to deal with the Chinese Communists in a way not open to Democrats—who, after all, had "lost" China to Communism, at least in the hard-line Nixon view—Republican Nelson Rockefeller had been able to spend money as Governor of New York on a profligate scale which Democrats could only watch with wonder.

As Governor, Rockefeller committed astronomical sums for the projects which attracted his interest—some wholly frivolous, like the billion-dollar Mussolini-modern mall at the state capital in Albany, others highly commendable (if expensive), such as $1.8 billion in construction projects designed to upgrade the state university system.

In working out his enthusiasms, Rockefeller set the forces in motion which discredited financing by New York State and New York City and by other local governments generally. Faced with an inconvenient nineteenth century provision of the New York constitution which required voter approval for state bond issues, Rockefeller, advised by then successful bond lawyer John N. Mitchell, devised the "moral obligation" bond which did not directly commit the "full faith and credit" of the state—a commitment requiring voter approval—but merely provided that future legislatures, assuming they were so minded, would backstop the obligations of various independent "moral obligation" authorities.

By the time Rockefeller went to Washington in 1974, the independent authorities had issued roughly $5 billion of "moral obligation" bonds—far in excess of the amount of bonds outstanding which did have the "full faith and credit" backing of the state. Between 1972 and 1974 alone, the independent New York Housing Finance Agency issued "moral obligation" bonds in the amount of $1.7 billion—more than the total of "full faith and credit" long-term bonds sold by all fifty states combined during the period. Other "backdoor" techniques (i.e., techniques not requiring voter approval) were also used. These included the leasing of capital projects by governmental units from independent authorities, with the independent authorities issuing bonds supported by the expected lease rentals. Again, voter approval was not required either for the governmental lease commitments or the authority bond issuances. With this financing added, more than $8 billion in bonds had been issued by 1975 without the formal credit of New York State behind them. See Humphrey S. Tyler, "The Steady Growth of Backdoor Financing," *Empire State Report*, June 1975, p. 211.

the nation's capital markets and choked the nation's public and private capacity for research and development as well.

As the footnote on the previous page details, Rockefeller as governor had presided over the issuance of billions in so-called moral-obligation bonds, not backed by the credit of New York State. The day of reckoning came in 1975, when one of Rockefeller's independent authorities, the Urban Development Corporation, required legislative appropriations to meet its borrowing obligations. The UDC collapse led to a reappraisal of the whole moral-obligation concept and its implications for the credit of New York State—could or would the state fail to recognize its nonbinding moral obligations? The result was a tightening bond market, a hike in interest rates, increasing liquidity and refinancing problems and a further blow to the shaky credit standing of New York City. All these factors were well known in Washington and the appeal of "backdoor" financing proposed to fund the Energy Authority programs was, to say the least, at a very low point.

Thus a sensible and probably workable idea fell victim to Rockefeller's uncritical and ill-timed attempt to smother it with money.* Both Treasury Secretary William E. Simon and Alan Greenspan, Ford's Chairman of the Council of Economic Advisers, allegedly opposed the authority plan in the Executive Branch and enthusiasm in the Congress was all but nonexistent.

3. *The Scapegoat Approach*. When in doubt about the causes of a crisis, find a scapegoat. Obviously the major oil companies would qualify in the case of the energy crisis as candidates for "having the black mustache pasted on";[13] fully 25 percent of the respondents in a Gallup poll taken shortly after the 1973 embargo blamed the oil companies for the crisis (as compared with only 7 percent who blamed the Arab countries).[14] Indeed, consumer advocate Ralph Nader questioned the existence of a real crisis at all, terming it "an energy crisis for consumers who are being subjected to billions of dollars of unarmed robbery by the oil companies in collusion with government support."[15]

Suspicion of the oil industry certainly contributed to Congress' resistance to President Ford's proindustry program. It also produced a tax law reform—repeal of the depletion allowance—which probably would not have been possible without the hostility to the oil companies created by the price increases.

* The indomitable Rockefeller renewed his Energy Authority proposals in testimony before the Senate Finance Committee on September 13, 1977.

Depletion allowances had been a part of the Internal Revenue Code since enactment of the first income tax in 1913. Depletion was thought of for wasting assets, such as oil, as the equivalent of depreciation for normal capital assets.

With a capital asset such as a plant or a piece of expensive machinery, a taxpaying owner is permitted to deduct the cost of such asset in determining his taxable income over the useful life of the asset. A new plant, for instance, might be "written off" over twenty years— i.e., one twentieth of the cost would be deducted as an expense in each year in determining the owner's taxable income.

In its earliest form, the oil depletion allowance was also based on the costs and risks of finding and developing a new field. But practical difficulties arose in computing "cost" depletion so that, in 1926, the Congress adopted a system of percentage depletion, whereby the depletion deduction was based on a percentage of gross receipts. This percentage was fixed at 27.5 percent for almost fifty years, until reduced to 22 percent by the Tax Reform Act of 1969.

The benefits of depletion are starkly illustrated in the following example, using the post-1969 rate:

	With depletion	*Without depletion*
Gross receipts from sales of oil	$200,000	$200,000
Cost	120,000	120,000
Net income	$ 80,000	$ 80,000
Percentage depletion (22% of gross receipts)	44,000	—
Allowable depletion (maximum of 50% of net income)	40,000	—
Taxable income	40,000	80,000
Tax (48% corporate rate)	19,200	38,400

In this example the producer's tax bill was cut in half. According to the theory—stoutly defended over the years by the oil companies— these tax savings were necessary to support highly expensive, and often unsuccessful, exploration and development activities.

This justification seemed less acceptable in the context of the high crude-oil prices prevailing in 1975. With prices at record levels, the industry presumably received an incentive to explore and develop on the basis of the increases alone. Yet it continued to receive the depletion incentive as well—an incentive which itself increases as prices increase, since it is based on a percentage of gross receipts.

The incentive of depletion was also perceived to be inefficient. Based on oil production (or more precisely, sales of actual oil), the allowance in reality encouraged drilling in known reserves and pumping from existing wells. Indeed, a study made for the Treasury Department in 1969 had concluded that depletion cost the government $1.4 billion in lost tax revenue a year while increasing oil reserves with a value of only $150 million a year.

And the percentage method often enabled producers to recover their costs over and over again. The 22 percent allowance was available every year as long as oil supplies continued—in contrast to depreciation, which permits an owner to recover his cost for an asset only once over the life of that asset.

In the spring of 1975, the Congress voted to repeal depletion for the large oil producers and to phase it out for so-called "small" producers.

The energy crisis had thus produced a tax change that had eluded reformers for years. While long overdue as a matter of tax equity, repeal of depletion had little to do with developing an energy policy.[16]

Two other proposals were considered in 1975 that reflected Congressional antipathy to the oil companies. In October, the Senate voted down an amendment to require the major oil companies to concentrate on only one aspect of the business—production, refining or marketing—and to divest themselves of assets relating to the unretained parts.

The surprise was not that the amendment, the principal sponsors of which were Senator James G. Abourezk (Democrat, South Dakota) and Gary W. Hart (Democrat, Colorado), was defeated but that the vote was a relatively narrow 54–45. Forty-five Senators, in other words, went on record as being willing to "dismember" (the industry's word) the major oil companies—a situation which, Robert Sherrill wrote, probably caused "the smell of rich sweat" in countless board rooms.[17]

A second amendment, sponsored by Senator Edward M. Kennedy (Democrat, Massachusetts), was also narrowly defeated. His amendment would have required the majors to divest themselves of activities unrelated to the oil business, such as Atlantic Richfield's ownership of Anaconda Copper and Mobil's ownership of Montgomery Ward. It would also have required divestiture of uranium reserves and mills and coal reserves owned by oil and gas companies. At the time, oil and gas companies owned approximately 51 percent of United States uranium reserves, 62 percent of uranium milling capacity and 44 percent of leased coal reserves.[18]

Despite desultory hearings over the years into the question of oil company divestiture, no convincing argument was made that the Abourezk-Hart amendment would in any way alleviate the energy crisis. More detailed study might well have produced such arguments but, in the posture presented, the amendment seemed merely an attempt to take advantage of the existing climate in the Congress by making the oil industry a scapegoat.

The Kennedy amendment, too, had a scapegoat element, although two plausible reasons were advanced to support it: that prohibiting non-petroleum diversification would require the oil companies to devote their increased revenue to new exploration and drilling, and that prohibiting ownership of uranium and coal resources would prevent the manipulation of such resources in a way designed to favor oil, as long as petroleum supplies lasted.

The petroleum industry, of course, countered that its business expertise was really in the field of energy, as opposed to petroleum alone, and that its companies would be the logical developers of other energy sources.

Who had the better of the argument in this debate was not really known in 1975 and, indeed, would require more extensive study even today before a definitive evaluation of the Kennedy proposal could be made.*

4. *The Anarchic Approach.* The attempts of the Congress to formulate an energy policy in 1975 were pitiful, even ludicrous, and took virtually all the year. (By the Congress one really means the Democratic majority, since the Republicans were by and large wedded to the price-raising approach of the President.)

Rejecting President Ford's pricing proposals, the Democratic leadership in the House and Senate put forth their own program in March. Fearful that the increased prices that would have resulted from the

---

* The Carter Antitrust Division concluded in March 1978 that the United States coal industry was "workably competitive" and that there was not any need to require oil companies to get out of the coal business. Edward Cowan, "Antitrust Aides See No Need to Split Up Oil and Coal Sector," *New York Times,* March 31, 1978, p. 1.

President's program would feed both recession and inflation,* the Democrats focused on deterrents to consumption—a 5-cent increase in the Federal gasoline tax (with tax rebates or credits for some minimal use of gasoline by individual consumers), excise taxes on industrial fuel consumption and a sliding scale of penalties to compel the automotive industry to produce more efficient cars over a ten-year period. They also proposed creation of a National Energy Production Board to conduct all negotiations for purchases of foreign crude oil. Decontrol was specifically rejected.

The House Ways and Means Committee substantially altered the leadership proposal. By the time the Committee version reached the House floor, the gasoline-tax feature had been altered to provide for a maximum 20-cent tax, the amount of the tax to be imposed over a five-year period to depend on gas consumption; if the public voluntarily cut consumption within prescribed limits, the tax would not be imposed. An additional 3-cent tax was proposed to finance government research and development efforts. More significantly, the fuel-efficiency provisions, which would have penalized the auto industry if miles-per-gallon performance were not improved, were substantially watered down under pressure from the industry and the automotive unions. And the proposal for a National Energy Production Board was dropped just before the bill came to the floor, to secure the support of oil-state Congressmen, who viewed it as a first step toward "nationalizing" the oil companies.

The Ways and Means bill also introduced the concept of import quotas, as opposed to import duties or fees. The amount of imported oil would be limited, to help ensure that the conservation measures led to a decline in consumption of foreign, rather than domestic, oil and to reduce the impact of the OPEC world price on the U.S. domestic price of oil.

Then the roof fell in on the Democrats. More than fifty amendments were considered in the floor debate, including an amendment that passed by a vote of 345–72, striking out the 20-cent gasoline tax, the key feature of the House bill. A subsequent amendment struck out the 3-cent tax as well.

* A projection by Chase Econometrics, Inc., as to the effects of "old" oil decontrol over two years estimated a 1.7 percent increase in the Consumer Price Index by the end of the two years, an increase of 430,000 unemployed and a gross national product $20 billion less than that projected for the end of the second year. Quoted in 121 *Congressional Record* (1975), p. H4952.

The bill was thus stripped of its conservation features, though the quota arrangements—which were designed to complement the conservation of energy induced by the taxes—and the watered-down inducements to automotive fuel efficiency remained.

As amendment after amendment eviscerated the Ways and Means bill, Republican Congressman Robert Bauman of Maryland said that the spectacle was one of watching a "leaderless two-thirds majority rape an artichoke, peeling off leaf after leaf of the original energy-saving proposal."[19]

In late December, the Congress finally did pass the Energy Policy and Conservation Act. As already noted, this Act required a roll-back in the domestic oil price from $8.75 per barrel to $7.66, with maximum increases thereafter up to 10 percent a year until expiration of the law in 1979—increases that would have the greatest impact after the 1976 elections.

The Act also provided loan guaranties to small coal operators; standby authority for the President to impose allocations, rationing and import restrictions; mandatory mileage standards requiring automobiles to achieve 27.5 miles per gallon by the 1985-model year; and authorization for a strategic petroleum reserve projected to grow to one billion barrels by 1983. The Act also authorized the General Accounting Office to audit oil company records.

Incentives for conservation, by way of tax increases, substantial price increases or rationing, were absent. So was any incentive to encourage new production or the development of alternative fuel sources.

While the Act was not the "Orwellian Leviathan" that the *Wall Street Journal* found it to be, imports of foreign oil continued to increase after its enactment, as both the *Journal,* which opposed the Act, and *The New York Times,* which favored it, predicted.[20] By 1978, an estimated 42 percent of the country's petroleum consumption came from oil imports, compared with 35 percent in 1973.

The course of energy legislation in Congress in 1975 in part reflects an institutional failure. There was no central focus in either chamber for energy legislation—the Ways and Means and the Interstate and Foreign Commerce Committees proceeded on a separate, uncoordinated basis in the House, and no fewer than nine committees in the Senate considered bits and pieces of the overall program.

The Congressional problem was further aggravated by the diametrically opposing positions taken by the White House and the Congress. The Congressional majority was simply unwilling to accept the price-raising proposals of the President or the grandiose development plans of the Vice President. This left the Congress in the position not of reacting to the President's program but of devising a program of its own. This posture put the Congress at a disadvantage, as Congressman Bill Frenzel (Republican, Minnesota) noted:

> Normally, on basic policy, the Congress works from an Executive proposal modifying, amending, substituting, as it sees the need. Normally, it does this reactive job well.
>
> On the contrary, the Congress usually falls in [*sic*] its face when it attempts to build its own plan.[21]

In the final analysis, however, blame must rest with the members of Congress and their leadership. Proponents of energy legislation in 1975 steadfastly refused to impose meaningful conservation measures on either the individual consumer or on industry—any plan for rationing was scarcely discussed—or to exercise the imagination required to construct a program for the development of alternative energy sources.

Seven · Does Congress Work?

All members of Congress have a primary interest in being re-elected. Some members have no other interest. Their participation in decisions of great national importance is dependent entirely upon the reaction they expect from their own district or state. When seniority pushes them to a position of influence in some special area of the government, they may begin to make decisions without regard to district reaction (because the district knows nor cares little about it), but the irresponsible congressmen who reach these positions of power use them primarily for their own personal political ends.

         —FORMER CONGRESSMAN FRANK E. SMITH[1]
         (Democrat, Mississippi)

Ralph Nader has called the Congress the "broken branch" of government. Its response over the years on the aid-to-education issue and its response to the energy crisis in 1975 appear to justify Nader's crack.

Recent institutional reforms in the Congress give some hope that it is now more capable of dealing with the country's domestic problems. And the members, younger and supposedly brighter, should in theory be more capable of dealing effectively with the increasing complexity of social and economic policy questions.

Pointing the other way is a disturbing increase in "incumbency"— the repeated reelection of sitting members by wide margins—and an equally disturbing tendency of Congressmen to play it safe on controversial issues likely to jeopardize their chances for reelection.

In the House of Representatives, the power of the autocratic committee chairman, if not broken, has at least been diminished. Through rules changes made in 1975, committee chairmen are now subject to election by the majority-party caucus. The result has not been a wholesale unseating of the incompetent, the senile and the venal, but the four defeats the caucus handed sitting committee chairmen in 1975 and 1977 have served notice that autocratic highhandedness or incompetence, if excessive, will be curbed. The House also has, after a series of colorless and feckless speakers, a Speaker in Thomas P. O'Neill who is neither.

The democratization of committee assignments— including assignments for junior members to the conference committees on crucial legislation—combined paradoxically with a stronger and more powerful Speaker, offer encouragement that the stage has been set for effective House action on major legislation.

The Senate also moved tentatively in the direction of reform in 1977. Under the leadership of Senator Adlai E. Stevenson III (Democrat, Illinois), the committee system of the Senate was reformed, with the number of committees being reduced from thirty-one to twenty-five, and the number of committee and subcommittee assignments for each member being reduced from an average of eighteen to an average of eleven.

The 1977 Senate resolution restructuring the chamber's committees was passed 89–1, but the resolution was the subject of substantial modification before passage, reflecting intense lobbying efforts. Senator Stevenson's Select Committee had, for example, eliminated the Veterans' Affairs Committee in its first version of a revised committee structure, a step which had the support of the Veterans' Affairs Committee chairman, Senator Alan Cranston (Democrat, California). Lobbying by the American Legion and the Veterans of Foreign Wars, including personal calls on Senators by state leaders of those groups, led to restoration of the Veterans' Affairs Committee.[2]

Despite the fact that the ultimate streamlining was not quite as spare as originally planned, the committee reorganization in the Senate as enacted did provide real reform, which may promote efficiency in the future.*

---

* Reduction in the number of committees may come in the House in the near future. A preliminary report of a House Commission on Administrative Review concluded in 1977:

> Members have too many assignments, and jurisdictions are too confused for the strains and conflicts members currently endure to be substantially alleviated by piecemeal and procedural reform. Only marginal improvements can occur until a basic restructuring of the committee system takes place.

"Study Gives Committee Reform a Push," *Congressional Quarterly,* September 3, 1977, p. 1855.

A little-remarked aspect of the 1977 reforms, which also may have a significant future impact, was the repeal of Clause 6 of Senate Rule XVI. Originally adopted in 1921, when the Committee on Appropriations was given jurisdiction over all money bills, Clause 6 provided that certain committees could each appoint three members—ex-officio, but voting—to the Appropriations Committee when appropriations concerning matters within the jurisdiction of those committees were being considered. With two exceptions, the privilege of naming extra members to the Appropriations Committee was confined to committees in being in 1921.

One Washington observer of the operation of Clause 6 noted the result:

> Both by accident and by design, it [Clause 6] favors the pork-barrel agencies over the social agencies. It means two or three extra votes for the Pentagon, farm subsidies, public works, military construction, space extravaganzas, and atomic-energy subsidies. There are no extra votes for housing, schools, health, mass transit, consumers, crime prevention or other social programs. . . .
>
> In every case those selected are the senior members. With some honorable exceptions they are special pleaders for the agencies represented by their legislative committees.[3]

The most encouraging reform in the Congress has been the drastic change in the appropriations process made by the Budget and Impoundment Control Act of 1974.[4] The 1974 Act was inspired by the decline in Congressional influence on budgetary matters and in particular by the arrogance of President Nixon in "impounding" (i.e., not spending) funds appropriated by Congress for programs of which Nixon did not approve. Under the Act, the fiscal year of the Federal government was changed from July 1–June 30 to October 1–September 30 (starting with fiscal year 1977, which began on October 1, 1976).

What theretofore had been an uncoordinated process of adopting fifteen separate appropriations bills (and still further separate bills to provide for the taxes to meet expenditures) was consolidated into a coordinated, coherent process. To describe the process briefly, by January 15 prior to the opening of each fiscal year, the Congressional Budget Office (created by the Act), the Office of Management and Budget in the White House and the Congressional Joint Economic Committee must prepare studies concerning spending, economic assumptions about unemployment, inflation and the like, culminating in the submission by the President of his budget fifteen days after the Congress convenes in January. The various Congressional committees then study the administration budget and the Congressional Budget Office submissions looking toward adoption on May 15, on the basis of a report from the House and Senate Budget Committees (also created by the Act), of a concurrent resolution that tentatively sets spending outlays, budget authority, the limit of the surplus or deficit in the overall budget, the proposed amount of any increase or decrease in taxes and any increase required in the public-debt limit. Before adoption of this resolution, neither the House nor the Senate may consider spending bills or changes in revenue or the debt limit.

From May 15 through the seventh day after Labor Day, action is taken on individual appropriation bills, using the specifications of the first concurrent resolution as a guide. By September 15, the Congress must adopt a second concurrent resolution, which "reaffirms or revises" the parameters of the earlier resolution. Between then and September 25, individual appropriation or tax bills out of line with the second resolution must be reconciled. Congress may not adjourn until this process is complete.

The 1974 Act is not revolutionary, but if its procedures work in practice, rational order, and not uncoordinated chaos, may emerge. As *Congressional Quarterly* noted:

> The process requires members of Congress for the first time to vote on a deficit. Instead of treating spending and tax measures individually and separately, Congress is forced to compare total spending with total receipts. In doing so, Congress must confront such fiscal policy issues as the effect of the budget on inflation, unemployment and economic growth.
>
> The Budget Act also required members for the first time to make choices and thereby set priorities. For example, if Congress calls for more spending for health programs, it now must increase revenues through higher taxes, accept a larger deficit or balance the addition by cutting other programs.[5]

A "dry run" of the new process in 1975 generally proved successful. Attempts from the left to increase appropriations for the school-lunch program over the first concurrent resolution limits and from the right to increase funds for weapons procurement were both defeated. Senator Edmund S. Muskie (Democrat, Maine) and then Congressman Brock

Adams (Democrat, Washington), chairman of the Senate and House Budget Committees, successfully led an uneasy coalition through the various votes and procedures required to implement the process, despite objections by conservatives and such interest groups as the AFL-CIO to changes in the chaotic (and hence more manipulable) status quo. "To the surprise of many, Congress has taken the new procedures seriously. ... [the new process] should enable Congress to allocate the nation's resources among competing objectives more judiciously, with a more appropriate economic impact, and with a closer eye to its sense of the nation's priorities."[6]

The Act also requires the Congress to take into account tax "expenditures" as well as direct spending by the government, recognizing that spending policies of the Federal government can be budgeted directly or by means of tax "expenditures."* The net effect of this analysis should be to require a broader and more intelligent view of policy matters. For example, the question of real-estate tax shelters for investment in low-income housing may be considered not only within the larger context of closing tax loopholes but also within the context of whether such shelters (tax "expenditures") have a higher or lower cost-benefit ratio than direct government subsidies for such housing.[7]

In 1976 and 1977, several budget resolutions passed the houses of Congress by very close votes and in one instance (in April 1977) the preliminary resolution was defeated in the House by a coalition of liberal Democrats opposed to the proposed level of defense spending and Republicans displeased with the size of the projected budget deficit. (A compromise resolution was passed a week later.)

"The process has a long way to go before becoming a Washington institution," a reporter commented in 1977. But he also noted the commitment to the process by the Congressional leadership and many committee chairmen, and he observed that "memories of uncoordinated spending are fresh enough to make legislators fear that failure will mean that too much money will go where they believe it is needed least."[8]

In 1977, the Congressional budget managers avoided a confrontation over the Food and Agriculture Act of 1977.† The Act, as adopted, was estimated to cost (exclusive of its Food Stamp features) some $700 million over the ceiling for agricultural subsidies set in the second

---

* See Appendix A for examples of estimated tax "expenditures" for fiscal 1979.
† See pp. 34–35, *supra*.

concurrent resolution. Rather than confront Senator Herman E. Talmadge (Democrat, Georgia) and other friends of the farmer with a so-called "reconciliation instruction," which would have mandated a reduction of $700 million in agricultural appropriations, they amended the resolution itself to permit the greater spending on agriculture.

Changes in the budgeting process and other structural reforms, salutary as they may be, will not restore the "broken branch" to health without a change in attitude on the part of both Congressmen and the electorate.

In a recent poll commissioned by the House, a majority of the public said that a Congressman's most important duty was making sure his district gets its fair share of government money and projects. The polled voters also said that a Congressman's votes should reflect the majority view of his district, even when that view might be at variance with his perception of the national interest or his own conscience.[9]

The authors of the *Federalist,* defending the direct election of the House of Representatives, argued that motives of a "selfish nature" would bind a Representative to his constituents:

> His pride and vanity attach him to a form of government which favors his pretensions and gives him a share in its honors and distinctions. . . . It must generally happen that a great proportion of the men deriving their advancement from their influence with the people, would have more to hope from a preservation of the favor, than from innovations in the government subversive of the authority of the people.[10]

This observation was prescient. Both the Congressman and his constituents have become increasingly more interested in the "preservation of the favor" than in attempts to perceive and act in accordance with the overriding national interest or to come to grips with major social and economic issues.

The time is past when the average voter confronts the Federal government only on income-tax day. The medical and educational programs already discussed, and intensified Federal regulation of pension plans, hiring practices and safety and health standards have vastly increased the opportunity for—and the necessity of—contact between the voter and the Federal bureaucracy. And with that contact has come the need for a friend in Washington who can advise and expedite and intervene as an informal ombudsman when things go wrong or astray.

That friend in the usual case is the local Representative or Senator.

As the result, a bargain is struck whereby the Representative or Senator functions as a sort of super caseworker, tracking the misplaced Medicare claim or helping to untangle the knots of immigration policy, for example. In return, the Congressman is reelected to office, where he can enjoy the "honors and distinctions" of government and draw a respectable annual salary of $57,500.*

Since the 1950s, there has been a steady decline in the number of House seats in which the margin of victory was less than 20 percent of the vote. Incumbency is favored in both the House and the Senate, and the so-called "swing ratio" (the percentage increase in House seats a party obtains when it receives a one percent increase in the popular vote nationwide) has dropped substantially.[11]

Political scientists have advanced several reasons for these changes,† but the most plausible seems to be the new status of Congressmen as nonideological, district-first custodians, returned to office for services rendered to their constituents. It would seem to be no accident that staff allotments in the Congress increased by 50 percent between 1967 and 1973.[12] And the lesson of 1966 cannot be lost on the seekers of reelection, that lesson being that Republicans gained the largest number of seats in the House in twenty-five years after the "Xerox Congress," the Congress which passed more programs than any since the beginning of the New Deal.

Unhappily the district-first attitude is found even among the much-heralded "new blood" that is supposed to revitalize the legislative branch. Echoing the *Federalist*, Alan Otten of the *Wall Street Journal* wrote in 1977:

---

* A survey by the Presidential Commission on Federal Salaries, reported in 1977 but made before the $12,900 Congressional pay increase in 1977, showed that new Congressmen averaged a 2 percent increase in salary when they entered Congress. Judges, by contrast, took an average 33 percent salary cut on assuming office. T. R. Reid, "The Rich Man's Club," *Washington Post*, March 14, 1977, p. 1.

† The explanation with the most ironic twist is that incumbents in the House have been able to exert their influence when district lines have been redrawn by state legislatures. In 1946, a majority of the Supreme Court, in *Colegrove v. Green*, 328 U.S. 549, disassociated the Court from interfering in the "political question" of redistricting. In 1964, the Court reversed itself, and decreed that districts must be apportioned as nearly as possible in accordance with the principle of "one man, one vote." *Wesberry v. Sanders*, 376 U.S. 1. By outlawing the "gerrymander" and the "safe" district, this decision was expected to increase the responsiveness of House members. Edward R. Tufte has argued that the redistricting that has taken place "has given incumbents new opportunities to construct secure districts for themselves." "The Relationship Between Seats and Votes in Two-Party Systems," *American Political Science Review*, June 1973, p. 553.

Most new members love the job, and want to keep it. They like the prestige; the pay is good; the work's not that hard for a vigorous young person. "Let's face it," a sophomore Democrat says. "A lot of us are on a real ego trip. The direct mail, the mobile office back home, all the drudgery of casework—that's our ticket to keep on taking that trip."

"It's all well and good for these [new] guys to give first-rate service to their constituents," one senior Democrat told Otten. "But their work as legislators and as educators is third-rate, and that's not well and good."[13]

A second consequence of the district-first attitude is the preservation of government programs of marginal utility but with a high degree of visibility or support back home—Corps of Engineers projects, Civil Defense outlays, support for the Reserves and the National Guard.

Taking this last example, $1.7 billion was included in the President's Budget for the Army and Air National Guard and the Army, Navy, Air Force and Marine Reserves in fiscal 1977. It is doubtful that any former Reservist or National Guardsman in possession of his faculties and a minimum commitment to the truth could say that, based on his experience, these reserve forces have any capacity to defend this country anywhere, at any time or in any way (except conceivably with long sticks, in hand-to-hand combat). Yet the myth is perpetuated that the reserves are "ready," or at least are in the process of getting ready.

In actuality the Reserve–National Guard system is a social-welfare program, providing supplemental income (a day's military pay for an evening's drill) to its members, many if not most of whom would be below or close to the poverty line if required to earn a living without the extra income the Reserves or National Guard provides. And, in the case of higher officers, one should not overlook the ego fulfillment that dressing up in a uniform and "commanding" may instill.

Can the Reserves and National Guard be justified as a defense proposition? Probably not, since objectively it would seem impossible to give adequate military training on a sporadic once-a-week or two-weeks-in-the-summer basis. Can they be justified as social-assistance programs? Most assuredly not, for the criteria for public assistance do not apply.*

---

* Incredible as it may seem, the House of Representatives in April 1977 voted to authorize $44.8 million more for another defense-related boondoggle, civil defense (i.e., fallout shelters and the like), than the Pentagon had asked for, making the total sum, $134.8 million, the highest civil defense expenditure in a decade. Representative G. William Whitehurst (Republican, Virginia) defended the increased authorization as necessary to implement a program to provide fallout shelters within a day's walking

But any cut in Reserve appropriations will be opposed by the Congressman facing homeward.

Similarly, it is difficult to pretend that most of the scrub-pine military bases in the country are necessary for the national defense. What they are essential to are the economies of nearby communities. Keeping many of these installations open is not a matter of military policy but of economic policy. But why keep them open for the wrong reason? If a military post has no defense purpose, it should either be closed or operated for a useful purpose, such as job training, the rehabilitation of juvenile delinquents or the like. But try and convince the district-first Congressman of this.*

The third and most troubling consequence of the district-first attitude is a failure to view the country's larger problems in a national perspective.

The argument has been made historically that national prosperity depends upon the prosperity of all sections of the economy and regions of the country. The national economy is only as strong as its weakest link. Over the years, this has meant a massive transfer of wealth, through Federal programs, from tax-rich areas to tax-poor areas. Depending on one's perspective, liberals from tax-rich areas have been willing to help the poorer areas—or have been too ineffective to prevent such transfers, as through farm-support programs, for example.

Today, when the relative needs of various regions of the country have changed, there does not seem to be a like willingness to spend tax dollars where they are most needed—namely in the decaying urban centers of the great cities. As we have seen in the case of Title I of

---

distance of major urban areas, based on the assumption of "a three-day notice of nuclear attack." "We were wondering," the *Washington Post* editorialized, "whether there might be something in the bill that required the Russians to give three days' notice—and perhaps also file an environmental impact statement—before launching a nuclear attack." "On the Beach Again" (Editorial), *Washington Post*, April 28, 1977, p. A18.

* In his 1976 campaign debate with Vice President Mondale, Republican candidate Robert Dole did the unthinkable by explicitly linking defense spending with jobs:

In the area of defense . . . he [Mondale] votes for every budget cut. I think he's voted to cut the budget . . . some $16 billion against the B-1 bombers, which means a lot of jobs. . . .

I'd like to add up the number of jobs Senator Mondale has cost this country in defense plants, defense jobs, in all his anti-defense votes. It'd be hundreds and hundreds of thousands, and he knows it.

"Transcript of Debate Between the Vice-Presidential Candidates," *New York Times*, October 16, 1976, pp. 8–9.

ESEA, aid formulas targeted to reach the greatest concentrations of deprived children—that is, urban concentrations—are distorted so that virtually all school districts share in Federal assistance. Adequate funding for all is next to impossible; efficiently targeted funding is also next to impossible if each Congressman insists that the formula somehow be skewed so that his district shares in the limited resource pie.

No one can expect voters consistently to vote against their immediate self-interest as they perceive it. And no Congressman could long survive by ignoring the opinions of his constituents. But is it too much to ask both voter and Congressman to avoid the narrower focuses of the district-first mentality and to be receptive to larger solutions to national social problems? Or for a Congressman to make a minimal effort toward educating his constituents to the sometimes indirect and subtle stake his district may have in the solution of social problems?

Ironically, the district-first Congressman who excels in performing services for his constituents, thereby assuring continued reelection, may have created a situation where he can exercise independent judgment on important issues. But that has not been the pattern to date.

In terms of its internal reforms and its new leadership, the Congress is now positioned to make responsible contributions to the general welfare. The success of the Congress is, however, going to depend on the ability and the will of its members, and what the voters are willing to demand—or perhaps not to demand—of their Congressmen.

Eight · The Presidency: Republicans

*Can you tell me one single program . . . in the past 30 years of benefit to the
people that's identified with the Republican party or its leaders?*
—JOHN F. KENNEDY, October 1962[1]

In April 1976, the Gallup Poll took one of its periodic surveys to
determine what the public thought was the most important problem
then facing the country, with the following results:

High cost of living	38%
Unemployment	24%
Dissatisfaction with government	13%
Corruption in government	4%
Crime	8%
Drug abuse	3%
Foreign affairs	5%
Moral decline	4%
Race relations	3%
Other	27%
No opinion	3%

Each poll respondent was asked as a follow-up question which
political party could best handle the problem or problems the respondent had named. A clear plurality in every category, whether grouped
by age, race, occupation, income or residence (the one exception being
enrolled Republicans), named the Democratic Party over the GOP.
Overall, 39 percent favored the Democrats and 18 percent the Republicans, with 31 percent saying it made no difference and 12 percent
undecided.[2]

An earlier 1975 survey, commissioned by the Republican National Committee, no less, found that only 27 percent of the electorate thought the Republicans "competent" and only 25 percent found them "trustworthy."[3]

These results are at odds with former Senator Hugh Scott's observation that Republicans are "the best stock. We are the people who represent the real grit, brains and backbone of America."[4]

A review of the domestic problems named in the Gallup survey and the response to them of the three Republican Presidents since 1945— Dwight D. Eisenhower, Richard M. Nixon and Gerald R. Ford—perhaps indicates why the Gallup results turned out as they did.

High Cost of Living—Inflation

Few issues have stimulated Republican orators more than the "thievery" of inflation.[5] Yet the flood of Republican oratory has simply not been translated into effective action, as evidenced most recently in the record of the Nixon and Ford administrations. From January 1969, when Richard Nixon took office, through 1976 the Consumer Price Index (despite the Nixon wage-and-price-control program) had increased by more than 50 percent with a corresponding decrease in the purchasing power of the dollar by more than one third.[6]

The Democrats have been far from guiltless in the matter of countering inflation; Lyndon Johnson's simultaneous funding of Great Society programs and the expanded Vietnam war effort had a marked upward effect on price levels. And Democrats have been willing to tolerate a greater degree of inflation to stimulate economic growth than have the Republicans.

Whatever the Democrats' indifference to inflation, it has been more than made up for by the Republicans. Inflation has traditionally been a Republican issue and at the center of Republican concern, presumably because of its effects on basic elements of the Republican constituency: lenders repaid by borrowers in dollars with cheapened purchasing power and the affluent (and relatively affluent) retired living on fixed incomes or fixed-income investments, the value of which depreciates in times of inflation.

President Eisenhower defined the problem and the conventional Republican response to it in a 1953 speech:

From the day that the new administration came into a position of responsibility and authority, every single proposed expenditure of government, indeed some of those already in progress, have been under constant examination by men who are experts in the business—by business men. These are men who believe that the soundness of your money is absolutely essential to our form of government. These are men who believe that unless you have a sound and stable value to your money, then there is no point in your taking out an insurance policy, or investing in a savings bond, or doing any of those other things which in the American way means putting aside some money for a rainy day, or against the time of danger. If that money deteriorates while it is in your bank, or in your bonds, or in your pocket, the incentive for saving is removed.

And so this very great issue has been tackled from every single standpoint. First of all, the new administration is trying to cut costs in the effort to get rid of recurring deficits in our national budget—in spite of the necessary and staggering costs of providing for security in this modern world.

Now, if we can work toward eliminating that deficit, one of the most terrific incentives for the cheapening of your money will have been removed. No one will pretend that the recurring deficits are the only reason for inflation, but they are an important one. It is not too much to say that with recurring deficits, you must have inflation, because the only way to meet the debt is to secure more money, which means cheaper money —printing press money.[7]

The Republicans' approach to inflation has been puzzling, for often demands for cutting government spending as a means of reducing inflationary pressures have been accompanied by equally strident demands for tax cuts, which orthodox economic theory would say should increase such pressures. Immediately after World War II, for example, the Truman administration was faced with increasing inflation resulting from consumer demand pent up during the war. With demand outpacing production and prices rising, the Republican position was to call for an immediate end to the World War II controls on wages and prices and, in 1947, to pass a major tax cut. Truman, in vetoing the tax cut, was required to read a lesson in basic economics (at least as "basic economics" was then understood) to the Republican Congress:

The time for tax reduction will come when general inflationary pressures have ceased and the structure of prices is on a more stable basis than now prevails. . . .

A time of high employment and high prices, wages, and profits, such as the present, calls for a surplus in Government revenue over expenditures and the application of all or much of this surplus to the reduction of the public debt.... If the Government does not reduce the public debt during the most active and inflationary periods, there is little prospect of material reduction at any time, and the country would, as a result, be in a poorer position to extend supports to the economy should a subsequent deflationary period develop.

With the present huge public debt, it is of first importance that every effort now be made to reduce the debt as much as possible....

The integrity of the public debt is the financial bedrock on which our national economy rests. More than half of the American people are direct owners of Government securities. A major portion of the assets of banks, insurance companies, and trust funds is invested in Government bonds. To maintain the integrity of the public debt, we must now reduce it by substantial amounts.[8]

The Republicans are right in saying that the present level of inflation is intolerable, being far above the 2-to-3 percent annual level that most economists assume to be necessary for economic growth to continue. The situation is further made intolerable by the fact that unemployment has persisted at record levels, defying the economic precepts that appeared to be unquestioned at the time of Truman's veto message —inflation will decline as unemployment rises or, put another way, inflation cannot be abated without significant unemployment.

Lyndon Johnson's deficit spending is one reason advanced by the GOP for the present inflation. But it seems a little hard to blame Johnson for the state of the economy more than ten years later; besides, as J. K. Galbraith has pointed out, there was a surplus in the national income accounts in fiscal 1969, which turned to a deficit only when the Nixon administration allowed the surtax to lapse, and the price index had risen from a base of 100 in 1967 only to 106.5 in January 1969, when Nixon took office.

"In fact," Galbraith states, "the fiscal position inherited by the Nixon Administration was, as such matters are usually described, remarkably sound. This was not so true of the efforts of its economists to make economic causation a branch of archaeology."[9]

Another "devil theory" used by the Nixon-Ford administration to explain away inflation was the worldwide increase in petroleum prices that began in 1973. To the extent that prices have risen to reflect increased costs of fuel there has been an undoubted inflationary effect. But, as both Galbraith and former Professor Richard N. Cooper of Yale have noted, the increased revenues to OPEC countries, to the extent not recycled into the world economy, have had a deflationary effect on the oil consuming countries (including the United States), acting much as a sales tax would operate in curbing purchasing power.[10]

Economists have been puzzled by the simultaneous existence of high unemployment and high inflation. Among the theories advanced have been that important sectors of the economy are no longer subject to supply-and-demand principles. Manufacturers are able to raise prices even though consumer demand has decreased and operations are at less than capacity; this has certainly happened in recent years with automobiles, steel and many chemicals. Likewise, big labor is able to negotiate substantial wage increases, even though there is significant unemployment. But most economists do not really seem certain as to the total impact of such price behavior or labor demands.*

If the economists are in doubt, the Republicans are not: the root cause of inflation remains, as it always has been, government spending. In vetoing the Health, Education and Welfare appropriation passed by Congress in 1970, President Nixon aptly expressed this view:

> In the past decade, the Federal Government spent more than it took in —$57 billion more. These deficits caused prices to rise 25% in a decade.[11]

President Ford adopted the same view, "stonewalling" Congress by vetoing virtually every bill which would involve spending above the levels set by the White House. From August 1974 until he left office, Ford vetoed 62 public bills. This was consistent with the Nixon formulation of the problem, which would virtually eliminate *any* new spending, since the administration and the Congress should oppose spending programs that "would help some people but that would raise prices for all people."[12]

The Nixon-Ford position had venerable, if dubious antecedents. Calling for a balanced budget and *increased* taxes in the depths of the Depression, Herbert Hoover had said:

> The first requirement of confidence and of economic recovery is financial stability of the United States Government. . . . We must have insistent

* But see the views of Arthur Okun described on pp. 250–51.

and determined reduction in Government expenses. . . . Rigid economy is a real road to relief. . . . Our first duty as a nation is to put our governmental house in order. . . . We cannot squander ourselves into prosperity.[13]

The Nixon-Ford approach to inflation had at least the following deficiencies:

1. It failed to make any distinction between inflation at a time of full production and inflation at a time when the nation's industrial plant was not operating at full capacity. Government spending will obviously fuel inflation if industry is operating at capacity, since demand will be increased by such spending at a time when more goods cannot be produced to meet it. This is the situation that exists in wartime and existed in the years immediately after 1965 as the result of the production demands created by a combination of the shooting war in Vietnam and the nonshooting war on poverty. It is not at all clear that increasing government spending to stimulate consumer demand will be inflationary if industry is not operating at capacity, particularly if such spending is targeted to depressed economic sectors and areas.

2. It failed to recognize that expenditures in the private sector, as well as government expenditures, can stimulate inflation. Capital expenditures by industry have precisely the same effect as expenditures by government—they increase purchasing power. Yet the Republican anti-inflation program never sought to restrain private investment; only public investment should be curtailed. This is apparently on the assumption that private investment, no matter for what frivolous purpose, is always superior to public investment, however worthy its social objectives may be. There was no thought of assigning priorities to investment, public and private, on the basis of need or objective.

3. If union wage demands are in fact a significant cause of inflation, the Republicans hardly made an attempt to discover the dimensions of the problem or to do anything about it. This is perhaps understandable in view of Republican attempts to win political support from unions the wage demands of which, at least in normal times, could be expected to have the greatest inflationary effect, such as former Secretary of Labor Peter Brennan's construction workers and the Teamsters.

4. The obsession with government spending did not permit the exploring of new and imaginative measures that might relieve the hardships caused by inflation, such as the "indexing" of pensions and fixed-

income securities, or adjusting income-tax payments to avoid taxation at higher progressive rates on increases in income attributable to inflation rather than increased "real" earnings. Such concepts have been adopted abroad, most notably in Brazil, but they clearly must be introduced into an economic system under government aegis, not piecemeal on a private basis.

5. If increases in productivity result in lowering product prices and permit wage increases which do not require corresponding price increases, encouragement of productivity gains should be a part of anti-inflation policy. With much fanfare, President Nixon appointed in July 1970 a National Commission on Productivity, consisting of a distinguished panel of industry, labor, public and government members.[14] The accomplishments of this Commission, which continues today as the National Center for Productivity and Quality of Working Life, have been modest, to say the least. Under a strengthened Congressional mandate in 1975, the Commission is now charged with encouraging "productivity growth consistent with the needs of the economy, the environment, and the needs, rights and best interest of management, the work force and consumers."[15] The Commission represents a start, but little more, in exploring the whole area of productivity, and certainly does not hold out to the smaller entrepreneur, unable to afford his own research and development on productivity problems or to acquire expertise in dealing with such problems, the sort of technical assistance that is routinely provided to the farmer by the Department of Agriculture.*

6. The single-minded cut-spending approach ruled out price and wage controls as a tool for containing inflation or, perhaps more important, as a threat to compel "voluntary" compliance by industry and labor with price and wage guidelines. President Nixon, who said in 1970 that "wage and price controls only postpone a day of reckoning of a very important part of freedom,"[16] of course reversed himself the following year with the Phase I, II, III and IV controls, which extended to April 1974. President Ford reverted to the traditional Republican

---

* Productivity, as measured by output per hour of all workers in the private sector, grew at a rate of 3.2 percent during the period 1947 through 1966, then dropped sharply to an average 1.6 percent from 1967 to 1976. The Bureau of Labor Statistics projects average annual growth at 2.4 percent for the period 1973–80 and 2.7 percent from 1980 to 1985. Ronald E. Kutscher, Jerome A. Mark and John R. Norsworthy, "The productivity slowdown and the outlook to 1985," *Monthly Labor Review*, May 1977, pp. 3–4.

antipathy to controls, bolstered by the conclusion that the Nixon controls had not worked:

> The free economy over the years has proven to be the best answer [to inflation], and our experiences in the last several years with wage and price controls has [*sic*] not been a very good one.[17]

Faced with double-digit inflation in 1974, the Ford administration, while rigidly adhering to its strategy of resisting government spending, did propose other anti-inflation measures, most of which on their face seemed doomed to failure: the quickly abandoned WIN (Whip Inflation Now) button campaign; what amounted to an all-American essay contest in which private citizens were asked to send ten suggestions for fighting inflation to the President;[18] and the appointment of a confusing proliferation of committees—the Council on Wage and Price Stability, the White House Labor-Management Committee, a new Economic Policy Board and a National Commission on Supplies and Shortages.

Substantive Republican attempts to deal with inflation have simply not matched the purported concern for halting inflation displayed in Republican oratory. Given the gap between rhetoric and performance, it does not seem unfair to conclude that the Republicans' anti-inflation approach of cutting government spending is often really a respectable camouflage for opposing social programs. Certainly it was in social programs, and not the defense budget, where cuts were made and increases stopped, all in the name of fighting inflation. And particular social programs at that. In his 1970 State of the Union message, President Nixon discussed inflation at great length, concluding that "we must balance our Federal budget so that American families will have a better chance to balance their family budgets." The very next subject discussed in the message was an increase in the Federal budget to "declare and win the war against the criminal elements."[19]

As Adlai Stevenson once remarked, Republican discussions of inflation seem filled with "exaggeration, misstatement and fallacy" and often make discussion "an exercise not of reason but of ideology."[20]

Unemployment

In view of the unemployment figures, it is hardly surprising that public confidence in Republican ability to reduce unemployment was low in the Nixon-Ford years. Republicans' fear of inflation appeared to make them incapable of adopting policies designed to stimulate the economy and increase jobs.

In fairness, one must say that the lowest annual unemployment rate in the postwar period (2.9 percent in 1953) occurred in the first year of the Eisenhower administration. But Eisenhower seemed completely unable to cope with the unemployment problem when it became more acute. In fact, it was considered something of a wonder that he endorsed the concept of unemployment insurance at all, although such a system had been in existence for twenty-five years when he came into office.

"I believe that our citizens," Eisenhower pronounced in 1954, "now *generally* accept the principle that insurance against loss of income due to unemployment . . . should be provided under law. This is a practical and orderly way to alleviate such personal hardships in a free, private enterprise economy."[21]

Such a grudging acceptance of the unemployment-insurance concept was as close as Eisenhower came to proposing measures for increasing jobs. Following the Lincoln maxim that Eisenhower was fond of quoting—that the government should only do for people what they cannot do for themselves—he apparently concluded that people could not provide their own unemployment insurance, but could somehow provide or create their own jobs.

With Richard Nixon, one had the feeling at times that he perhaps preferred to have a large unemployed population, straining governmental unemployment and welfare resources. Elimination of indolent welfare recipients would have deprived him of one of his more colorful issues.*

---

* Those who remember the Nixon Family Assistance Plan may disagree with this conclusion, but I do not feel Nixon's conduct concerning the FAP contradicts it. In August 1969, Nixon offered an imaginative and enlightened outline for welfare reform which in effect provided for a guarantee of income for a family of four of $1,600 a year. This complicated plan, a respectable and major step toward welfare reform, was generally acknowledged to be the handiwork of Daniel Patrick Moynihan, then a Counselor to the President. The FAP proposal twice passed the House, but never reached the floor of the Senate. Moynihan himself has laid the blame for this legislative defeat at the door of a cabal of Southern conservatives, who thought the proposal did too much, and liberals, who thought it was too meager. See Moynihan, *The Politics of Guaranteed Income: The Nixon Administration and the Family Assistance Plan* (New York: Random House, 1973). But the fact is that Nixon never really pushed the plan or challenged its Senate opponents. With typical hyperbole, he called it "one of the dozen or half-dozen most important pieces of domestic legis-

This is a possible explanation for his veto in 1971 of amendments to the Economic Opportunity Act, which would have provided extensive day-care and child-development facilities for the children of working mothers, and poor, urban mothers heading up families at that. The ostensible reasons given for the veto were his fear of a swollen bureaucracy, the relegation of the states to a secondary role, and the commitment of the "vast moral authority of the National Government to the side of communal approaches to child rearing over against the family-centered approach."[22]

The Republicans have not played favorites in their disdain for creating jobs. Not only have they refrained from job-stimulating fiscal policies, they have avoided programs which would have aided segments of the public that one would have normally thought to be part of the Republican constituency. As Lyndon Johnson once pointed out, nearly ten million Americans left the nation's farms for its cities in the 1950s. Noting that the Republicans were in power for much of this period, Johnson asked rhetorically: "Did you hear the Republicans urging the country to find jobs and to provide training for rural people who had no skills when they came to the city and wanted to work? Did you find them pressing for help to depressed areas, so that the people might be encouraged to remain in rural America, instead of crowding into the cities?"[23]

Given the unemployment rates in the middle 1970s, even Republican policy-makers acknowledged that *some* measures perhaps should be taken to relieve joblessness. But the combination of a dread fear of inflation (heightened by the then current rate of inflation) and a general indifference to relieving joblessness produced some strange proposals, none more so than the plan of Dr. Arthur Burns for *lowering* the minimum wage.

---

lation in American history" (clearly a ghost-written description, since Moynihan refers to the plan in the same terms on page 4 of his book), but his own actions did not accord with his extravagant description. The failure of the FAP was not a subject of Nixon's campaign oratory in 1972 and, by 1973, he denied that his Secretary of Health, Education and Welfare, Casper Weinberger, was correct in saying that the Nixon Administration had never been "comfortable" with FAP, declaring simply that the Senate was only willing to pass a bill embodying the plan on a basis (of higher benefit levels) that "we could not possibly afford." All evidences of horse-trading and compromise by the President to enact this "important piece of domestic legislation" are utterly lacking. See Special Message to the Congress on Reform of the Nation's Welfare System, August 11, 1969; Special Message to the Congress on the Administration's Legislative Program, September 11, 1970; and Press Conference, March 2, 1973.

Burns, President Eisenhower's principal economic adviser and Nixon's choice as head of the (independent) Federal Reserve Board, made a distinction in 1975 between "voluntary" and "involuntary" unemployment. In his view, it was proper for the government to assist the "involuntary" unemployed, that is, those who are willing to work below the minimum wage but are prevented from doing so by the Federal minimum-wage law. Even Dr. Herbert Stein, chairman of Nixon's and Ford's Council of Economic Advisers, while citing Burns's analysis with approval, conceded that the voluntary-involuntary distinction was one that "no public official has dared to breathe for about forty-five years." Given its overtones of Dickensian wage slavery and the line at the plant gate as the best way of keeping down wages (inflation again), one can easily see why.[24]

To the "involuntary" unemployed worker, Burns would have offered public employment—"for example, in hospitals, school, public parks or the like"—at a rate of pay "somewhat below" the Federal minimum wage. His plan would not reach the "voluntary unemployed"—i.e., those unwilling to work for subsistence wages—"but there is also no compelling reason why it should do so. What it would do is to make jobs available for those who need to earn some money."

To minimize the net cost of this plan, Burns would have sharply reduced "the scope of unemployment insurance and other governmental programs to alleviate income loss."

Burns's "dismal-science" approach is rather much in contrast with the conclusion reached by Elliott Liebow, an anthropologist at the National Institute of Mental Health, who has extensively studied the human costs of unemployment. Discussing substandard wages, Liebow writes:

> The man who works hard but cannot earn a living has put himself on the scales and been found wanting. He says to society, "I have done what needed doing. Now, what am I worth?" and society answers, "Not much, not even enough to support yourself and your dependents." But the man who does not seek out or accept such a job [Burns's "voluntary unemployed"] may, for a while at least, fool himself or his fellows into thinking that he has not climbed onto the scales at all.
>
> By itself . . . work does not guarantee full and valued participation in society. Participation . . . requires, reciprocally, an acknowledgment by society that the contribution is of value. That acknowledgment, typically in the form of wages, lets the man know that he is somebody. . . . But the

man who cannot find a job, or the man who finds one but is still unable to support himself and his family, is being told in clear and simple language, and loud enough for his wife and children and friends and neighbors and everyone else to hear, that he is not needed, that there is no place for him.[25]

At last forced to cope with joblessness and inflation, the Republicans have turned adversity to advantage by proposing solutions to these problems that in effect represent sideswipes at the progress that has been made with respect to environmental protection and industrial safety. As Dr. Burns has also said:

Progress towards full employment and price stability would be measurably improved, I believe, by stretching out the timetables for achieving our environmental and safety goals.[26]

Crime; Drug Abuse

Richard Nixon said that crime would double in the United States in four years if he were not elected in 1968.[27] He was elected, and crime did not double. But it nonetheless increased substantially from 295 violent crimes per 100,000 population in 1968 to 397 in 1972 and 425 by the time Nixon left office in 1974.[28]

The Nixon administration proposed measure after measure to curb "crime in the streets" and to preserve "law and order," but once again Nixon appeared to be more concerned with the appearance of his appeals to the public than with a thoroughgoing attack on factors that might be thought to reduce crime, such as combating unemployment and reforming the criminal-justice, bail and penal systems. There was much oratory, much razzle-dazzle, but very little that went to the substance of crime prevention.

Nixon, for example, reorganized Federal drug-law enforcement efforts in a reorganization plan submitted to Congress in 1973. The Bureau of Narcotics and Dangerous Drugs, the Office of Narcotics Intelligence and the Office for Drug Abuse Law Enforcement were transferred into the Justice Department, along with 500 Customs Service agents from the Treasury and 900 inspectors from the Immigration Service. The highly touted reorganization did not work. Two years after it took place, a Senate subcommittee concluded that smuggling of all types of narcotics and street sales had increased (the estimated smuggling rate of heroin being some 10 to 20 million tons a year). This despite a budget of $10 million for purchasing information and evidence (i.e., illegal drugs) alone, compared with a similar budget for such purposes of $750,000 in fiscal 1967.[29]

Another major aspect of the Nixon war of the "peace forces" against the "criminal forces" was the Law Enforcement Assistance Administration. The LEAA had been established by Lyndon Johnson under the Omnibus Crime Control and Safe Streets Act of 1968. This act in turn had been the outgrowth of a report of a Presidential Commission on Law Enforcement and Administration of Justice,[30] which had called for Federal assistance to state and local governments in seeking new and innovative means of fighting crime and improving the court and corrections systems.

Johnson, while critical of amendments that broadened the 1968 Act's provision for the use of wiretapping and eavesdropping, nonetheless hailed it as a measure that would "help to lift the stain of crime and the shadow of fear from the streets of our communities."[31]

The 1968 Act and the LEAA did nothing of the sort. The Act provided for grants to the states for use by them and by local governments in improving law enforcement. The initial hurdle confronted was the unimaginative embarrassment of the states, which could not think what to do with the money. At the end of 1971, only 25 percent of the grants disbursed for fiscal years 1969, 1970 and 1971 had been turned over to local communities; several states simply invested the money and kept the interest earned.[32] Local communities, while more eager to spend, lacked guidance from LEAA as to what was expected of them. The result was an "extraordinary concentration on the purchase of hardware," including tanks for riot prevention and highly sophisticated surveillance equipment developed in Vietnam. Outside "consultants," often inexperienced and untrained, were hired. Upgrading of police training and expenditures for corrections and the courts were, predictably, neglected. The state of Arkansas, for example, despite a court finding that conditions in seven of its prisons required improvement for the protection of the Constitutional rights of prisoners, spent 7 percent of its initial LEAA grants for corrections, 37 percent for new hardware.

Since the beginning of LEAA, grants have been used to perfect shoes with changeable soles for policemen, to study the need for a loose-leaf encyclopedia on law enforcement, to provide Dale Carnegie courses for policemen in Kentucky and to fund a program of the Junior Leagues to enable its postdebutantes "to serve as catalysts in mobilizing community participation in organizing efforts to seek continued justice improvements."[33]

Grants under the 1968 Act were supposed to be matched by state governments, to be expended in programs that could be continued after the grants ran out and to be subject to prior Federal approval. President Nixon found these restraints too confining and, in 1971, proposed making Federal funds available on a "special revenue-sharing" basis (i.e., without restriction), giving local governments the "benefits of Federal assistance without the burdens of assistance built into the present grant programs."[34]

Other observers felt that more, not less, supervision was needed. A spokesman for the Committee for Economic Development told a Congressional committee in 1973 that LEAA had been "a grave disappointment, both in respect to the setting of rational standards and goals, and in the weakness of evaluative efforts."[35]

If the Congress would not unfetter the LEAA grants to the states, as it refused to do despite his 1971 appeal, Nixon could do the next-best thing and refuse to administer any standards. The results were summed up in 1973 by Sarah C. Carey, Assistant Director of the respected Lawyers' Committee for Civil Rights Under Law:

> [In] the four years since its creation, LEAA has imposed few standards, guidelines or restraints on the states to govern the expenditure of their block grant funds and has been loath to assist them in evolving viable planning mechanisms at the state and local levels. The agency has simply failed to administer the funds that it controls for research (The National Institute), for discretionary programs, and for manpower training in a manner that shows the way to the states in designing new approaches to old problems. The federal agency . . . has even refused to conduct evaluations and has not required the states to assume that obligation, making it almost impossible to determine what has worked.[36]

With such lack of supervision, it is also not surprising to find that the LEAA has had one of the worst civil-rights enforcement records among Federal agencies.[37]

Analyzing the LEAA in 1974, the General Accounting Office found that LEAA's efforts to provide seed money to projects had not worked and that projects simply stopped when the seed money ran out because of inadequate guidelines for establishing and continuing innovative projects.[38]

In 1976, President Ford requested that LEAA be extended for five years; Congress responded with a three-year extension to September 30, 1979. Spending appropriations continue at a rate of roughly $800 million a year.

One of the Nixon administration's most touted anticrime measures was the euphemistically titled District of Columbia Court Reform and Criminal Procedure Act of 1970, which endorsed "preventive detention" (the jailing of suspects for up to sixty days before trial without bail) and "no-knock" searches (which permitted policemen to enter private homes without a search warrant), a combination that led Senator Sam Ervin to call the act "a bill to repeal the Fourth, Fifth, Sixth, and Eighth Amendments to the Constitution." The Congress could act only in the area of "street crime" in the District of Columbia, but Nixon pressed for this highly repressive measure for its "symbolic" value.[39]

A postscript to the Nixon war on crime: In October 1974, Congress repealed the "no-knock" provision applicable to the District of Columbia; the vote in the Senate was 89–0. It "won't affect us one way or another," was the comment of District of Columbia Police Chief Jerry Wilson.[40]

Dissatisfaction with Government; Corruption in Government

As for Republican handling of corruption in government, in all decency there is nothing further one should say. Given Mr. Nixon's penchant for "firsts" and for describing accomplishments in superlatives —"I have traveled to more countries than any President who has ever held this office, seventy-four"*—it is irrestible to point out that he *was* the first President to resign (following the first twentieth-century Vice-President to resign), that more of his onetime cabinet members and more of his staff were indicted than in any previous administration (and probably all administrations combined), that Nixon was served by

---

* Remarks at Union Hall of United Steelworkers of America, Dundalk, Maryland, October 24, 1970. The ultimate Nixon "first" probably occurred on a visit to a sewage treatment plant in Hanover Park, Illinois: "I think you would be interested to know that during my years of traveling as a political official and as a campaigner, I have been to many facilities. This will be my first tour of this kind of a facility." Remarks, Hanover, Illinois, February 6, 1970.

more Attorneys General than any previous President (7 percent of the total since Edmund Randolph, in fact), et cetera, et cetera.

"Dissatisfaction with government" most likely covers a multitude of sins, but it seems reasonable in the Presidential context to construe it as meaning dissatisfaction with a lack of leadership. Such a lack can be found only too readily in the Republican Presidential record, taking "leadership" in the sense of using the Presidential forum as a means of raising, sharpening and defining issues, of educating the public to the complexities of issues, of persuading a majority to support just compromises of divisive issues.

Eisenhower

Aside from his farewell address, in which he warned of the dangers of "unwarranted influence" by the "military-industrial complex,"[41] it is hard to find exhortations of leadership in the public statements of President Eisenhower that go beyond the obvious and the platitudinous. A review of the transcripts of the Eisenhower press conferences brings home with striking force his ingrained and basic desire to avoid controversy. His self-imposed "rules" as to what questions he would answer, while sometimes plausible in the context of a given question, created a high and formidable screen behind which Ike could shield his opinions. When it suited his convenience, the past, the present and the future, as well as the Congress and the Judiciary, were all subjects which he would not discuss, under his self-imposed "rules."

Agreements made by Roosevelt and Truman with the Soviet Union were among such subjects, as he told reporter May Craig at a news conference on February 25, 1953:

> Oh, I think I have made it quite clear, Mrs. Craig, before a number of such press conferences, that I have no interest in going back and raking up the ashes of the dead past.

A Reconstruction Finance Corporation recommendation to the President that the government sell its synthetic-rubber plants to private industry was another untouchable topic when, on March 5, 1953, a reporter asked him about it:

Well, the recommendation hasn't reached me yet; therefore I don't know any of the arguments on either side of the question.

In answer to a question by Merriman Smith, of the Associated Press, at a news conference on June 17, 1953, Eisenhower ruled that it was improper for him to say whether a speech he had made at Dartmouth College had been meant to be a criticism of Senator Joseph R. McCarthy (Republican, Wisconsin):

Now, Merriman, you have been around me long enough to know that I never talk personalities. I think that we will get along faster in most of these conferences if we remember that I do not talk personalities; I refuse to do so.

At a news conference on March 10, 1954, he ruled out a question concerning Adlai Stevenson's criticism of the "new look" defense program:

Well, of course, I comment on nothing that other individuals say.

In response to a news reporter's question concerning a critical speech by former President Truman, Eisenhower had this to say on May 12, 1954:

I wouldn't answer anyone who finds it proper to criticize me and my actions. . . .

On April 29, 1954, Eisenhower dealt with a newsman's question regarding legislative restrictions on the President's authority to send troops to Indochina:

Well, I am not going to talk about Constitutional interpretations, because it scarcely needs to be said I am not a lawyer. . . .

When, at a news conference on January 21, 1959, a reporter asked him about the Supreme Court's desegregation rulings, he said:

I do not believe it is the function or indeed it is desirable for a President to express his approval or disapproval of any Supreme Court decision.

On April 29, 1954, at a news conference, Eisenhower was asked whether he would veto certain proposed farm legislation. He replied:

> I have several times said that I never prophesy in advance what I am going to do about vetoing bills. . . .*

At a news conference on January 30, 1954, he was asked a question relating to a substitute proposed by Senator Walter F. George for the so-called Bricker Amendment, which dealt with United States treaty obligations, and he answered:

> Well, I'll tell you, at this moment I am not going to talk about the details of the thing because, as was suggested a few minutes ago, these things are complicated; they are very complicated and they need long study.

At a news conference on February 26, 1958, Clark Mollenhoff asked a question relating to the propriety of alleged approaches to the Civil Aeronautics Board by Sherman Adams, Assistant to the President. Eisenhower's answer was:

> I don't want anything more about that.

Eisenhower's innate small-town conservatism always seemed to hold him back from exercising Presidential leadership in advancing social programs. Eisenhower, who had warned against the potential for "paternalism" and "socialism" in Federal aid to education in 1949 when he was President of Columbia University, was not prepared to arm-twist the Congress to achieve the margin of victory for his education program in 1957 when House Democrats withdrew objections to his program and urged its passage.† His recommendations on aid to education, as in so many other areas, "ranged from study to first-echelon action, then back to second-echelon study after first-echelon inaction."[42]

William V. Shannon has disputed Arthur Larson, the "quondam philosopher of 'Modern Republicanism,'" in Larson's conclusion that Eisenhower "for the first time in our history discovered and established

---

* To be fair to Eisenhower, Harry Truman too claimed that he never commented "on legislation that is not before me on the desk, and that hadn't been passed by the Congress as yet." News Conference, March 18, 1949. But this never stopped him from discussing the subject matter of legislation.

† See pp. 91–92, *supra*.

the Authentic American Center" and that the Eisenhower administration expressed an "American Consensus."

> The steady decay of the Republican party at the state and congressional-district level throughout the Eisenhower years is enough to discredit this thesis [Shannon wrote in 1958]. Parties which have formulated a widely accepted consensus on the big contemporary issues and are united behind a great leader do not show these alarming signs of disaffection and disrepair.
>
> There is an American Consensus on the issues, but it was developed by Franklin Roosevelt and developed further in some respects by Truman. Eisenhower has been content to leave it undisturbed.

Shannon concluded that the Eisenhower Presidency was a transitional one:

> He has not shaped the future nor tried to repeal the past. When he leaves office in January 1961, the foreign policies and the domestic policies of the past generation will be about where he found them in 1953. No national problem, whether it be education, housing, urban revitalization, agriculture, or inflation, will have been advanced importantly toward solution or its dimensions significantly altered.[48]

That sometime closet Republican, Daniel Patrick Moynihan, gives added credence to Shannon's analysis. Attempting to find achievements of Eisenhower to extol, Moynihan described his Interstate Highway System building program as a "massive event, the equivalent in ways of the building of the railroads."[44] In ways.

Nixon

Lyndon Johnson once called Richard Nixon a "chronic campaigner"[45] and a review of his record as President—leaving aside Watergate-related actions and statements—shows a dedication to neither principle nor program but a concern with shifting tactical maneuvers designed to appeal to a particular bloc within the electorate at, as they liked to say, a particular point in time. Even as steadfast a supporter as conservative speechwriter Patrick Buchanan appears to support this position. Jonathan Schell, in his first-rate study of the Nixon administration, *The Time of Illusion,* quotes Buchanan, in a memorandum to Nixon:

> We suffer from the widely held belief that the President has no Grand Vision that inspires him, no deeply held political philosophy that girds, guides and explains his words, decisions and deeds. The President is viewed as the quintessential political pragmatist, standing before an ideological buffet, picking some from this tray and some from that. On both sides he is seen as the textbook political transient, here today, gone tomorrow, shuttling back and forth, as weather permits, between liberal programs and conservative rhetoric. As someone put it, "the bubble in the carpenter's level."[46]

Since the President himself did not have a firm vision of a program, there was no question of educating the public about issues or leading the people to a consensus on issues. Quite the contrary, the shifting positions, the view of issues from a tactical rather than a substantive point of view, the conflict between deed and word can only have served to confuse and further disillusion the public.

"The Nixon administration was characterized by, among other things, fragmentation," Schell writes. "What the Nixon men thought was unconnected to what they said. What they said was unconnected to what they did. What they did or said they were doing at one moment was unconnected to what they did or said they were doing the next moment."[47]

In his first inaugural address, Nixon spoke of the need to "lower our voices," to avoid "inflated rhetoric that promises more than it can deliver; from angry rhetoric that fans discontents into hatreds; from bombastic rhetoric that postures instead of persuading."[48] These strictures soon gave way to what Spiro Agnew called "positive polarization," an all-consuming tactic to divide the Democrats by, as Buchanan put it, throwing the dice, cutting the country in half, and picking up "far the larger half" in the ensuing chaos.[49]

Such a tactic explains Nixon's executive order in 1971 that directed that the policy on abortions in military hospitals must correspond to the laws of the states where such hospitals are located. The order was accompanied by a statement that "the country has a right to know my personal views," such views being that "from personal and religious beliefs I consider abortion an unacceptable form of population control," which he could "not square with my personal belief in the sanctity of human life."*[50]

In 1971, before the Supreme Court's decision in *Roe v. Wade*,[51] abortion was an ugly, divisive issue in the United States, bringing out the worst stridency of militant and largely right-wing Catholic groups and militant and largely left-wing elements of the women's movement; the only conceivable common bond among the combatants was a possible allegiance to the Democratic Party.

The battle over abortion laws was a state battle; there was and is no Federal criminal penalty for performing an abortion. A President would thus have been well advised to stay out of the fray and let the fight go on in its proper arena. Certainly Eisenhower would have found a "rule" allowing him to stay out.

Nixon was willing to expend a part of his good-will chips as President in exacerbating the debate to shore up his support with a particular block of voters and to divide Democrats from Democrats, just as the Republicans seemed willing to make abortion a campaign issue in 1972 and 1976.

Similarly, the President told a convention of Roman Catholic Knights of Columbus in August 1971 that they could "count on my support" to keep private and parochial schools open.† This was a truly devious and ambiguous statement, since it certainly must have aroused hopes for Federal assistance to parochial schools, yet stopped short of taking a

---

* For a savage parody of this statement, see Philip Roth, *Our Gang* (New York: Random House, 1971), pp. 2–10.

† Remarks to the 59th Annual International Meeting of the Knights of Columbus, New York City, August 17, 1971.

Nixon's preinaugural Task Force on Education explicitly warned about taking positions in the education area that might reopen the church-state controversy or undo the tenuous compromise on church-state matters contained in the Elementary and Secondary Education Act of 1965 (see Chapter Four). Task Force reports are often neglected or forgotten, but seldom has a report had such a perverse effect as this one. It recommended making the Commissioner of Education a cabinet-level post; Nixon systematically downgraded the authority of his Commissioner. It warned against substituting a general school-aid concept for the Elementary and Secondary Education Act and called for greater local accountability in using Federal funds; Nixon proposed "special revenue sharing" to provide unrestricted general-purpose funds to local schools. It called for emphatic statements to the effect that the administration would not accept a lower standard of compliance with Supreme Court desegregation orders; Nixon spoke out frequently against "busing for racial balance." It urged special assistance to urban schools and expanded school assistance; Nixon cut appropriations and impounded funds. See the text of the Report reprinted at 115 *Congressional Record* (1969), pp. 6103 ff.

stand that would have committed Nixon to a flatly unconstitutional position.

Schell concludes that the Knights of Columbus speech was not simply a crude attempt to get Catholic votes, but an effort once again to split the opposition, quoting Buchanan as saying that the speech "divides the Democrats who run the New York *Times* from the Democrats who run for office in Queens and the North Bronx."[52] As one observer noted:

> If Richard Nixon had been a genuine conservative, he might have made the 1970s a period of peace, social consolidation, government tightening and reorganization and moral stability. He might even have achieved "The Emerging Republican Majority," which Kevin Phillips prophesied in 1970.
>
> Instead, Nixon kept the war and the turmoil of the anti-war demonstrations going for another four years, exacerbated racial, regional and generational antagonisms for his own short-run ends, overreached himself on government reorganization and program consolidation ... and presided over political crimes and irregularities.[53]

Ford

Gerald R. Ford was schooled for Presidential leadership in negative, minority politics. Ford repeatedly won office as a Congressman from a Michigan district uncritically appreciative of his stolidity and decency. Never challenged on the issues, he was able to mouth without challenge the clichés of laissez-faire capitalism and WASP individualism—and to mouth them in rhetoric unequaled in recent Presidential history for its vapidity and banality.* As a minority Congressman, and as Minority Leader of the House, his duty was to oppose—to oppose spending, to oppose experimentation, to oppose any policy or program that conflicted with the traditional Republican pieties.

Inevitably Ford brought this sense of negativism to the White House —it was the only political attitude with which he was comfortable and, after all, one that had brought him from back-bench obscurity to the Minority Leadership to the Presidency.

His decency and honesty calmed the country after the Nixon trauma. In this instance adherence to the pieties worked; therefore, why

---

* He occasionally has competition for this prize from his successor, President Carter.

wouldn't the other verities—thrift, self-reliance, governmental frugality —work in solving economic and social problems? If only the activist assault could be contained, wouldn't everything turn out for the best?

The result, of course, was a profoundly negative interregnum—government basically by negative veto, except for an occasional policy initiative reactionary in result and probably in intent. Let the good honest local doctors and hospital administrators, rather than the Federal bureaucracy, decide how funds earmarked for medical care should be spent—possibly a viable alternative if all doctors were like his affable golfing companions from Grand Rapids, but naïve and inefficient in the hands of the predatory sharks often found running nursing homes and Medicaid mills. Give enterprising local businessmen their head— again free of government interference—and they will hire the unemployed. A nice idea, but one that overlooks the woeful lack of training and ability among the "structurally" unemployed, kept from the uplift ladder by barriers of discrimination, inexperience in the world of work and inadequate education.

The novelist John Hersey, who spent a week observing Ford in the White House in 1975, perhaps caught the failure of this decent man imprisoned in the conditioned negativism of a thousand provincial Republican fund-raisers and a thousand losing battles in the Congress. Hersey was "shocked" by the President's preoccupation with cutting spending as plans to relieve joblessness were discussed at a cabinet-level meeting he attended:

> Why am I shocked? Because in this discussion I have seen a first glimpse of another side of the man who has been so considerate, so open and so kind to me as an individual—what seems a deep, hard, rigid side. Talking here, he has seemed a million miles away from many Americans who have been hardworking people all their lives and are now feeling the cruel pinch of hard times. What is it in him? Is it an inability to extend compassion far beyond the faces directly in view? Is it a failure of imagination? Is it something obdurate he was born with, alongside the energy and serenity he was born with?[54]

Race Relations

A case study of the deficiencies of Republican leadership can be found in its leaders' responses to civil-rights problems. If ever there was an issue where articulate leadership was needed, it is this trouble-some, emotional area. Eisenhower, Nixon and Ford were willing, at the drop of a hat, to support the Red Cross or Billy Graham's Crusades. But one looks long and hard for executive encouragement or support for those men and women of good will, white and black, who, years after *Brown v. Board of Education*, attempted to carry out its mandate and to save the public schools from senseless destruction. To the contrary, the racists, the red-necks and the obstructionists were encouraged in their efforts to prevent school integration by indifference in the White House, or worse, covert support from the White House.

President Eisenhower felt that "it makes no difference" whether he endorsed the Supreme Court's decision on segregation.[55] Even making allowance for the low state of white consciousness concerning civil-rights matters in the early 1950s, Eisenhower's views appear today at best archaic, at worst incredible. Consider, for example, his remarks to a United Negro College Fund luncheon in 1953:

And now I want to tell you a little bit of a story that just happened the day before yesterday. I was down at Annapolis, and I inspected a Marine Guard. As I went around, I noticed there were several Negroes occupying different positions in this Guard. One of them had on the chevrons of a non-commissioned officer. I talked with the commanding officer of this group. I said, "Now here occurs one of those things that was always advanced as an argument when we were working for the cause of eliminating segregation in the armed services—it was said that white men would not willingly serve under a Negro superior." And here I noticed that it was evidently not true. The officer smiled, and he said: "I must tell you that this man, when it came to the making of non-commissioned officers, could not pass the rigid mental examination we gave. But his personality was so fine, his qualities of leadership so evident, his character and reputation in the company so great that we had to make special arrangements so that it was unnecessary for him to pass completely the mental examination."

As I see it, you people today who are supporting the Negro College Fund are not only supporting the idea that men are equal, but you are making it unnecessary for a man to appear in a competitive place in our country, whether it be in governmental service or anywhere else, and have less opportunity than has his brothers for the mental training that would have given him exactly the same opportunity in that company as any other. It spoke to me very eloquently of this lad's very exceptional qualifications.[56]

In fairness, the first civil-rights act in eighty-two years, establishing on a permanent basis a Commission on Civil Rights (as opposed to the temporary Committee on Civil Rights set up by Truman without legislative authority in 1946), was requested by Eisenhower in 1956 and passed in 1957. But this legislation was largely a creature of the Congress, with Eisenhower moving "very reluctantly."[57]

The Republicans' leader in 1964, Senator Barry Goldwater, would not even concede the validity of the *Brown* decision, let alone methods to carry it out. In his book, *The Conscience of a Conservative,* he said:

> It may be just or wise or expedient for negro children to attend the same schools as white children, but they do not have a civil right to do so which is protected by the federal constitution, or which is enforceable by the federal government.[58]

Coming to Nixon, we again find him dividing the country on the issue, rather than promoting any sort of consensus. As part of his "Southern strategy," Nixon reduced the integration question to one of "busing"—a constant theme in his discussion of civil rights and school integration.* Even when forced to acknowledge that Supreme Court decisions must be upheld, he seemed incapable of finishing a declarative sentence on the subject without a qualifier to give hope to his Southern supporters: "I believe in carrying out the law even though I may have disagreed, as I did in this instance with the decree that the Supreme Court eventually came down with."†

---

* Nixon was capable of playing racial politics on both sides of the street, albeit always cheaply. As Vice President, he bragged at a Republican Lincoln Day dinner that it had been a Republican Chief Justice who had ordered an end to segregation, thereby performing "a disservice to the Eisenhower administration and a shocking undercut to the prestige and impartiality of the Supreme Court." "Nixon in New York" (editorial), *San Francisco News,* February 15, 1956, quoted in 102 *Congressional Record* (1956), p. 2786.

† Press Conference, December 8, 1969. The case referred to was *Alexander v. Holmes County Board of Education,* 396 U.S. 19.

The New York Times reported that Nixon considered four "options" regarding busing: (1) a speech reiterating his opposition and raising "broader educational issues" as well; (2) more Justice Department intervention against busing; (3) legislation restricting the busing remedy; and (4) an antibusing Constitutional amendment. Tom Wicker raised the question of why Elliot Richardson or someone else around the President did not raise a "fifth option" that would go something like this:

> A speech or a series of speeches by the President expressing the view that while he personally favors others means of desegregating schools and considers busing in some ways harmful, he views segregated schools as even worse and realizes that at present there is no feasible alternative to some busing for purposes of racial desegre-

Nixon's emphasis on the "neighborhood school" and opposition to "busing for racial balance" became code words for antiblack attitudes that were finally clarified in 1972, when he asked Congress to declare a moratorium on busing orders by the Federal courts. (He really favored a Constitutional amendment to do this, but thought this would take too long and could not be adopted before "hundreds of thousands of school children will be ordered by the courts to be bused away from their neighborhood schools . . . with no hope of relief.")

Nixon asked that the busing moratorium be accompanied by the passage of his "Equal Educational Opportunities Act of 1972," which would provide aid to upgrade inferior schools:

> What I am proposing is that at the same time we stop more busing, we move forward to guarantee that the children currently attending the poorest schools in our cities and in rural areas be provided with education equal to that of good schools in their communities.[59]

In other words, Federal funds should be expended to vindicate the concept of separate but equal schools, which was specifically held to be unconstitutional in the *Brown* case.

Nixon's bill, despite its high-sounding title, was both cynical and vicious—cynical because it was probably unconstitutional, interfering as it would have done with the vindication of constitutionally protected civil rights and the jurisdiction of the Federal courts; vicious because buried in the text of the proposed bill were provisions to reopen outstanding busing orders—even in communities where such orders were settled and accepted—and to inhibit prospective civil-rights plaintiffs by making them potentially liable for their opponents' attorneys' fees if such plaintiffs lost. As a practical matter it would have prevented experiments in school pairing or the creation of educational parks and would have prevented the courts from shaping remedies combining busing with other desegregation techniques.

Two committees of the Association of the Bar of the City of New York jointly condemned Nixon's bill as "indefensible" legislation, the net result of which would be to "further divide our nation, to encourage

---

gation; that the evidence is overwhelming that the "quality education" he seeks cannot be achieved without substantial school desegregation; that therefore there will have to be some busing until other means of desegregation make it unnecessary.

Tom Wicker, "In the Nation: The Fifth Option," *New York Times*, February 22, 1972, p. 37.

racial strife, and to interfere with the realization of what are generally recognized to be desirable educational goals."[60]

Nixon's strained distinctions between *de jure* segregation and *de facto* segregation; his permitting the Attorney General to advocate a watered-down version of the Voting Rights Act of 1965 when that act came up for review in 1970; his attempt to appoint G. Harrold Carswell to the Supreme Court; his opposition to lawfully entered Federal court desegregation orders and to the withholding of funds from school districts that did not comply with such orders; his permitting the Justice Department to contest a court ruling that segregation "academies" may not receive a tax exemption—all these actions made his position "perfectly clear" to those hoping that the tide of integration was not inevitable.

Nixon was also the master of taking actions little noticed by the general public—or the press—but certainly noticed by those zealots of the right who monitor every action of government in a search for reassurance or support. Consider, for example, the administration's prohibition of university-based desegregation centers from assisting the Federal courts in developing school desegregation orders. Under Title IV of the Civil Rights Act of 1964, financial assistance to aid local desegregation efforts was authorized. Under Title IV, a number of centers at major universities, principally in the South, were established to act as clearing houses for information on desegregation experiences, to provide training programs for personnel from districts about to desegregate. But in 1972, these centers receiving Title IV funds were explicitly forbidden by the U.S. Office of Education to make their expertise available to the Federal courts.[61]

Finally, we come to Gerald Ford, who continued the Nixon pattern—criticism of the courts and of busing orders, all carefully interspersed with lip service to the concept of desegregation. At the height of his nomination campaign against Ronald Reagan in June 1976, President Ford proposed an antibusing law that would have required a court, before entering a busing order, to determine "the extent to which acts of unlawful discrimination have caused a greater degree of racial concentration in a school or school system than would have existed in the absense [*sic*] of such acts." The remedy of busing could be used only to eliminate "the degree of student racial concentration caused by proven unlawful acts of discrimination." Further, busing orders would be subject to review after three years and could not be maintained in effect for more than five years.[62]

The Ford proposal makes the impossible assumption that factors causing *de jure* segregation can be precisely isolated from those causing *de facto* segregation, a task roughly equivalent to determining which drop of water fell into the rain barrel first.

The proposal also appeared to be patently unconstitutional under Supreme Court decisions, which have consistently held that if *de jure* segregation is found the remedies for curing it may extend beyond the *de jure* circumstances.

In issuing busing orders, Ford said, "some judges of lower Federal courts have gone too far." Yet, when pressed, Mr. Ford's counsel was "unable to cite a single specific case" supporting Ford's conclusion.[63]

The Civil Rights Commission took issue with Ford. In a 1976 report, the Commission said:

> School officials and other local leaders are dependent on the tone set by leaders at the national level. The Commission believes, for constitutional reasons, that efforts by either the executive or the legislative branches to curb the power of the courts, in the final analysis, will not prevail.... Furthermore, these attempts contribute to the position of some individuals that desegregation can be avoided. This Commission ... takes issue with the President and those Members of Congress who seek to curb the rule of the courts. The President's recent submission of the School Desegregation Standards and Assistance Act of 1976 falls within this category.[64]

One civil-rights worker in Atlanta, noting the trend to *re*segregation in Southern schools and the failure of the Federal government to monitor compliance with integration orders, remarked that "things started coming apart after the Nixon administration said, 'Watch what we do, not what we say,' and then did nothing ... But the Ford administration has made things even worse by neither saying nor doing anything. There just isn't any affirmative action or any monitoring going on out there on the part of Washington, not any more."[65]

Moral Decline

Stemming "moral decline" is probably not a function that politicians can perform particularly well. About all that an elected official can really do is set a decent example and avoid hypocrisy. Eisenhower and Ford may have partially achieved this; Nixon assuredly did not.

Nixon's self-righteous moralizing, offensive enough in its original context, becomes ludicrous with the hindsight we now possess. Consider, for example, the peroration of his 1970 State of the Union Message:

> Even more than the programs I have described today, what this Nation needs is an example from its elected leaders in providing the spiritual and moral leadership which no program for material progress can satisfy.[66]

Most politicians are easily tempted to give moral lectures; the *Congressional Record* for any day is full of them. Eisenhower, Nixon and Ford were all particularly given to preaching, none more so than Eisenhower, who, campaigning in 1952, recalled "some of the maxims written at the top of the copy books we used in grade school . . . the standards by which, in those days, greatness was judged. Listen to some of them," the candidate said approvingly. "Honesty is the best policy; a man is known by the company he keeps; he that goes aborrowing, goes asorrowing; birds of a feather flock together; I would rather be right than President. Where do we stand today, where does our government stand when measured alongside the moral principles—the sacred honor—of our founders?"[67]

It is hard to imagine such oratory having much effect. Perhaps milder exhortations more closely related to political issues might have had some. Consider, for example, John Kennedy's practical variation on being one's brother's keeper:

> When you have 7 percent unemployed, you have 93 percent working. . . . Some Congressmen can come back . . . and tell you that there is a great sense of urgency in this matter. Others who represent other areas may not feel it . . . [but] anyone who honestly is seeking a job and can't find it deserves the attention of the United States and the people, particularly those who are fortunate enough to work, and that includes us all.[68]

Or Harry Truman's muscular Christian appeal to the Federal Council of Churches:

> To raise [the standard of living] should be, and is, the constant aim of your government and the underlying basis of its policies. It would make

the effort so much easier if people and nations would apply some of the principles of social justice and ethical standards which have come down to us from Biblical times. All the questions which now beset us in strikes and wages and working conditions would be so much simpler if men and women were willing to apply the principles of the Golden Rule. Do as you would be done by. Consider the gleam in your own eye and pay less attention to the mote in your brother's.

If we really believed in the Brotherhood of Man, it would not be necessary to pass a Fair Employment Practices Act.

If certain interests were not so greedy for gold, there would be less pressure and lobbying to induce the Congress to allow the Price Control Act to expire, or to keep down minimum wages, or to permit further concentration of economic power.

A truly religious fervor among our people would go a long way toward obtaining a national health program, a national housing program, a national education program, and an extended and improved social security program.[69]

Nine · The Presidency: Democrats

Its shortcomings, eccentricities and anachronisms notwithstanding, the Democratic Party has been the instrument of a remarkable amount of change from the days of the New Deal. I would hope it can do so again. In any case, there isn't anything else.

—JOHN KENNETH GALBRAITH[1]

Franklin Roosevelt's New Deal, codified and refined in the Second Bill of Rights, was only the first of a series of programmatic agendas advanced by the postwar Democratic Presidents. Harry Truman's Fair Deal, John F. Kennedy's New Frontier and Lyndon Johnson's Great Society all were attempts to distill questions of economic and social reform into an overall program. And President Carter, while he has not seen fit to give his program a name, has inundated the Congress with a whole series of messages calling for new legislation.

A programmatic approach to economic and social problems has been typical of the Democrats. In Presidential politics they have, unlike their Republican rivals, generally avoided one-issue or narrowly focused campaigns. The basic themes of every postwar Republican campaign (with the exception of 1976) can be summed up in a catch word or phrase: "statism" (1948); the "Truman-Acheson-Hiss" foreign policy (1952);* "Quemoy and Matsu" (1960); "socialism" (1964); "law and order" (1968); and "acid, amnesty and abortion" (1972).

The Democrats' programs, with the notable exception of the Great Society, have never come to fruition.

---

* To be fair, this characterization was then Vice Presidential candidate Richard Nixon's, not General Eisenhower's. One should also not forget President Nixon's off-year favorites in 1970: "smut" and the "flow of pornography." See Statement About the Report of the Commission on Obscenity and Pornography, October 24, 1970.

Ironically, the most farsighted, comprehensive program was put forward not by a Democratic President, but a Presidential candidate—Adlai Stevenson. In 1956, he tried to bring a domestic focus to the campaign with carefully crafted speeches and position papers on a wide range of topics. *The New America,* a compilation which appeared in 1957, is an unheralded and seminal work in our political history, brimming with ideas that were translated into action long after 1956, if at all: ending the draft; banning atomic testing; lowering income-tax rates; giving corporations tax credits for dividends to stockholders; sharing tax revenues with the states; easing the local property-tax burden; prohibiting discrimination against the aged; developing American shale-oil resources; increasing productivity to curb inflation.

President Eisenhower never gave Stevenson a chance. He began his first speech of the campaign with a theme that he simply would not leave thereafter: "I want to talk of one word—and many things. The word is Peace. And the many things are its many and momentous meanings."[2]

Before Stevenson, passage of broad-gauged civil-rights and immigration legislation, Federal aid to education and national health insurance had all eluded Harry Truman, although all were central to his Fair Deal.

Truman, in adopting Roosevelt's Second Bill of Rights as the basis for postwar domestic policy, had gone Roosevelt one better by advocating "Twenty-One Points" for Congressional action in his special message of September 6, 1945.*

"Not even President Roosevelt ever asked so much at one sitting," House Republican Leader Joseph W. Martin complained. "It is just a case of out-New Dealing the New Deal."[3]

Whatever the breadth of his proposals, Truman had to fight, and fight hard, for each scrap of progressive legislation that cleared the Congress. His legacy is in fact limited to the Employment Act of 1946,† the Public Housing Act of 1949, a bill increasing the minimum wage in 1949 and one increasing Social Security benefits in 1950.

John Kennedy's exposition of the New Frontier was masterful. With-

---

* The challenge of Truman's "Twenty-One Points" was outdone only by his challenge to the Republican majority in the Eightieth Congress, issued in his acceptance speech at the Democratic convention in 1948, to reconvene in a special session (which Truman called) and enact the Democratic platform. Address in Philadelphia Upon Accepting the Nomination of the Democratic National Convention, July 15, 1948.

† See pp. 26–28, *supra.*

in six months of taking office, Kennedy sent a dozen messages to Congress dealing with such domestic concerns as health, education, natural resources, highways, housing, agriculture and taxation, together with seven plans for reorganizing various segments of the Federal bureaucracy. The messages are models of expository prose—well-written and free of clichés; hortatory, yet never preachy; cogent in their reasoning, yet never cold; intelligent in their marshaling of facts, yet never lacking in compassion for the victims of deprivation. But again the legislative product was meager, and there was little indication at the time of his death that prospects would greatly improve. Pioneering, if very limited, efforts to attack unemployment through targeted and "finely tuned" programs—the Area Redevelopment Act of 1961, the Manpower Training and Development Act of 1962 and the Public Works Acceleration Act of 1962*—together with lesser housing, social security and tax legislation, and the symbolically important Equal Pay Act of 1963 (providing for equal pay for women workers), were his legislative achievements.

Even with numerical Democratic majorities in the Congress (for part of the time, in the case of Truman), Truman and Kennedy suffered at the hands of a shifting but nevertheless innately conservative coalition in the Congress, composed of Republicans and Democrats alike, suspicious of both governmental intervention and social innovation and ready to coalesce to negative Presidential initiatives that threatened one or another buttress of the status quo.

But even if they could not translate their grand vision into law, the programmatic approaches of Truman and Kennedy—and Stevenson—had lasting value, for their stated positions served to educate the public and to stimulate discussion and a focusing of the various economic and social issues addressed.

As one analysis of Harry Truman's administration has noted, his "best proposals proved to be a form of public education that prepared the way for enactment of similar programs in more favorable times" and "helped to prevent repeal of the New Deal and preserved its vision of mild welfare capitalism."[4] The same could be said of Kennedy and Stevenson.

* See p. 228 fn.

Johnson

Lyndon Johnson was the exception to all the rules. In the 1965 session of the Eighty-ninth Congress alone, the Johnson Administration sponsored 87 major pieces of legislation (by its own count) and got 84 of them passed, including bills establishing Medicaid, Medicare, ESEA, the Department of Housing and Urban Development and the National Endowments for the Arts and the Humanities, and others demonstrating the wide-ranging concerns of the Great Society for such problems as denial of voting rights, air and water pollution, billboard advertising, drug abuse and crime.[5]

Small wonder that Barry Goldwater called this Session the "Xerox Congress"![6]

The Johnson record in getting Great Society legislation through Congress is perhaps equaled only by the First Hundred Days of the New Deal, though the Johnson accomplishment was perhaps even more remarkable, since it did not occur in a period of economic crisis.

There is no denying the Johnson achievement. With more than a little hyperbole, Professor Eric Goldman notes that Johnson "presided over an America that—without a single break of as much as a month—was the most generally prosperous nation in all of man's five thousand years of recorded history."[7]

Johnson, probably both out of ego and personal conviction, equaled or bettered the legislative record of FDR. No one would call his administration, as some had called Kennedy's, the third term of the Eisenhower administration. He would do what he knew best—manipulate the Congress.

In all of this, one must conclude that Johnson was sincere and was acting from deep conviction, whatever deviousness and dissembling may have attended his tragic Vietnam policy. It is hard to doubt the sincerity and conviction of a man who could speak thus to the Congress:

> My first job after college was as a teacher in Cotulla, Tex., in a small Mexican-American school. Few of them could speak English, and I couldn't speak much Spanish. My students were poor and they often came to class without breakfast, hungry. They knew even in their youth the pain of prejudice. They never seemed to know why people disliked them. But they knew it was so, because I saw it in their eyes. I often

walked home late in the afternoon, after the classes were finished, wishing there was more that I could do. But all I knew was to teach them the little that I knew, hoping that it might help them against the hardships that lay ahead.

Somehow you never forget what poverty and hatred can do when you see its scars on the hopeful face of a young child.

I never thought then, in 1928, that I would be standing here in 1965. It never even occurred to me in my fondest dreams that I might have the chance to help the sons and daughters of those students and to help people like them all over this country.

But now I do have that chance—and I'll let you in on a secret—I mean to use it. And I hope that you will use it with me.

This is the richest and most powerful country which ever occupied the globe. The might of past empires is little compared to ours. But I do not want to be the President who built empires, or sought grandeur, or extended dominion.

I want to be the President who educated children to the wonders of their world. I want to be the President who helped to feed the hungry and to prepare them to be taxpayers instead of taxeaters.

I want to be the President who helped the poor to find their own way and who protected the right of every citizen to vote in every election.

I want to be the President who helped to end hatred among his fellow men and who promoted love among the people of all races and all regions and all parties.

I want to be the President who helped to end war among the brothers of this earth.[8]

Citing the drop in the number of poor people in America from 40 million in 1961 to 24 million in 1969, Arthur Okun concludes that "Lyndon Johnson's domestic programs must have been doing something right!" But Okun also points out that the political climate after Johnson was "chilled by disappointment about the housing, manpower, urban, and education programs of the 1960s," concluding that the main fault of such programs lay in "overpromising" rather than "underperformance."[9]

It is here that the Johnson program failed. It did overpromise; it did create expectations that were not fulfilled. Combined with the Vietnam War, it heated up the economy in ways that led, under the inept Nixon-Ford leadership that followed, to economic chaos.

To Johnson, his legislative proposals were not simply a program of social legislation, but a *war* on poverty:

This administration today, here and now, declares unconditional war on poverty in America.

Or:

I request the doubling of the War Against Poverty. In addition I request legislation to improve our ability to conduct that war.

Or:

Just as Abraham Lincoln abolished slavery 100 years ago, it is the dedicated purpose and objective of the Democratic Party in our time to abolish poverty in the United States of America.[10]

"War"—and "unconditional war" at that—is a strong metaphor. It simply was not possible to deliver results as fast as the metaphor implied.

There likewise came to be a triumph of quantity over quality in the "war." As noted earlier, Johnson loved to cite statistics; the more programs the better. In his 1968 State of the Union Message, he exultantly pointed out that a new college was being founded in America every week,[11] a breathtaking statistic but, on reflection, one that does not in and of itself really say much about improving the quality of education.

Experimental programs were attempted on a grand scale, leading to grand-scale failures, grand-scale disappointments. The advice of the late Seymour Harris was not followed:

A small and experimental beginning [to the economic opportunity program] is wise. Ultimately, much larger outlays will be necessary. But to move too fast in the early stages, with inevitable blunders, might well hurt, if not destroy the program. Moreover, there is the usual hurdle of Congressional approval, which can be gained with a modest program in the early stages and with larger outlays later when the program begins to prove workable and effective.[12]

Johnson sought—and got—large outlays at the outset. Perhaps he did this simply because of the Texas habit of thinking big, but more likely for two other reasons. First, his knowledge, based on his own

Congressional experience, that his legislative advantage could not last, that there was not time for the modest program now and the larger outlay later. And second, his desperate desire to keep with him those who were deserting and opposing him over Vietnam. Give the liberals a program so vast in scope, so massive, so responsive to expressed liberal concerns, and they would have to follow along on the other war.

Eli Ginzberg and Robert Solow have eloquently summed up the problem of overselling the Great Society:

> It is hard enough for a reformist government to set realistic goals. It is almost impossible for it to limit itself to realistic promises. Here the social engineers of the 1960's clearly failed. The Administration's spokesmen promised to undertake and win the war on poverty, to assure every American family an adequate home, to relieve old and poor people of the financial burdens of illness, to widen the educational opportunities of poor children, to speed the integration of the black community into the mainstream of American life, to provide skill training so that men and women on the periphery of the economy could get better jobs. A democracy with a two-party tradition is inured to exaggerated promises and claims, especially in an election year. But the mid-1960's saw the President, his advisers, and the Congressional leadership wantonly blur the distinction between campaign promises and legislative commitments. From one point of view, the Great Society programs were doomed from the moment of their enactment: There was no prospect that any government could deliver on such ambitious promises, certainly not within the time limits that an impatient public would allow.
>
> It is easy to see how damaging this kind of puffery can be to the good name of sensible social policy. . . . One has the impression that nothing less than a Crisis can any longer attract political attention. . . . One can hardly respond to a Crisis with small-scale experimental programs that will test out the nature of the problem and accumulate some knowledge that can ultimately lead to the design of better policy. A Crisis has to be met on a grand scale. . . . This sort of atmosphere is hardly conducive to the rational allocation of public funds and administrative capacity. . . .
>
> It is important that the leadership's promises of results from intervention be realistic rather than extreme. A public which has been encouraged to expect great things will become impatient, critical, and alienated if the progress that is achieved falls far short of the rosy promises. A wise leadership is careful to promise no more than it feels reasonably sure it can deliver within a reasonable time.[13]

One is greatly tempted to speculate on what might have been if the tide of events had permitted Lyndon Johnson to orchestrate fully his Great Society, to deliver fully on his expansive promises. What if there had been no Vietnam War? What if he had run for reelection and won in 1968? Would he have conducted his War on Poverty at the same helter-skelter pace? Would the chaos and confusion have continued, or would his separate programs have been coordinated into a unified whole?

There is evidence both ways, but it is not unrealistic to think that the country would have seen a period of rational and efficient consolidation. Johnson, after all, was the President who (at least by his own account) reduced the White House electricity bill from $5,000 to $3,000 a month.[14] He is also the President who said, within his first month in office, that "I want to spend everything that is necessary to spend to keep moving our country forward progressively. In order to do that, I don't want to waste a dime," and that "nine out of ten government employees do a full day's work for a day's pay—but I want that tenth man to measure up also."[15]

In a message to Congress in March 1967 entitled "The Quality of American Government," Johnson recognized that the focus had shifted from adopting programs to implementing them:

> Because of the social and economic legislation passed by the 88th and 89th Congresses—legislation unmatched in all the annals of our history—this Nation now has programs which can lift the quality of American life higher than any before us have known.
> What remains for us now is to improve the quality of government itself —its machinery, its manpower, its methods—so that those programs will touch and transform the lives of the people for whom they were intended.

It is sad that the "quality of American Government," a theme that meant to Johnson the ability of government to serve the people, took on a wholly different meaning to those protesting the quality of the Johnson administration's policies in Vietnam. It is sad to recall that the Gulf of Tonkin "crisis" and the signing of the Economic Opportunity Act occurred in the same seven-day period in August 1965. It is sad that one must only speculate about whether the Great Society would have improved the quality of American life under the protean guidance of an undistracted Lyndon Johnson, and sadder to do such speculation confronted with the all but total dismemberment of the Great Society by his two successors, who were quick enough to see the inconsistencies, discontinuities and failures of the Johnson design, but who lacked either the imagination or the will to build upon it.

The Johnson approach to leadership on domestic issues resulted in a severe setback for social progress in this country. But his achievements will provide the basis for a truly "great society" at the hands of a President bold enough, wise enough and progressive enough to utilize the Great Society lessons and experience in fashioning a new social program.

McGovern

Before coming down to the present and the problems of Jimmy Carter, a special word is necessary about George McGovern. The Senator, who began his come-from-behind campaign for the Democratic nomination in 1972 as a one-issue candidate, sought to broaden his appeal with a social program that was, to be most charitable about it, inadequately researched and thought out.

"The case made in behalf of taxing the rich and aiding the poor during the election campaign of 1972 provided an object lesson in how *not* to present a program of equalization to the American people," Arthur Okun has observed. "Ironically, the cause of reform received a serious setback from those who sought to advance it. With friends like that, it needed no enemies."[16]

McGovern's infamous $1,000-per-person "demogrant" is worth a moment's attention. As originally proposed by McGovern, it called for a grant of $1,000 for every man, woman and child in the United States. This $1,000 would be added to the income of the recipient and, to the extent the recipient had sufficient other income, would be returned to the Federal government in whole or in part through the income tax.[17] In other words, the program would not cost $200 billion (200,000,000 citizens times $1,000) but something less, depending on the income level at which the income tax would retrieve the "demogrants" from their recipients.

Unfortunately, McGovern never spelled out what "less" might be. One aide alleges that he "coasted to California without anyone knowing what his positions were, including himself." When asked in his first debate with Senator Hubert Humphrey in California what the cost of his "demogrant" plan would be, "McGovern looked startled, as though, in the midst of a biology exam, he'd been asked to conjugate a French verb. . . . 'I honestly don't know,' he said. 'I don't have the figures.' "

The same campaign worker alleges that McGovern, under pressure to come up with a figure in the second Humphrey debate, simply made one up.[18]

In addition to the fundamental question—How much would it cost? —there obviously were other implications of the "demogrant" plan that simply were not thought through at all. For example, would payments be made in one lump sum, quarterly or monthly? Assuming that an annual payment were used, how could the temptation be avoided to spend the money as soon as received, leaving (for the poor) the question of basic support for later or (for the nonpoor) the question of paying the income tax on the amount received and spent? One wry observer predicted that the country would be deserted after the annual "demogrant"; the entire population would be on twenty-one-day excursion tours to Europe. Could the program really rely on proper budgeting by recipients?

McGovern, down to the present, has been ambiguous about his disastrous proposal. In a television speech in October 1972, in which he tried to clarify his economic program, he acknowledged that it was "true that in my search for a way out of the welfare mess I once discussed a plan—a plan by some of the nation's leading economists—for a $1,000 grant to every citizen that would be taxed back from those who do not need it. But it is also true, and it is a matter of public record, that I have rejected this idea, just as Mr. Nixon advocated and then rejected a similar guaranteed-income plan."[19]

Yet in his annotations to his collected campaign speeches, he states that "a number of my supporters tell me in retrospect that I never should have changed the '$1,000 Plan.' They have a point. The plan was a complicated but basically sound idea."[20]

More recently, the Senator said that "the largest share of responsibility" for the 1972 loss was his own and that one of his "mistakes" was "inadequate preparation" of his $1,000 guaranteed annual income.[21]

Senator McGovern also spoke in extremely vague terms about tax reform, declaring among other things that, through taxation, he would limit inheritances to any individual to $500,000 during his lifetime.

As T. H. White noted, such a scheme was "revolutionary" at a time when "half a million dollars is about the value of a good family farm in the Midwest."[22] The proposal also met with a surprising "storm of protest" from blue-collar workers. "The possibility of 'making it big' seems to motivate many Americans, including some who have not made it at all," one economist has written. "The silent majority did not want the yacht clubs closed forever to their children and grandchildren, while those who had already become members kept sailing along."[23]

Estate and gift taxes today account for approximately 1.5 percent of Federal tax revenues, and impartial tax experts are of the view that "the revenue potential of structural reform in the estate and gift taxes is not large."[24]

Was Senator McGovern proposing his ceiling on inheritances as a means of raising revenue, in which case his proposal would not have been very effective, or was he proposing some basic change in the social distribution of wealth in America? He never articulated the reasons for his policy but, in the process of enunciating it, he managed to create the impression—which may not have been the correct one—of desiring "revolutionary" change.

His proposal is reminiscent of former British Prime Minister Harold Wilson's highly criticized wealth tax which, by taxing concentrations of personal wealth over time at more than 100 percent, would confiscate the holdings of the "upper classes" in the United Kingdom without really contributing significantly to the national tax revenues. The end result is, of course, to raise the *percentage* of private wealth held by lower-income groups without any increase in real wealth. The wisdom of Mr. Wilson's policy has been sharply questioned, and one could say the same about Senator McGovern's proposal. A "revolutionary" policy which has real social consequences can at least be defended; a policy which has only symbolic value and merely heightens social tensions is something else entirely.

Senator McGovern also spoke frequently in the 1972 campaign about closing "loopholes" in the individual and corporate income taxes, which would result in being able to reduce the maximum individual tax rate from 70 percent to 48 percent, and at the same time increase tax revenues by $22 billion. One has to have the suspicion that the $22 billion figure was again pulled from the air, since it is hard to see what "loopholes" could realistically be closed to raise $22 billion, plus the $3.3 billion raised in fiscal 1972 at tax rates from 50 percent to 70 percent,[25] that would have been eliminated under McGovern's plan.

Under the "tax-expenditure" concept, which considers as government expenditures taxes that are not collected because of income-tax exclusions, deductions or credits, an estimated $135 billion of "tax expenditures" were to be made in fiscal 1979, as detailed in Appendix A. Reviewing these "tax expenditures"—or *loopholes,* if you will—it is almost impossible to come close to $22 billion—let alone $22 billion plus $3.3 billion—in savings without drastically altering fundamental precepts of the income tax that would have a profound impact on the taxpaying public and various sectors of the economy, such as abolishing the deductions for mortgage interest, property taxes and charitable contributions.

Even allowing for the generalities permitted in a political campaign, it would have been instructive to know where Senator McGovern's multibillion "savings" were to come from.

One cites this sad record not to belabor McGovern—surely he has been belabored enough—but to indicate that vague policies emanating from a good heart do not constitute a viable political program. Nor are they a substitute for decently researched programs or for leadership in educating the electorate in the intricacies of social policy. As the late Hubert Humphrey observed in 1939, in his Master's thesis at Louisiana State University on the New Deal:

> The modern democratic statesman realizes now more than ever before that if government is to be able to meet its appointed tasks, it must become more practical, more efficient, and more responsive to needs. Simple honesty in the carrying out of plans or policies is not enough.[26]

Carter

While he has not put a label on what he is doing, President Carter is clearly following the programmatic tradition of his Democratic predecessors. By late 1978, he had delivered major messages on Social Security reform, energy policy, tax reform, the welfare system, hospital costs, education, civil-service reform, urban policy and national health policy.

Early indications are that Carter will make out no better than his predecessors with Congress. Certainly his proposals for Social Security reform and a national energy policy were largely ignored, and there appears to be no disposition to move forward toward acting upon other messages.

Carter has been faulted for his dealings with Congress. This is in part a valid criticism and in part not. Except for Lyndon Johnson, no modern Democratic President has had particularly rewarding relations with the Congress on domestic matters. Even Franklin Roosevelt was unable to obtain passage of any major piece of domestic legislation after the "court-packing" episode of 1937 and the abortive "purge" of recalcitrant Congressmen in the 1938 elections.[27] So, to say that Carter is not producing results in the Congress is to place him in a long, if unfortunate, Democratic tradition.

But that is perhaps too simple an answer. As discussed in Chapter Seven, structural reforms have occurred in the Congress to lessen the power of a conservative Republican-Southern Democratic coalition. A decently liberal majority on most issues should be attainable. This would require an assiduous and shrewd reaching out by the President to the much-vaunted "new blood" in the Congress—the younger, supposedly more intelligent and liberal new members. And it would require weaning them away from the comfortable tendency, noted in Chapter Seven, to become highly paid custodians oblivious to current issues.

It also would require a reappraisal of the programmatic approach to economic and social problems. One of the weaknesses of a comprehensive program is that priorities among facets of that program are not set. Time and effort are spent devising an overall program that is all things to as many as possible; less time, if any at all, is spent deciding whose claims are more important. Great attention is given to assembling the team; little attention is given to the batting order.

If the President does not firmly set his priorities, his program will go the way of the Fair Deal or the New America; it will be an estimable blueprint for discussion and debate, but not for legislative action.

A need to set priorities is especially acute in the late 1970s, when few expect a return to the days when reformers could assume virtually unlimited national growth to provide the revenue base for new programs. Everything cannot be done—and nothing will be done unless in accordance with explicit and understandable priorities.

The Presidential messages which bear the imprint of Secretary of Health, Education and Welfare Joseph A. Califano, Jr., have to date been especially impressive. An intimate of President Johnson, Califano appears to share the Johnsonian desire to accomplish significant reform and, in his own right, possesses a refreshing optimism that problems can be solved. The proposals for hospital cost-containment,* and welfare reform, for example, are realistic and hard-headed and address themselves to very real current problems. They are by no means retreads of earlier schemes taken down from the shelf.

President Carter has seemed determined to make legislative proposals on all the major subjects touched on in his 1976 campaign, presumably on some theory that to do otherwise would somehow violate his pious undertaking never to lie to the American people. But to assume that the hasty production of a series of legislative messages fulfills his campaign promises is at best naïve, at worst cynical.

Many of the Carter messages are shaping up as a plausible blueprint for action on social and economic issues. But they will remain just that —a blueprint—unless the President's relationships with Congress take a new tack and he more clearly outlines, and sticks to, a well-ordered set of priorities.†

* See p. 255, *infra*.

† Now that jams, jellies and knitwear are largely made in factories, the last authentic American cottage industry is publishing. Hence by the time this manuscript has been ministered to with all deliberate speed, this analysis of President Carter's program may be quite outmoded. It would certainly be best for the country, if not necessarily for the author, if this were so.

Ten · The Presidency: Some Higher Common Denominators

The issue is not government big or small. The issue is government that works.
—HUBERT HUMPHREY[1]

One of the unhappier legacies of both the Vietnam War and Watergate has been the ever-increasing popularity of the notion that Presidential power is inherently bad.

The perceived abuses of power by our national leaders have broken down the distinction between the *existence* and the *use* of power. If power is used wrongly, the argument goes, the power itself must be eliminated; restriction and regulation of its use are not sufficient.

Simplistic notions of a limited Presidency have arisen in this context. Eugene McCarthy, for example, has written that "leadership should be almost a residual function of the office." In his view, "leadership" will simply well up from the populace below:

> Even though the President must sometimes give firm leadership, he should understand that this country as a rule does not need so much leadership, because the potential for leadership in a free country must exist in every citizen. Sensing the will of the people, the President must be prepared to move out ahead so that the people can follow, giving direction to the country and guiding it, largely by way of setting people free.[2]

It is ironic that the New Left conception of power dovetails nicely with the traditional right-wing view that power *per se* is a bad thing and corrupts absolutely—at least when exercised in domestic affairs;

without power there cannot be leadership, and without leadership troublesome social policies are unlikely to be codified into even more troublesome legislation.

If recent history teaches us anything it is that meaningful social programs can be formulated and executed only if there is forceful Presidential leadership, and possibly not even then. Congress, through the hearing process, can contribute in a very important way toward the gathering of information and the exploration of policy alternatives, but it simply has not proved an efficient vehicle for developing coherent policy. The factionalism of the interests represented in Congress inhibits policy initiatives, as we have seen in the cases of aid to education and energy policy. And the indifference to major issues among Congressmen content with their role as "district-first" custodians* makes Congress still less effective as a partner in policy-making.

The Supreme Court may hand down decisions that profoundly affect the course and direction of social policies, as in the case of the desegregation decisions since 1954.† Its role remains, however, more one of setting the ground rules under which social-policy struggles are played out. And, given the increasingly cautious and conservative cast of the Court's majority, positive and progressive "judicial legislation" is simply not a realistic prospect in the immediate future.

The institutional and practical limitations of the Congress and the Supreme Court leave Americans who are concerned about domestic political issues no alternative but to look to the President and the Executive Branch as the prime instruments for progress and social change in this country.

"I'm the only President you've got," Lyndon Johnson was fond of saying. Liberals, or reformers, or even technocrats, could well paraphrase Johnson's dictum and acknowledge that the Presidency is probably the only effective institution they have got for generating social and economic reform.

"Residual" exercises of leadership, as suggested by Eugene McCarthy, simply will not suffice to marshal public opinion, to cajole Congressmen and to manage administrators. Certainly with our more intractable problems the President may require all the resources of his office to gain even the semblance of a handle on them. Curtailing the President's powers is hardly the answer. To the contrary, one would

* See Chapter Seven.
† See pp. 118–24, *infra.*

hope that our Presidents will always have a full awareness of their resources and use them to the full at the right times and for the right purposes.

The key here is "the right times and the right purposes." If he truly understands his office, a President will be wise enough to know that not all social problems compel or demand the exercise of Presidential power; that an economical and wise use of such power is likely to be more productive than attempts to use it at all times and for all purposes; and that, even when exercised, such exercise may take many more modest forms than the full-blown "crisis" response with which we are all too familiar.

A President should also be wise enough to perceive that the non-exercise of his power can have as many implications for social policy-making as a full push on the throttle. The famed Nixonian concept of "benign neglect," for example, by definition did not involve the exercise of Presidential power, but its policy implications were probably more vast than almost any positive action the Executive Branch might have taken in the area of civil rights.

Properly comprehending the uses and limits of power is not an easy intellectual exercise. Nor is it easy for politicians to articulate, or the public to perceive, the delicate balance between the abdication and the abuse of power. Simply because the subject is a difficult one does not, however, justify curtailing power, denying that it exists or pretending that it really reposes in the bosoms of the yeomanry.

An informed affirmation of the existence and legitimacy of Presidential power should be accompanied by public insistence that such power be exercised *openly* and *intelligently*. This is the true lesson of Vietnam and Watergate, and there is probably no political doctrine anywhere, and certainly not one acceptable to most Americans, that would deny the need for both openness and intelligence.*

"OPENNESS"

In the 1976 campaign, there was much talk about an "open Presidency," by which presumably was meant the opposite of the secrecy and deviousness which characterized the Nixon administration.

---

* An exception may be the novel proposition advanced by Senator Roman Hruska in the fight over G. Harrold Carswell's nomination to the Supreme Court in 1970 that "mediocrity" was entitled to representation on the Court.

Watergate had not been the only impetus to "openness"; the Freedom of Information Act of 1966 had already given citizens the means of cracking much Executive Branch secrecy. This Act made it very hard as a practical matter to keep a secret. Jody Powell, President Carter's Press Secretary, recognized the inevitability of this in 1977 when he said:

> The fact is that it's pretty difficult to keep a secret anyway around here. And I've always believed the old saying that bad news never gets better with age. Generally you're better off getting it out and getting it over with.*[3]

If "openness" is construed merely as having the President administer his office on camera, with his most trivial actions photographed and ballyhooed, the concept of "openness" is a dubious one. The populace would be bored in no time.

After announcing that he would open Cabinet meetings to the press, President Carter had second thoughts, based on the nearly unanimous opposition of his Cabinet members. The risk was that televised Cabinet meetings would become a "subterfuge," with closed, secret meetings held whenever serious business was to be discussed.†

"Openness," properly viewed, has at least three elements: a healthy relationship with the press, a commitment to discuss issues in precise and frank terms, and a willingness to listen to the viewpoints of divergent groups within American society.

Both the Presidency and the press as institutions will continue, regardless of the relationship between the President and reporters—assuming, that is, that the President does not use the powers of his office illicitly to intimidate the press and that the press adheres to basic standards of professionalism and fairness in covering the President.

After the Nixon paranoia about journalists, it is hoped that the cautious good will that characterized President Carter's relations with the press in his first months of office will continue. The model for

---

* Mr. Powell did not appear to follow his own good advice in the Bert Lance fracas of 1977.

† There may be an analogy here with the German experience under a "reform" corporation law which requires worker representation on the boards of directors of publicly held German corporations. One gathers that it is usual to hold any substantive discussions (with the worker members absent) before formal board meetings, the meetings themselves (at which the worker members are present) reduced to mere ratifying sessions.

such relations might well be the healthy balance that existed between Harry Truman and the press: on the one hand, a President who knew who he was and understood what the job of the press was; on the other, a press corps warily respectful of the Presidency but approaching the President with a certain amount of unsolemn "Front Page" humor.

Consider this interchange at a news conference in 1948, when two running jokes between Truman and the White House correspondents—the question of whether Truman would run in 1948 and the matter of his controversial White House balcony—collided in this way:

Q. Mr. President, since your last press conference, there have been some more presidential candidates come out in the open, even Governor Dewey. So far, there have been no Democratic candidates. [*Laughter*] Have you any idea when there will be any announcement?

THE PRESIDENT. No, I haven't the slightest notion.

Q. Will there be any?

THE PRESIDENT. Oh, eventually of course there will be one before the Democratic convention meets in Philadelphia, but I don't see that there is any hurry about any announcement. [*Laughter*]

Q. Just one, Mr. President?

Q. I notice you said one.

THE PRESIDENT. I didn't say that—everybody in the United States has a right to be a candidate for President if he wants to be, on either party ticket.

Q. Or a third party ticket?

THE PRESIDENT. Or a third party ticket. He would have a better chance, however, if he were on the ticket of the other old parties.

Q. Mr. President, do you imply that some don't have to pick a ticket until pretty late in the day?

THE PRESIDENT. Some of them don't—they vacillate. Could name a great many who are newcomers to both parties. But some of them, of course, will try to get back on the bandwagon and in the parties where they really belong.

Q. Anyone particularly in mind, Mr. President?

THE PRESIDENT. You can draw your own conclusions. [*Laughter*]

Q. Do you think that there will be an announcement before the Democratic National Convention?

THE PRESIDENT. Oh, undoubtedly there will be, by someone. I know somebody will be a candidate on the Democratic ticket.

Q. Do you plan to do much traveling this year, sir? [*Laughter*]

THE PRESIDENT. No, I don't. I may go down to Key West again for a rest.

Q. Does that mean a back porch campaign?

THE PRESIDENT. It probably might, Miss May. A front porch campaign. No, that's the front of the White House. [*Indicating*]

Q. Really. Yes.

THE PRESIDENT. That's the front of the White House. The Chesapeake and Potomac Canal used to run along down there—[*indicating*]—and John Quincy Adams used to go down there and swim every morning. Some lady reporter had been trying to get an interview with him for a long time.

Q. Anne Royall.

THE PRESIDENT. She went down and sat on his clothes and let him talk to her. [*Laughter*] I thought you would be interested in that.[4]

Or the nonparanoid qualities displayed in these remarks to a delegation of the American Society of Newspaper Editors, at a time when Truman was regularly being beaten about the head on editorial pages around the country:

Just not long ago I passed the hundredth press conference, and one of the lady reporters there—just about as scarce as the lady editors in here today—asked me what I thought of the press and my treatment. I was glad to tell her that I thought the press had been extremely kind to me, and that the young men who represent you gentlemen here had done a good job in reporting, in that they had conveyed the facts as nearly and as truthfully as they could be conveyed under the circumstances, and that I was exceedingly happy that this country had a press that could say and do what it pleased under the law.

And it is a situation that does not prevail in very many countries. I don't know of any country where the head of a state is willing to submit himself to a gang of gentlemen—[*laughter*]—who ask him any sort of a question they please. I always try, so far as I am capable, to give a truthful answer, and as nearly as I can to state the facts. . . .

I am appreciative of the press this United States has, and of its present management. I think they have been as fair in stating the facts as it is possible for them to be. As I have said time and again here to the young men who represent you here in the White House, that I didn't care much what was said on the editorial page if I got the facts on the front page! And that has been the case. And that has been particularly true of this announcement of the foreign policy with regard to Greece and Turkey. I think the press has given the country a completely clear and fair statement of that situation, and the necessity for it.[5]

Whether answering the questions of reporters or speaking directly to the people, both the President and those speaking for him must be precise and frank in their discourse. The public issues facing the country are quite complex enough without doubletalk, obfuscation or appeals to prejudice and emotion.

"Let's talk sense to the American people!"—Adlai Stevenson's campaign slogan in 1952—has a nostalgic ring today. But after the verbal deception of Vietnam and Watergate, it is not at all nostalgic to insist on plain speaking and basic integrity and precision of language.

The politician using inflammatory code words such as "busing" and "law and order" should be held to a higher degree of precision in his discussion of race relations and criminal justice. And that abomination, "national security," which has been used to justify everything in the post–World War II era from the school-lunch program to illegal searches and seizures, should cease to be justification for anything except the most basic elements of national defense.

A plain-spoken President might, for example, attempt to clear the air on the complicated and emotional issue of abortion this way:

I am personally [for, against] abortion. But, regardless of my personal views, I am opposed to legislation—State or Federal—which attempts to circumvent the standards set forth by the Supreme Court in *Roe v. Wade*. To enact legislation which is unconstitutional can only falsely raise the hopes of those who support it, giving them a temporary victory but ultimately a defeat which will enhance the bitterness and ugliness surrounding this issue. This bitterness, in addition to promoting further division among the American people, is likely to spill over and become disrespect for the Supreme Court. This is precisely the result desired by many alleged "antiabortion" supporters—they care little if at all about the question of abortion; they care a great deal about discrediting the Supreme Court, for, if the Court can be discredited in one area, its decisions in others—civil rights, civil liberties, education and labor—can be discredited as well.

I am also opposed to a Constitutional amendment to ban abortions or to legislation denying public-assistance funds for abortions. Abortions will take place, as they have since the earliest days of medicine, whatever the Constitution and the legislatures say, and they will be performed on girls and women of all religions and all races. The only question is whether they will be performed on the butcher's table or in the hospital operating room. Making abortion illegal can only create contempt for the law and magnify human misery.

The decision to have an abortion is an intensely private matter of conscience. Those who oppose abortion are entitled to respect for their views. They should, and must, be free to hold their views and, through the churches and their writings, to expound those views. The responsibility for disseminating such views is, however, that of the church, not the government.

On this matter of conscience, Government must be neutral. In delivering health care and social services the Government must neither advocate nor condemn abortion. It cannot as a practical matter deny public-assistance funds to those desiring abortions; to do so would be to revive all the evils associated with illegal abortion. But Government must never condition public assistance on having an abortion and, indeed, must insure that alternatives to abortion are readily and freely available to the pregnant woman. Abortion must never become a short-cut to solving more basic social problems.

This Administration will fight to preserve the neutrality of the Government and of the laws in this matter. It will fight as well those who seek, by creating divisiveness, to divert the attention and support of the people from other pressing social issues with which Government is legitimately concerned.

If two elements of "openness" involve speaking, the third involves listening. The President must listen to the views of divergent groups within the society and maintain a receptivity to new ideas.

Hearing the views of groups that have learned to use their voices—organized labor, for example—is easy. Searching out and discerning the views of less organized groups is more difficult, either because of a lack of authentic spokesmen or fragmentation within the interest group.

To take a case in point, thirty years ago it would have been difficult for a political leader to know what black thinking might be on a particular issue. Black leaders, centered in the National Association for the Advancement of Colored People, while men of wisdom and integrity, did tend to express views calculated to create a minimum of disturbance. Blacks themselves tended to insist on individualism and to deny their leaders authority—an outgrowth, one supposes, of the basic organizing principle of slavery, which divided and conquered by pitting black man against black man in bidding for the master's favor, and the curious assimilation by blacks of the textbook American doctrine of laissez-faire individualism.

One of the great changes that occurred in the 1960s was the emergence of black leaders with real followings, of leaders who could purport to speak for a constituency. Indeed, the problem for a time was—and still is, to some extent—the existence of too many voices, ranging from Roy Wilkins on the one hand through Jesse Jackson to Stokeley Carmichael and Huey Newton at the other extreme. But a receptive President would have no trouble learning the concerns and problems of blacks, though he might have to sift through a number of divergent presentations of those concerns and problems.

"Openness" can also mean listening to, and utilizing the abilities of, groups that might otherwise be excluded for "ideological" reasons. In a Democratic context, "openness" would mean improved relations with the business community. While President Carter in the early months of his administration has appeared to express far too much concern for the feelings of business, the thrust of his initiative is undoubtedly correct.

The failure of an administration, Democratic or Republican, to deal effectively with business is simply not good for the economy. As one analyst of the New Deal has observed:

> Even large government investments were only stimulants. They could be resisted by countervailing factors that inhibited private spending. It seemed that between 1933 and 1937 the New Deal floundered between ever more daring banking and budgetary measures on one hand and ever more uncertain and stubborn business leaders on the other. Every new economic stimulant acted as a depressant on the minds of the affluent. *This was aggravated by the almost total lack of dialogue between the government and business.*[6]

Two unfortunate and equally wrong-headed tendencies have usually dominated the relationship between government and business in recent years. One, the traditional what-is-good-for-General-Motors view, which assumes that the man of business is especially wise and knowing, is patent nonsense. A sufficient number of take-charge business types have fallen on their faces in Washington to demonstrate that. Businessmen as a class are probably no smarter or no dumber than any other group, and probably perform in government as well or as badly as the representatives of any other group.

But the other extreme, that any probusiness decisions by government are inevitably antisocial, and that businessmen are necessarily either bunglers or seekers of special favor, is equally inaccurate.

The dilemma for a President is to find the intelligent, pragmatic, sophisticated businessman—to find the Douglas Dillons and to leave Maurice Stans and his ilk back at the store. And when listening to the views of business, to isolate and ignore what is self-serving.

A good example of the dilemma is the current question of whether private business will be able to raise the investment capital needed to expand and, where necessary, replace plant and equipment in the years immediately ahead. What is the dimension of the need? A total of $4.5 trillion from now until 1985, as estimated by former Treasury Secretary William E. Simon, or something less? Are the private capital markets adequate to meet the need? Or must there be government incentives, such as tax credits for plant investment (which, by reducing a corporation's tax bill, give it more cash for use in expansion) or tax breaks to encourage individual savings and investment? Are the fears expressed by businessmen as to the potential adequacy of capital real, or do they simply mask special pleading for tax favors?[7]

In reaching conclusions on questions such as these, proper answers are more likely to be arrived at on the basis of analysis that does not assume that the business community's position is enshrouded with special wisdom or, at the other extreme, represents a veiled attempt to bilk the public once again.

Businessmen do have themselves to blame in large part for suspicions of publicly expressed business viewpoints. Frankness has not been a trademark of business dialogue with the public; slick public relations more often than not has. As Thomas A. Murphy, Chairman of the Board of General Motors, recently observed:

> Credibility requires that we in business should not ignore or excuse demonstrated instances of misleading advertising, misrepresented warranties, and other questionable practices. We cannot overlook the admitted wrongdoing of some of our country's largest and most respected corporations. No one believes that business is blameless in every respect. For us to try and make it seem to be is worse than ineffectual: it only

deepens disbelief. It suggests that we in business can no longer distinguish between what is right and fair and honest and what is not.[8]

The capital-resources question is the sort of problem President Kennedy had in mind when he gave a commencement speech at Yale University in 1962. History may well mark this speech as the most important of Kennedy's Presidency, calling as it did for a nonideological approach by government and business to economic problems.

Kennedy observed that "the great enemy of truth" is not the lie but the myth—"persistent, persuasive, and unrealistic. . . . Too often we hold fast to the clichés of our forebears," he said. "We subject all facts to a prefabricated set of interpretations. . . . Mythology distracts us everywhere—in government as in business, in politics as in economics." In his judgment, the dialogue between government and business was "clogged by illusion and platitude" and failed "to reflect the true realities of contemporary American society." He went on to say:

> What is at stake in our economic decisions today is not some grand warfare of rival ideologies which will sweep the country with passion but the practical management of a modern economy. What we need is not labels and clichés but more basic discussion of the sophisticated and technical questions involved in keeping a great economic machinery moving ahead.

Economic policies presented "subtle challenges for which technical answers, not political answers, must be provided." Government and business may disagree, but government and business should be discussing such problems "in the most sober, dispassionate, and careful way if we are to maintain the kind of vigorous economy upon which our country depends."[9]

A modern President would be well advised to seek "technical" and not "political" answers to economic questions and to open the process of seeking such answers to those from the business community who are prepared to put aside the ideological baggage of the Rotary Club and the National Association of Manufacturers and to recognize, for example, the business sense of the following proposition of Adlai Stevenson:

> As a business matter every dollar we spend on educating American boys and girls will be returned—with interest—in terms of their increased productivity; and further . . . if we decide to skimp on education, every

dollar we save will probably be lost twice over in terms of things like the costs of juvenile delinquency, boys unable to meet the standards for military service, the unavailability of scientists and engineers, and increased relief rolls.[10]

Another aspect of "openness," and at first blush perhaps a surprising one, is the need for Presidential receptivity to the views and concerns of local workers of his political party. The nature of Presidential campaigning has changed much in recent years, with a candidate's pollsters and media experts infinitely more important to a successful result than grass-roots precinct leaders. Successful Presidential politics has been geared more and more to the cleverness of a candidate's personal organization than to the zeal of lowly doorbell ringers who work for all candidates of a party through thick and thin and without any particularly critical judgment of the individual office seeker. And the growing number of Federal and state campaign-finance laws, providing public funds to conduct both Presidential and other campaigns, has lessened the need for broadly based fund-raising activities.

The result has been a weakening of the ties between the President and the party hierarchy, which starts with the precinct worker and ends with the national chairman. In many ways this is probably an improvement, removing the President or the Presidential candidate from parochial and pedestrian concerns. At the same time, such distance cuts off a President or a candidate from another source of access to public thinking. The ward heeler depends for his success on being responsive to the needs and desires of his local constituency and, in the process, must make some judgment among the competing needs and priorities of that constituency. The result is not necessarily a distilled form of wisdom readily served up to a President, but it is another source of input that a President should not be too aloof or too independent to tap.

By treating his party as a viable institutional entity and according access to its leaders, the President may greatly help local officials elected by his party who, without a broad base of support, often seem tempted to "buy" that support at public expense. This is particularly true of elected Democrats running our major cities. Former Mayor John V. Lindsay of New York, for example, never certain of the traditional Democratic coalition as a base for support, purchased such support from municipal workers through a series of wage settlements that proved to be disastrous.

Local officeholders of either party now face, and will continue to face, problems requiring courageous and often unpopular solutions. To the extent that they are members of the President's party, his support of them and of party leaders can strengthen their often vulnerable positions and, at the same time, provide him with another means of access to the public.

Poll results about voter attitudes may take on greater meaning and usefulness if read in conjunction with the advice of those actively exposed to living, breathing voters who express those attitudes.

Finally, the President should establish rapport and maintain contact with the young people of this country. Not only does this make political sense, with 40 percent of the adult population being between the ages of eighteen and thirty-four, but the performance record of concerned young people in America has been impressively good in recent years. The major initiatives for ending the war in Vietnam, for civil rights and for consumer and environmental protection, for example, received their strongest impetus from the young.

Rapport with the young does not mean publicized visits to the Washington Monument, embarrassing attempts to be "with it," or pandering to what are perceived to be—usually without great reason—the unique concerns of young people. What it does mean is bringing young people into the decision-making process—seeking out the views, say, of young doctors on the delivery of health care or young lawyers on the operation of the criminal-justice system.

Public-opinion polls on thorny social issues consistently show the attitudes of the young to be more flexible, more tolerant and less hardened than the views of their elders. A wise President will take advantage of this, both because it is right to do so and because it is good politics.

"INTELLIGENCE"

Insistence upon an intelligent President does not necessarily mean insistence on an extraordinary I.Q. or an Ivy League education. Richard Nixon strove for, and largely achieved, a number of academic successes; Franklin Roosevelt did not. Adlai Stevenson flunked out of the Harvard Law School; Gerald Ford graduated from Yale's.*

"Intelligence" in this context can better be defined as (1) an awareness of the national character of the Presidency, (2) a shrewdness (and lack of personal jealousy or suspicion) in the selection of his principal advisers, (3) a refined sense of judging the "ripeness" of problems for governmental attention and (4) a commitment to wise planning and efficiency in government.

Affording access to local officials and party leaders should be beneficial, as suggested above; harboring romantic presumptions that state and local governments are best equipped to solve problems is not. In other words, an intelligent President will look upon "revenue sharing" with local governments as it has developed in recent years with great skepticism.

Federal grants to the states and to local governments—"revenue sharing," if you will—are not new, beginning at least as early as the Morill Act of 1862, which provided Federal support for the state land-grant colleges. By 1972, the Federal government had 650 specific grant programs for providing aid to state and local governments.

This "excessive categorization" of grants often overlapped and led to a situation in which Federal bureaucrats negotiated with their grassroots counterparts, bypassing governors and mayors in the process.[11]

The fiscal difficulties of the states, and the increasing evidence that the Federal government has a limited capacity for administering (as opposed to financing) programs, led a number of economists in the late 1960s to consider the consolidation of the existing grant programs,

---

* A semirelevant aside: "Intelligence" in a President also does not mean dressing up his speeches with snippets of poetry. President Kennedy, in his flirtation with Robert Frost, started the whole thing. And President Carter continues the trend as a public exegete of the works of Dylan Thomas. Now the most slack-jawed hack running for sheriff feels compelled to tell us that he has many miles to go before he sleeps (blithely unaware that the preceding line of "Stopping By Woods on a Snowy Evening" refers to "promises to keep"—dangerous ground for a politician). Or he quotes the current favorite, Yeats, particularly the half-line from "The Second Coming," "the centre [invariably misspelled] cannot hold."

Instead of reciting, and misquoting, our Presidents might ponder Yeats's "On Being Asked for a War Poem":

> I think it better that in times like these
> A poet's mouth be silent, for in truth
> We have no gift to set a statesman right;
> He has had enough of meddling who can please
> A young girl in the indolence of her youth,
> Or an old man upon a winter's night.

or the substitution of direct, unrestricted payments by the Federal government to state and local units. Most notable of the proponents was Walter Heller, who appears to have coined the term "revenue sharing" in his Godkin Lectures at Harvard in 1966. Convinced that the Supreme Court's reapportionment decision* would revitalize state and local government, and that a substantial "peace dividend" at the end of the Vietnam War would be available to fund revenue sharing, he advocated unrestricted per capita grants to the states from a percentage of Federal income-tax revenues. The Federal government's efficient and progressive taxing system would provide economic sustenance to the states (and, through them, to local governments), enabling them to function in the Brandeisian sense as "laboratories of the Federal system." The dilemma posed by Richard Goodwin concerning the nation's problems—"We are not wise enough to solve them from the top, nor are there resources enough to solve them from the bottom"— would be unknotted by giving this new fiscal base to Federalism.[12]

Heller himself admitted that the question of unrestricted grants was not an easy one, but he concluded in 1968 that the needs of local governments were sufficiently pressing to override doubts about local competence or efficiency.

President Nixon had no doubts at all in advocating revenue sharing, which was finally enacted into law in the State and Local Fiscal Assistance Act of 1972. This Act provided for payments to state and local governments of $30 billion over the fiscal years 1973 through 1977, the funds to be used for "ordinary and necessary" capital expenditures of any type, or for maintenance and operating expenditures relating to public safety, environmental protection, public transit, health, recreation, libraries, social services for the poor or aged and financial administration. Nixon's pledge that there would be "no strings" on these so-called "general" revenue-sharing funds—"When we say no strings, we mean no strings"[13]—was borne out by the Act. Except for restrictions on using revenue-sharing funds to match other Federal grants, the only substantive restriction was one prohibiting discrimination in the operation of local programs.

To encourage community participation in decisions as to the use of revenue-sharing funds, each government unit was required to submit a report of planned use to the Secretary of the Treasury, to publish

* *Baker v. Carr*, 369 U.S. 186 (1962).

the report in a general-circulation newspaper in the geographic area affected and to "advise the news media" of such publication.

The allocation formula for determining each state's allotment took into account the state's own taxing efforts and the income of its population.

Once revenue-sharing dollars are paid to a local government, it is thereafter impossible to trace them. For example, assume that a city government has $100 million to spend and then receives $10 million additional through revenue sharing. It then spends $10 million on new libraries and $100 million to dig a hole to China. Have the revenue-sharing funds been used for the commendable purpose of erecting libraries or the frivolous one of digging the China hole?

Despite the problem of tracing funds, local governments were required to report how revenue-sharing funds are used. The tabulation for fiscal year 1975 shows that the largest single use was for public safety (24 percent), with almost one fourth of the amount in this category being spent for new equipment, such as police cars and fire trucks. The building and renovation of police and fire stations also constituted major expenditures in this category. Less than 4 percent of available funds was spent for social services for the poor and aged, less than 1 percent for libraries and less than 1 percent for housing and community development.[14] One wonders if police cars would have so readily replaced social services if local governments were spending their own funds. Certainly the provisions of the 1972 Act designed to increase public participation in determining how revenue-sharing funds should be spent were simple-minded. To think that publication of a "planned-use report" amid the legal notices in a newspaper would stimulate grass-roots discussion of revenue-sharing funds is ludicrous. And even if there should be public interest, it is an open question how such interest would be channeled.

President Carter, in his 1976 campaign, called attention to the skewing of the decision-making process inherent in revenue sharing. Noting in the last campaign debate that Congress had often passed programs to help "very poor people and neighborhoods in the downtown urban centers," only to find the funds appropriated channeled to the less needy suburbs "because of the greatly advantaged persons who live in the suburbs—better education, better organization, more articulate, more aware of what the laws are."[15]

In assessing the operation of general revenue sharing under the 1972

Act, the League of Women Voters, the National Coalition and others reported in 1974 that "citizen oversight" was not, and as the program is set up could not be, effective in monitoring the use of funds. This report said:

> One of the most striking aspects of the GRS [general revenue sharing] program is the absence of the usual checks on local governmental decision-making. . . . Federal oversight by the Congress or the Executive has been kept to a minimum. . . . The implicit check of voter approval of the measures and bond issues does not operate, since GRS reaches the local level "automatically." And the periodic check provided by local elections is ineffective in the context of multiple election issues, particularly since GRS money need not be raised locally and rarely amounts to as much as 7–8% of local city budgets in any event.

This same report concludes that, while local governments must certify that nondiscrimination requirements are being met, there is a "good bit of evidence that these assurances are unreliable. Indeed, by doing nothing to mitigate existing discrimination, GRS funds can be said to be contributing to its continuation." The report cites as an example the City of New Orleans, which allocated a quarter of its general revenue-sharing funds to its police and fire departments, where minority employment (21 percent in the police department, 2.9 percent in the fire department) was well below the minority population (50 percent).[16]

That nondiscrimination standards are not enforced is hardly surprising. Although more than 34,500 governmental units received general revenue-sharing funds in fiscal 1974, the civil-rights-compliance staff of the Office of Revenue Sharing during such year consisted of two people.

The gap between Professor Heller's idealistic economic Federalism and the Nixon-Ford general revenue-sharing program is wide. The Heller model envisioned strengthened local governments making efficient use of Federal money. The Nixon-Ford model represented a means of diverting Federal expenditures from programs with recognizable and socially useful standards and goals to a basically unregulated program that allows local officials to spend Federal money without reference to social utility. It also represented a convenient means of scrapping specific programs with goals found politically objectionable to Nixon and Ford in favor of the unfettered general revenue-sharing plan, under which benign local decisions were made concerning the allocation of funds—benign local decisions which in fact substituted police cars for day-care centers. The existence of general revenue sharing was used by the Nixon administration to justify cutbacks in existing social programs and the impoundment of funds for such programs. In the first quarter of 1974, for example, $1.5 billion were disbursed under revenue sharing, while a total of $1.6 billion appropriated for specific programs was impounded.[17]

No one can quarrel with the need for streamlining Federal grant programs to minimize overlapping and red tape and for the elimination of such programs when they have served their purpose. But to accomplish this by abdicating all controls over the expenditure of grants by state and local governments is to make "a really stupefying act of faith," as Arthur Schlesinger has put it, that local government is "more incorruptible, more efficient, or more expert than national government." Schlesinger goes on to observe:

It is the national government . . . that has vindicated racial justice against local bigotry. It is the national government that has protected the Bill of Rights against local vigilantism. It is the national government that has preserved natural resources against local greed. It is the national government that has civilized our industry, that has secured the rights of labor organization, that has defended the farmer against the vagaries of the free market. The growth of national power, far from producing government less "responsive to the individual person," has given a majority of Americans far more dignity and freedom than they could win in a century of localism.

It is little wonder that those who dislike civil rights and civil liberties, who want to loot our timberlands and break our unions and dismantle our regulation of business, should propagate the fraud of local government as the only true "people's government."[18]

While it is perhaps naïve to think that one could have an impact in any event, general revenue sharing effectively disenfranchises the Federal taxpayer. If Federal tax dollars fund a Federal program which is foolish and ill-conceived, the aggrieved taxpayer can at least protest to the President, a Cabinet officer, two Senators and a Congressman. If such tax dollars are funneled without restriction to a Mayor Rizzo or a Governor Wallace, and he uses them for a foolish and ill-conceived program, the taxpayer's protest becomes much more attenuated and ineffective (assuming he even has any notion of what has happened to the unrestricted Federal funds, which have disappeared into the Philadelphia or Alabama treasuries).

One can feel much more confident that medical reimbursements to chiropractors, jobs for political incompetents, racial favoritism in program benefits, expenditures for Mickey Mouse equipment and other examples of waste and quackery will be regulated more effectively if Federal standards are imposed and enforced with respect to money shared with local governments.

President Nixon, in signing the 1972 Act at Independence Square in Philadelphia (with Mayor Rizzo at his side), had the effrontery to declare that the Act would "renew" the Federal system envisioned by the Constitution.[19] With all due respect, the Act seemed more a renewal of the Articles of Confederation under which local decision-making was supreme and the Federal government was powerless to impose policies of national applicability.

President Ford requested, and Congress granted, an extension of revenue sharing in 1976. Under the 1976 legislation, $25.5 billion will be distributed to state and local governments from January 1, 1977, through September 30, 1980, on substantially the same basis as provided in the 1972 Act. The amendments made in 1976 can hardly be said to be responsive to the criticisms made of revenue sharing. The public participation procedures were modestly improved by requiring a public hearing on the planned use of revenue-sharing funds. But the only provision of the 1972 Act approaching a control on what funds are used for—the list of the types of permitted operating expenditures—was removed.

All opposition to the extension was beaten down with the argument that local governments needed the money and had come to rely on their revenue-sharing allocations.

An intelligent President must not be misled by the surface appeal of general revenue sharing and should attempt to confine it to existing—and probably permanent—proportions. This will be a formidable task as state and local governments try to meet their obligations from a shrinking—or (after Proposition 13 and its progeny) restricted—tax base.

He should also be wary of giving up the considerable leverage which the grant-making power affords to the Federal government to effect reforms in local governments. If properly used, the power of making grants conditional may, for example, be a means of compelling local tax reform and encouraging inner-city–suburban planning and cooperation. There is no reason why this power should, without a struggle, be ceded to state and local interests.*

A second aspect of "intelligence" is the ability to attract and retain competent advisers and to make use of them once they are in Washington.

There is heartening evidence that the old presumption that the President should have wide latitude in making his appointments and that the Congress, in the absence of grave reservations, will automatically defer to his selections is changing. Harry Truman was permitted to retain the venal General Vaughn on his personal staff and to appoint a number of mediocrities to the Federal bench. Eisenhower named a cabinet of eight millionaires and a plumber with no outcry other than a few feeble jokes; only his appointment of Clare Luce to be Ambassador to Brazil came to grief, and then only because she committed what was then the most cardinal sin for a prospective appointee— questioning the mental competence of a member of the Senate, Wayne Morse of Oregon.

The old ways show signs of disappearing. In the televised campaign debates of 1976, a surprising number of the reporters' questions related to the candidates' views on appointments, and President-elect Carter, starting with his selection of Vice President Mondale, engaged in a public, painstaking process in making his appointments.†

Whether Carter's public searching and the detailed invasion of the personal privacy of his appointees which he required produced a superior collection of advisers remains to be seen. It is certainly ironic, given the degree of public disclosure that Carter insisted upon, that Carter's first "scandal," concerning Bert Lance, should have involved

---

* Grants could also be conditional on the reduction of sales taxes by state and local governments as part of an anti-inflation program. See p. 249, *infra*.

† Another semirelevant aside: In describing members of their staffs, Presidents should use simple, direct titles like "Mister," "Ms.," "Miss" or "Mrs." or titles that go with the job ("Mr. Secretary," "Mr. Ambassador"), but please, unless the appointees involved are bona fide medical doctors, not "Doctor." The hoary and abused device of enhancing the prestige of anyone who has passed through a diploma mill by calling him "Doctor" should not be encouraged at the highest level of government. Enough of "Dr." Kissinger, "Dr." Burns and "Dr." Brzezinski. Someone should tell the White House press office that the practice smacks of either insecurity or elitism—take your pick. (The other alternative, of course, would be to adopt the custom of some third-world countries where everyone who has escaped a felony conviction for a decent interval is called "Doctor," thus making the whole silly practice meaningless.)

something less than complete and candid disclosure of Lance's troubled financial situation.

The elaborate selection process following the 1976 elections was politically necessary in 1976 and will probably set a pattern for candidates and Presidents in the future, as the result of at least five events which focused attention on the President's powers of appointment:

1. The ineptitude of the McGovern staff in the Eagleton and $1,000 "demogrant" fiascos of the 1972 campaign, which demonstrated the harm (in this case to the candidate but potentially to the country) that shoddy staff work can create.

2. The Nixon nominations of Haynsworth and Carswell to the Supreme Court, which dramatically showed that public and professional outcries can and probably should counterbalance the traditional acquiescence in Presidential appointments.

3. The publication in late 1972 of David Halberstam's study of United States involvement in Vietnam, *The Best and the Brightest,* which documented in extraordinary and powerful detail the ability of a homogeneous "Establishment" group of advisers to delude both themselves and the country about the conduct of public policy.

4. The illegal and quasi-legal behavior of the Nixon staff and Cabinet.

5. The sharp realization that a significant part of Richard Nixon's legacy survives his downfall as the result of his appointments to the Supreme Court.

Naming a potential Cabinet in advance of an election has traditionally been thought to be a sign of desperation or frivolity, as it was when Eugene McCarthy did it in 1968. But, just as the British voter knows pretty much who is likely to be in the Cabinet of the party he votes for, the same may soon be true for his American counterpart. At a minimum, it is likely that American candidates for the foreseeable future are going to have to commit themselves in advance at least to the basic principle of finding the best available appointees and of surrounding themselves with advisers not predominantly based in Cambridge, Massachusetts, Grand Rapids, Michigan, or the world of advertising and public relations.

Future Presidents will ignore at their peril the recent lessons of the use and misuse of staff, and of the importance of making first-rate appointments. In terms of staff, they might do well to return to the style of the Roosevelt White House where, in Professor Richard Neustadt's analysis, no one worked who was not essential to FDR as President. The staff was personal and not institutional, and when the words "this is the White House calling" came over the telephone it meant the President or someone acting "intimately and immediately for him" was calling.[20] Not, in other words, a plumber.

A third aspect of "intelligence," as applied to the Presidency, is a developed sense of the "ripeness" of issues for the attention of government. "Ripeness" is normally thought of as a doctrine applicable to the Supreme Court, whereby the Justices exercise their discretion in rejecting appeals until a legal issue is "ripe" for their decision.

A somewhat similar concept of "ripeness" should govern the President's sense of priorities in dealing with the nation's problems. Left to their own devices, both the public and organized pressure groups will demand Presidential attention for every social and economic problem, from health care to declining egg production.

A judicious President will carefully budget his own personal time, the time and energy of his staff, and his residual political capital with the public and the Congress, to focus immediate attention on the most pressing problems.

Choosing among "pressing" problems may be extremely difficult—should money go to health or to housing?—but choice is obviously necessary.

Failure to sort out issues and to define priorities can lead either to public disappointment, when a President has promised too much and delivered too little, or to neglect of *all* problems because the task of ranking them has not been undertaken.

In the period since World War II, ignoring—or exacerbating—social problems has in fact been either the stated or the implicit policy of the Republican Presidents Eisenhower, Nixon and Ford. And there is marginally respectable political thought for continuing that objective, as seen in the writings of the likes of Irving Kristol (the pre-Senator), Daniel Patrick Moynihan and his sometime collaborator, Nathan Glazer.

The social problems confronting the country are so massive and complicated, the argument goes, that ineffectual or helpless or incompetent government cannot possibly contribute to their solution. Witness the profound pessimism of Nathan Glazer in this regard:

> 1) Social policy is an effort to deal with the breakdown of traditional ways of handling distress. These traditional mechanisms are located primarily in the family, but also in the ethnic group, the neighborhood, and in such organizations as the church. . . .
>
> 2) In its effort to deal with the breakdown of these traditional structures, however, social policy tends to encourage their further weakening. There is, then, no sea of misery against which we are making steady headway. Our efforts to deal with distress themselves increase distress.[21]

An intelligent President rightly will dismiss such observations as rubbish. He will not hesitate to grapple with problems "ripe" for solution, neither throwing up his hands at the difficulty of it all nor cautiously waiting until the last shred of information is available concerning the matter at hand.

Most social problems "become more acute when neglected," Eli Ginzberg and Robert Solow have written. When government fails to recognize or neglects an incipient problem "it is likely to be forced later on to mount more ambitious programs of social intervention when the constraints of time, resources, and tolerance will be more painfully binding. Prolonged neglect is costly. Most social problems do not fade away."[22]

The most subtle exercise of all may be recognizing and making appropriate preparations for the incipient problems of the future. A wise President will insist that a portion of the resources at his command be dedicated to this sort of forward study.

This is also an area where the committees of Congress can exercise a creative role, holding hearings on subjects that today may seem esoteric but tomorrow may be difficult social realities.

As the next chapter argues, unemployment is a real and important issue that the country and the Federal government must face near term. There are, however, aspects of the employment problem that are not of such immediate concern, but could well become of concern in the future. One is the whole question of *under*employment, or the failure of the economy to properly utilize or upgrade the skills of workers. The question encompasses such matters as worker discontent with the monotony of the assembly-line, the dead-end job (which nonetheless must be filled in a functioning society), the Ph.D. driving a taxi.

It may well be that there is little or nothing that can be done about this aspect of the employment situation by way of executive orders or legislation. But the issue is real, and more information is needed about it. Utilizing the resources of the Federal government to gather such information is perfectly appropriate.

Another employment question worthy of study on a long-range basis is the desirability of continuing the civil-service system in its present form. Traditionally viewed as a means of protecting the government worker from political patronage, the system has become a means by which the government worker obtains "tenure" and cannot, as a practical matter, be fired. Thus, in 1976, less than 1/7th of 1 percent of Federal employees—fewer than 3,500—were discharged for inefficiency or "cause."[23] And in the Department of Health, Education and Welfare, for example, the President can make only 144 "political" appointments—in a Department of 145,000 employees![24] Does such a system unduly inhibit the implementation of policies set by the President? Does it affect the responsiveness of government personnel? Does their independence lead them to be better civil servants, or do they become time-servers, waiting for retirement? Have civil-service systems become "rigid, unresponsive, and uncontrollable administrative straitjackets"?[25] Given the experience the government now has had in administering anti-discrimination programs, would a general policy requiring balanced representation in career government employment among workers of varying political persuasions (Democratic, Republican, independent) serve as well as the "tenure" created by civil service?*

The Presidential commission and similar advisory bodies—as well as the Congressional committee—can serve as a useful political device in defining the dimensions of new problems, for suggesting alternative policy approaches and, at times, for helping to build a consensus on thorny issues when it does not exist.

But the merit of such commissions will depend on the intelligence

---

* President Carter's Message to Congress in March 1978 regarding the civil service contained a number of commendable proposals for reform: (a) a super-grade Senior Executive Service that the top 9,200 civil servants could join, (b) incentive pay for lower-level employees and (c) a fairer and speedier disciplinary system. Membership in the Senior Executive Service would be voluntary. Members could be transferred throughout the Executive Branch as and when needed, and would no longer receive automatic pay increases based on longevity. They would, however, be eligible for merit raises and up to 50 percent of them in any year could receive bonuses for superior performance. Federal Civil Service Reform, Message to the Congress, March 2, 1978.

of the President. Rightly used, the device is useful. Badly used, it is a means of evading present solutions to current problems that demand present solutions. (Witness President Eisenhower's calling of a White House Conference on Education in 1955, which effectively killed Congressional action on aid to education in 1954.*)

(The commission also has its uses as a means of rewarding the political faithful with appointments that have the trappings of prestige but do not really mean very much as a substantive matter. It is very useful to have a place to park hacks, where they can do relatively little harm. The Marine Mammal Commission or the Veterans Day National Committee would seem appropriate for this purpose.)

An intelligent President should make a genuine, honest and sustained commitment to planning and efficiency within the Federal government.

The pattern for all new Presidents, shortly after affirming their faith in God, is to renounce inefficiency. And there it stands. A real commitment by a President to efficiency, backed up by tough monitoring of ongoing programs, would be both novel and welcome.

"Why can't liberals start raising hell about a government so big, so complex, so expensive and so unresponsive that it's dragging down every good program we've worked for?" Senator Edmund Muskie asked in 1975. "Why can't liberals talk about fiscal responsibility and productivity without feeling uncomfortable? We're in a rut. Our emotional stake in government is so great that we regard common-sense criticism of government almost as a personal attack."[26]

To share or acknowledge Republican and right-wing criticisms of "waste" may gall a President, if he is a Democrat. But it may be necessary to attract and hold public support for social programs, quite apart from being "common sense." And it does not require the logical jump that many conservatives then make: X program is wasteful, therefore abolish it.

Nor does a commitment against waste require a domestic policy based on cost accountancy. Indeed, a vigilant attention to waste should not include cuts which are, on proper analysis, inefficient or more wasteful in the long run. As Adlai Stevenson said in 1956:

> It is economical to avoid waste and to examine every proposal with a careful, realistic eye as to its real merit and its financing. It is not economical to let needed public services deteriorate, to skimp on needed

* See p. 88, *supra*.

programs of general welfare, to be niggardly with the needs of future generations. For what, after all, is economy? It is not simply the accumulation of great unused storehouses of wealth. It is the wise use of that wealth, without waste, and with careful attention to the future's needs; it is the use of what we have to serve human living in the wisest way.[27]

The Congress, as we have seen, has made substantial progress in planning better the budget and appropriations process. It would be appropriate for the Executive Branch to make a similar commitment. A possible vehicle for this might be the proposed Balanced Growth and Economic Planning Act introduced in the Senate by Jacob Javits and the late Hubert Humphrey.* Because of the uncertainties of how a national planning mechanism would or should work, it would probably be unwise to cast the procedures envisioned by this bill into concrete, but they are certainly worth a try on an experimental basis.

The Humphrey-Javits bill would have established an Economic Planning Board in the executive office to collect and analyze economic data. Utilizing the studies of the Board, the President would be required every two years to submit a "Balanced Growth Plan" to Congress and the fifty governors. Congress would have power to review the Plan and to approve, disapprove or modify it. The Plan would identify national goals requiring action and the resources needed to achieve them, and would also recommend legislative and administrative action.

Once adopted by Congress, the Plan would be binding on the Federal government, but would be voluntary for the private sector and state and local governments.

Senator Humphrey saw this process as creating not a "planned economy" but a "planning economy" useful, for example, in reconciling "our concern about the environment with the legitimate needs of business" or attacking such problems as agricultural production:

> We could quit setting production objectives without consideration for transportation, fertilizer and energy requirements. We could quit regulating prices without apparent concern for energy needs or their impact on employment. We could begin to coordinate our shipments abroad with reserves at home. We are the only great nation in the world without

* This bill, introduced in the Ninety-fourth Congress, was not reintroduced in the Ninety-fifth Congress. Substantially similar provisions were at one time contained in the Humphrey-Hawkins full-employment bill, but they were largely eliminated in the compromise version of Humphrey-Hawkins worked out with the Carter administration in November 1977.

an explicit food policy. Yet an adequate food reserve program is the best way to stabilize food prices and keep our farmers solvent.[28]

There is sure to be opposition to any ambitious planning proposal—conservative economist Milton Friedman has warned against the creation of "another Federal agency to control our daily lives"[29]—but even President Nixon, in his 1970 Economic Report, pointed in the direction of greater planning efforts:

> We have learned that 1-year planning leads to almost as much confusion as no planning at all, and that there is a need to increase public awareness of long-range trends and the consequences for future years of decisions taken now.[30]

And the late Senator Humphrey's own arguments are compelling:

> The United States Government has become the last bastion of unplanned activity in the modern world. All other industrial nations plan and have planning systems. Businesses, universities, foundations and even individual families have realized that they have to plan in order to achieve their goals with the limited resources available. But the Federal Government continues to pursue an ad-hoc, piecemeal approach that is not only wasteful in its inefficiency but outright harmful in its short-sightedness.
> At present there are more than 50 Federal offices that collect and analyze economic data. Because no single office is responsible for overseeing and integrating their activities, the data collected often lack necessary detail or appropriate standards for comparison. In many cases the data are actually incompatible or contradictory.
> The confused and haphazard nature of this system makes it impossible to pursue coherent national objectives and our failure to clearly decide where we want our nation to go has wasted valuable resources.

Other planning devices that a strong President should seek include authorization from the Congress to the Executive to raise and increase taxes within prescribed limits and to make economic assistance available to local communities *automatically* in response to swings in the economy.

Congress has always jealously guarded its traditional prerogative of setting the levels of taxation and turned a deaf ear to President Kennedy's request for standby authority to cut or increase taxes to stimulate or slow down the economy. The fact remains that if tax adjustments are to be an effective part of fiscal policy, they are likely to be effective if made rapidly and not well into the ups or downs of the economic cycle, as is the case when authorization is required from a slow-moving Congress. The President's power in this area should be carefully circumscribed, but the potential of a more effective weapon against both recession and inflation is appealing.

In 1976 the Congress, as part of an antirecession public-works bill, embodied principles advocated by Harry Truman thirty years earlier.* Specifically, the bill recognized that Federal measures to stimulate the economy through expanded Federal activity are dampened if state and local governments, at the same time, cut back their activities. The bill provided for grants to state and local governments to maintain basic services, with the amount of funds available for such grants dependent on the level of the national average unemployment rate and the amount of each grant on the unemployment rate within the local government unit. The plan was experimental (although later extended in 1977) but was unique both in recognizing the need for "countercyclical assistance" and making such assistance available on an automatic basis in accordance with a predetermined formula.

"Openness" and "intelligence," in the broad senses described above, are central to a concept of the Presidency that sees that office as the most important institution for meeting the nation's domestic problems. There is need, however, for a third quality to make the Presidential engine run smoothly—an elusive quality best summed up as "compassion."

Compassion, or humanity, or good instincts, or bleeding-heart liberalism—call it what you will—uninformed by intelligence, will accomplish little. But in a desire to have a President with the technical competence to meet increasingly complex problems, we must not turn the equation on its head and ignore the continuing need for a President with a humane regard for the people of this country.

Identifying this elusive quality is difficult. How does one identify in advance a Franklin Roosevelt, enthusiastically poring over architectural drawings for projects that would put people back to work—

---

* President Kennedy succeeded in having legislation embodying this concept, the Public Works Acceleration Act (PL 87–658), adopted in 1962, but the Act expired two years later after expenditures of $843 million on 7,700 projects.

or, for that matter, a Richard Nixon, engineering "modified hangouts" in the Oval Office?

The hope is that American shrewdness will spot the phony before he reaches Pennsylvania Avenue, that the merciless public exposure to which our politicians are subjected will identify hypocrisy and meanness of spirit.

With our deepening concern for technocratic competence the matter of compassion in our leaders becomes even more important. We must forever strive to identify and elect leaders who understand that the Constitutional phrase is "we, the people of the United States," not "we, the government" and "they, the people."

Governmental solutions to our social problems are more likely to be both creative and lasting if the man ultimately responsible for them maintains his humanity; a man who has visited a patient in a nursing home will bring an added dimension to his review of computer printouts detailing the health statistics of the population over sixty-five.

And as the weave of our social fabric becomes more intricate, issues involving novel and troubling questions of human relations are likely to arise. The implementation of racial justice, the balancing of pluralistic values in arriving at a governmental abortion policy and the question of homosexual rights all come to mind. Solutions for these problems will never be simple or easy, but the nonplastic man is more likely to arrive at sensible results than the media manipulator, the poll watcher or the technocratic automaton.

The search for men of both compassion and brains is an extremely challenging one, and one quite likely to end at times in disappointment and frustration. When all is said and done, however, the excitement of that search is probably the most compelling and interesting feature of our national politics.

Eleven · Priorities

The Great Society must be a bold *society. It must not fear to meet new challenges. It must not fail to seize new opportunities. The Great Society must be a* compassionate *society. It must always be responsive to human needs. The Great Society must be an* efficient *society. Less urgent programs must give way to make room for higher priority needs. And each program, old and new, must be conducted with maximum efficiency, economy, and productivity.*
>   —LYNDON B. JOHNSON
>   Annual Budget Message to the Congress,
>   January 25, 1965

Assuming a will and a desire to do so, recognizing social and economic problems of concern in 1979 is relatively easy. Attempting to sort out the priorities for attacking these problems, and to formulate solutions, is much more difficult. Priorities can change, and change rapidly. A new wave of international crises, for example, could strike domestic concerns from a national agenda altogether. Foreign affairs, or a combination of foreign affairs and defense needs, could preempt both the energies of our leaders and the money in our fisc. Likewise, a series of polarizing riots and looting in our major cities could quickly turn public support away from measures to promote racial equality and to reform our welfare system.

Even under ideal circumstances, the process of accommodating competing demands is not easy when an agenda is being set for our diverse country and the often conflicting interests of 217 million Americans. But having led the reader this far down the garden path, it would be unfair not to show him the blueprints for the beautiful gazebo that is to be erected at the end.*

* The author recognizes that there is an aesthetic objection to agenda-making. Telling us what we should be doing in the future is a favorite preoccupation of foundation-

To help focus on the importance of setting priorities, as opposed to the mere recognition that certain problems exist and perhaps ought to be dealt with, it is perhaps useful to separate into three categories the social and economic issues troubling the country: *substantive issues,* such as unemployment, inflation and health care; *impact issues* that affect or are affected by solutions to substantive problems, such as racial equality, environmental protection and the viability of the family; and *procedural issues* of the sort discussed in passing in Chapters Seven and Ten, such as the Congressional budgeting process and government efficiency and planning.

Stated another way, substantive problems are those requiring government to develop and carry out affirmative programs to solve them; impact problems are those that must be taken into account as substantive issues are confronted; and procedural problems are those concerned with how government works, how it relates to the individuals and institutions of the nation.

If this classification is utilized, it means that the agenda-maker must construct an agenda with three subsets. As a first step, he must decide into which category an issue fits. This inescapably involves value judgments.

---

sponsored study groups. The impenetrable drafting-by-committee of such groups gives the art of agenda-writing a bad name. If the reader doubts this statement, he should examine the detritus collected and published under the aegis of the Critical Choices Commission. It will be recalled that Nelson Rockefeller founded the Commission in the early 1970s. There was not a little suspicion at the time that the real purpose was to provide Rockefeller with a forum for his perennial attempt to become the Republican Presidential nominee. This suspicion appears to have been confirmed, since the Commission ran out of steam at roughly the same time as Rockefeller's 1976 campaign. To put a good face on the deflated project, the position papers and other materials which happened to be available were gathered up and published in a widely unremarked series of extraordinarily boring books, with such titles as "Trade, Inflation and Ethics" and "Africa: From Mystery to Maze." It is hard to take seriously a series of studies which begins on the first page of an early volume with these portentous sentences:

No view of human nature is entirely false—else men would not hold it for long. But none is entirely true, either—else the philosophical question of "the nature of human nature" would have yielded a scientific answer and would have been settled beyond all argument. And these two propositions, once accepted, themselves add up to a third conception of human nature—as capable of knowing itself, but never finally; as capable of shaping itself, but never ultimately; as capable of being shaped, but never totally. This is a view that is congenial to the Judeo-Christian tradition, but quite uncongenial to various modern ideologies, whether of the right or of the left, which insist that man is either fully the master of his fate or completely a slave to it.—Irving Kristol and Paul Weaver, eds. (and joint authors of the foregoing), *The Americans: 1976—An Inquiry into Fundamental Concepts of Man Underlying Various U.S. Institutions* (Lexington, Mass.: Lexington Books, 1976), p. xvii.

For example, a dedicated environmentalist would insist that environmental protection be treated as a *substantive issue*, with the government developing positive programs to protect, preserve and improve our natural resources and air and water quality. There is certainly a respectable case for this viewpoint, as there are obviously straightforward programs and policies that the Federal government could and should adopt in the environmental field.

Treating environmental protection as an *impact issue* does not mean that the government should abandon potentially fruitful program initiatives, but it does mean that the primary thrust of the government's policy should be to react to programs designed to solve other problems to ensure, for example, that a national energy policy does not have damaging and irreversible consequences for the environment.

Similarly value judgments are involved in classifying inflation as a *substantive issue*. The traditional Republican approach to inflation discussed in Chapter Eight represents basically the treatment of inflation as an *impact issue*, the Republicans' primary thrust being to weigh social programs in the light of their potential inflationary impact.

Again it is obvious that the inflationary impact of plans for social action cannot be ignored; the Medicaid-Medicare experience* and the unfortunate resolution by Congress in 1977 of Social Security's funding problems† teach us that much. But by denominating inflation as a *substantive issue*, the dual judgment is implicitly expressed that the problem of inflation requires direct, programmatic action to meet it and, conversely, that the impact of inflation cannot be the ultimate determinative factor in policy decisions concerning such other problems as unemployment.

The categorization of issues suggested is workable only if used with the full realization that no issue falls neatly into a fixed category and that the classification of an issue can change over time (i.e., aid to secondary education as basically a *substantive issue* prior to 1965 and a *procedural issue* as the Elementary and Secondary Education Act of 1965 was administered thereafter), and that an activist government will attempt to attack substantive, impact and procedural issues— though not *all* such issues—at one and the same time. But analyzing

---

* See pp. 76–78, *supra* and 253–55, *infra*.
† See pp. 69–71, *supra*.

the primary category into which an issue falls, deciding under which subset of an overall agenda an issue belongs, can offer at least a clue as to the means by which such issue should be addressed.

SUBSTANTIVE ISSUES

Political party platforms, ingeniously designed to exert as wide an appeal as possible to the electorate, offer a good index of what are perceived as the nation's social and economic problems. The Republican and Democratic platforms of 1976 discussed the following major social and economic topics that could be classified as "substantive" domestic issues:

Unemployment
Inflation
The urban crisis
Antitrust enforcement
Aid to: Small business
    Veterans
    The handicapped
    The aged
    Farmers
Tax reform
Social Security reform
The minimum wage
The open shop
Neighborhood legal services
Welfare reform
Health care
Amnesty for draft resisters
Aid to education
Rural development
Housing
Assistance to the arts
Transportation
Abortion
Energy policy
The right of privacy
Indian rights and land protection

Most of these issues are worthy of inclusion on a social-policy agenda, although in some cases the proper approach may be to include them in a form different from that desired by their proponents. Thus, a special program of aid to schools in areas affected by defense installations might better be integrated into school aid administered under ESEA, and housing mortgage programs might better be considered as a matter of general applicability, not just as a special benefit for veterans.

Some of the issues can be or have been solved with a stroke of the pen. Political judgments are involved, but no particular expenditure of funds or detrimental implications for other policies. Amnesty for war resisters and legislation to protect the right of privacy are issues of this type.

Other problems probably can be solved within the context of existing agencies and appropriations. A careful selection of the head of the Bureau of Indian Affairs and a pointed indication of Presidential and White House concern for the Bureau's administration probably can do as much for Indian rights as proposals for ambitious new programs.

The real difficulties in agenda-making begin when new and large expenditures are called for, when competing groups in the society come into conflict over policy approaches and when the solutions proposed for one problem profoundly affect solutions to others.

Of the major substantive issues before the country, five stand out as needing serious attention here and now, without resort to fact-finding studies by commissions or interminable Congressional hearings: unemployment, inflation, the delivery of health-care services, a national energy policy, and welfare reform.

Unemployment

If progress in solving our social problems is to be a meaningful political goal, an absolute precondition to that progress is a committed, coordinated and sustained attack on unemployment. Piecemeal legislation creating modest training programs and pointing with pride to the increasing numbers employed simply will not do.

The first and fundamental economic right listed by FDR was the right to a useful and remunerative job. The correctness of that priority has not changed.

The principle that President Truman unsuccessfully fought for when the Employment Act of 1946 was passed—that every person desiring a job should have one—should, at last, after a third of a century, be recognized as a goal of national policy.

The availability of work is absolutely basic for the poor and for minorities; otherwise social gains will not come at all or will be tentative and illusory. It does precious little good to encourage a low-income family to purchase a home outside the ghetto, or a disadvantaged student to go to college, if the family breadwinner is thrown out of work. And "affirmative action" programs, based on new hiring of minority or women employees, simply cannot be effective in an environment where workers are being laid off.

The social cost of unemployment, and the interrelationship between joblessness and other social and economic problems, are summed up in the declaration of policy contained in the original version of the Humphrey-Hawkins Full Employment and Balanced Growth bill introduced in Congress in 1975:

(a) The Congress hereby declares that all adult Americans able and willing to work have the right to equal opportunities for useful paid employment at fair rates of compensation.

(b) The free exercise of this right by every American, irrespective of sex, age, race, color, religion, or national origin, is essential to personal liberties, individual development, the prevention of inflationary shortages and bottlenecks, and the well-being of families, organizations, the national economy, and society as a whole.

(c) Only under conditions of genuine full employment and confidence in its continuation is it possible to eliminate the bias, prejudice, discrimination, and fear that have resulted in unequal employment under unequal conditions of women, older people, younger people, and members of racial, ethnic, national, or religious minorities.

(d) To the extent that Americans may not be able to exercise this right, (1) the country is deprived of the larger supply of goods and services made available under conditions of genuine full employment, of the trained labor power prepared to produce needed goods and services, and of the larger tax revenues received at all levels of government, without any changes in tax rates, under conditions of genuine full employment, (2) inflationary shortages and bottlenecks are created, (3) the job security, wages, salaries, working conditions, and productivity of employed people are impaired, (4) families are disrupted, (5) individuals are deprived of self-respect and status in society, and (6) physical and mental breakdown, drug addiction, and crime are promoted.[1]

It is overly simplistic to assume that full employment can solve such problems as crime and housing segregation, but in logic there can be no question that reducing joblessness can do much to alleviate them.

If whites and blacks are competing at the bottom of the ladder for an insufficient number of jobs, if whites are urging "seniority" and blacks are calling for "affirmative action" to increase black employment, racial tensions can only be heightened; increasing the potential number of job slots available is bound to be less disturbing than a scramble for a shrinking number of places.

One should also keep in mind, as discussed in Chapter Three, that the highest unemployment is among the groups that can be expected to be the most impatient and volatile in the society—the young in general and the black young in the inner city in particular.

It would seem axiomatic that employed young people are less likely to commit crime than those who view the chance of getting a legitimate job—often their first job—as hopeless. If "idle hands are the devil's workshop" was printed at the top of General Eisenhower's copybook,* presumably even he would agree with this simple proposition.

The prospect of massive disaffection among American young people —both the untrained ghetto youth and the underutilized Ph.D.—is not pleasant. At a time when some predictions are that only one in ten Ph.D.'s will obtain faculty employment in the next decade, and when the surplus of trained secondary-school teachers may reach well over one million by 1980,[2] Americans should ponder the support Hitler and the National Socialists received from unemployed college graduates in Germany to realize the very dangerous potential of such disaffection.[3]

The late Dr. James B. Conant's warning of 1961 still has validity today:

> In a slum area where over half the male youth are unemployed and out of school we are allowing a grave danger to the stability of our society to develop. A youth who has dropped out of school and never has had a full-time job is not likely to become a constructive citizen of his community. Quite the contrary. As a frustrated individual he is likely to be antisocial and rebellious. Some of this group of youth will end as juvenile delinquents. No one would claim that providing full employment for youth in the large cities would automatically banish juvenile delinquency, for we all realize that the causes of this problem

* See p. 185, *supra.*

are complex and there is no one solution. However, I suggest that full employment would have a highly salutary effect. Moreover, I offer the following hypothesis for professional social workers and sociologists to demolish: namely, that the correlation between desirable social attitudes (including attitudes of youth) and job opportunities are [sic] far higher than between the former and housing conditions, as measured by plumbing facilities, heating, and space per family.[4]

The urgency of the problem of youth unemployment is illustrated in tortuous revisions of the Humphrey-Hawkins bill. As originally introduced in January 1975, the bill provided for reaching the goal of full employment—"a situation under which there are useful and rewarding employment opportunities for all adult Americans able and willing to work"—within five years. A revision of the bill later in 1975 by the House Committee on Education and Labor set as a goal 3 percent unemployment for all adult workers over sixteen to be attained within eighteen months after the first Presidential economic report called for by the Act. Widely criticized by economists and conservative politicians alike as an unrealistic attempt to "legislate employment," the revision of Humphrey-Hawkins introduced in January 1977 set as its goal the reduction of unemployment over four years to "not in excess of 3 per centum of adult Americans twenty years of age or older." No such target was set for unemployment among 16-to-19-year-olds, the goal being merely to lower unemployment to the adult rate "as rapidly as feasible."

The revision of Humphrey-Hawkins negotiated with the Carter White House in November 1977 changed the formulation again. The basic goal became the reduction of unemployment over five years to 3 percent among those twenty years old or older and to 4 percent among the entire labor force sixteen years old and older.* Both the January 1977

* Note to the unemployed 18-year-old voter: Before casting your next vote, you may wish to consider which version of Humphrey-Hawkins would have been most likely to benefit you. Using December 1977 figures, there were 6,337,000 persons sixteen years of age or older unemployed (6.4 percent of the civilian labor force), including 1,293,000 aged sixteen to nineteen (15.4 percent of all sixteen-to-nineteen-year-olds in the labor force). The number of those twenty and over who were unemployed was 5,044,000 (5.51 percent of those over twenty). Under the January 1977 version of Humphrey-Hawkins the goal for teen-agers would have been a reduction in the unemployment rate to the 3 percent goal set for those twenty and over "as rapidly as feasible." To meet this goal for sixteen-to-nineteen-year-olds, more than one million jobs would have had to be created or found for those in this age group. Under the November 1977 version, 3,615,000 jobs would be required to reduce the twenty and over rate to 3 percent, over and above which an additional 342,000 jobs would be necessary to reach the 4 percent goal for those sixteen and older—jobs that might or might

and November 1977 versions of the bill provided for special programs to reduce youth unemployment. But the January version did not set any goal for youth unemployment, and the November version set a goal that, as the footnote indicates, could have been met by a relatively small reduction in *adult* unemployment. Either treatment of the problem shows that even the most liberal advocates of government intervention in the employment process have conceded the severe difficulty of reducing youth unemployment.

The "urban crisis" is basically part of the unemployment problem. In fact, unless a concerted attack is made on joblessness, the efforts of New York and other cities to recover from their current financial straits may well be frustrated. Jobs in the private sector in the cities which can be filled by the poorly educated and unskilled have been steadily declining. City employment now means basically service employment, both public and private. To match a computer-programming job, which is typical of the service-industry positions available, with an unskilled resident of the ghetto, who is typical of the labor force available, is an impossibility. Businesses will continue to move out of the cities if proper matching cannot be done and the unskilled worker will continue to be an unproductive drain on urban resources unless and until he can be gainfully employed.

This problem of the cities is a structural problem that will, unless corrected, be around in good times and bad. It is difficult to see how the cities, looking to a shrinking tax base for revenues, can face the drain created on them when a substantial portion of their residents is unemployable by the standards of their sophisticated local job markets.

The "welfare mess" is likewise bound up with the availability of jobs. Proposals for welfare reform have tended to focus on the need for incentives to welfare recipients to work. But such incentives can be effective only if there are opportunities to work; to the extent that such opportunities exist, the number of people required to rely on welfare will be reduced. The lower the number of potential welfare recipients, the greater the chances for enacting welfare reforms that are financially realistic and administratively feasible.

While the ultimate goal of full employment is the same as it was

---

not go to those sixteen to nineteen years old. President Carter says he won't lie to you, but you might just take your pocket calculator along if you discuss this matter with him.

under the New Deal in the 1930s and as envisioned by FDR in 1944, it should be recognized from the outset that the problem being attacked today is quite different from the unemployment of the Great Depression.

In the Depression, unemployment was widespread, pervasive and not confined to any region or age group. The thrust of the New Deal was to revive the economy by any and all conceivable means; any positive result was almost sure to reduce unemployment. Putting people back to work was Roosevelt's theme. Today the theme might more properly be finding jobs for young people entering the labor market and training the unskilled of all ages whose skills have been made obsolete by technology.

Licking the unemployment problem today is both a matter of general economic strategy and of pinpointing the uneven pockets of unemployment and concentrating resources and programs there. All, of course, without fueling inflation (of which subject more later).

The traditional techniques of monetary policy—increasing the supply of money to encourage economic growth and expanded consumer demand through cheaper interest rates—and fiscal policy—providing tax incentives to encourage both business and consumer spending and increasing government expenditures generally to stimulate demand—are still valuable and important in fighting unemployment.

Indeed, in the best of all worlds, one would rely exclusively on such techniques to create a high-growth economy in which the private sector would solve the unemployment problem in its own way. Charles L. Schultze, Chairman of President Carter's Council of Economic Advisers, observed in 1976:

> However valuable some of the federal government's manpower training and other social programs may be, they cannot hold a candle to the efficacy of a tight labor market. Necessity is the mother of invention. When 4 million business firms are scrambling for labor in a highly prosperous economy, it suddenly turns out that the unemployable become employable and the untrainable trainable; discrimination against blacks or women becomes unprofitable. Instead of being the concern solely of bureaucrats in government training programs, the finding, counseling, training, and hiring of the disadvantaged becomes the goal of the entire profit-seeking private enterprise system.
>
> In the second World War, to choose a dramatic example, we pushed the unemployment rate below 2 percent. And the result of that tight

labor market was revolutionary. Black-white income differentials shrank faster than in any subsequent period; the income distribution became sharply more equal; employers scoured the back-country farm areas and turned poor and untrained sharecroppers into productive industrial workers, whose sons and daughters became the high school graduates of the 1950's and whose grandchildren will shortly begin to enter college in droves.[5]

Unfortunately, the high degree of stimulus required for such a happy turn of events is not really attainable, because of the potential for inflation that would be created. Monetary and fiscal policy should certainly continue to be oriented toward growth in the economy and probably represent the best means of creating positions for highly skilled and semiskilled workers who have lost their jobs through business cutbacks.

But the particular problems presented by disproportionate jobless rates among the young, the unskilled and minorities are more realistically going to yield to targeted fiscal incentives and training and job programs.

The gut issue for unemployment is the kids, 16 to 20 years old, in center cities [according to Irving Shapiro, Chairman of the Board of du Pont]. These are people who are uneducated, not trained to work, ill-equipped to ever get a job. And even if the economy is strong they'll be unemployed.

You have to zero in on these people and have programs that will train them, get them ready to enter the labor market, and make useful citizens out of them. If you don't, we're going to wind up with these people being social misfits for the rest of their lives.[6]

In 1977, as part of the Tax Reduction and Simplification Act of 1977, the Congress passed a tax credit for all employers, based on the number of new workers hired above a base level of 102 percent of the previous year's payroll. The credit per worker varies from $630 to $1,806, with a limit of $100,000 in credits to any single enterprise.

This credit, originally proposed by Chairman Al Ullman of the Ways and Means Committee and Senator Lloyd Bentsen, had great opposition from the Carter administration, big business and big labor.

Despite the opposition, Congress authorized the credit for two years. Was this a mere sop to small, labor-intensive Mom-and-Pop businesses, or the grant of a realistic incentive to create new jobs? It will be interesting to see, though at first blush the credit appears to be a tax break for Mom and Pop without compensating benefits. (GM, as well as Mom and Pop, can only utilize the credit up to $100,000.)

The 1977 credit illustrates at least two propositions: the problem of targeting programs to specific employment needs and the ignorance of what programs really promise effective results.

Public-works employment is another area where, almost half a century after the Great Depression, effectiveness remains something of a mystery. In 1976, the Congress passed a Local Public Works Capital Development and Investment Act[7] and appropriated $2 billion for state and local public-works projects. The Act was designed to create jobs in a hurry, particularly in construction. The Act required the Economic Development Administration to issue regulations within thirty days, to act on all applications for funds within sixty days, and to deny funds to projects that could not begin on-site operations within ninety days from approval.

Applications were received in October 1976, but four months later a *Wall Street Journal* reporter noted that "no worker has yet earned a cent, unless one counts the 265 people hired temporarily by the Commerce Department to figure out which cities should get the money."

The Act also allocated funds 70 percent to communities with unemployment above the national average and 30 percent to communities with rates below the average. With high-employment areas applying in greater numbers than low-employment areas, the chances of the less-needy areas getting allocations (albeit from the smaller 30 percent pool) actually turned out to be twice as great.

Later analysis of experience under the Act also showed that the public-works money tended to keep existing employees on payrolls—a not unworthy objective but not the one to which the Act was directed.

Public-works jobs are obviously expensive, since the costs of bricks and mortar, as well as wages, must be factored in. Congress estimated that the $2 billion appropriation would generate 300,000 jobs—half at work sites and half in material-supplying factories, or roughly $14,000 for each work-site job created; by July 1977, the experience in Baltimore had been that $36,000 was required to sustain each work-site job (again including project materials).[8]

Many of the shortcomings of public works jobs—particularly the time lag between appropriation and job creation and the (unintentional) favoring of high-employment areas—can be cured with experience. Indeed, the Congress made some attempt to do so when it eliminated the 70–30 percent allocation in the Public Works Employment Act of 1977,[9] under which $4 billion additional were appropriated for state and local public-works projects.

Similarly, questions have been raised about public-service jobs—jobs provided directly by state and local governments (with Federal assistance) and not involving the large expenditures for materials which public-works jobs require. Whereas public-works jobs are targeted primarily toward unemployed construction workers, public-service jobs are designed for the less-experienced and often chronically unemployed; jobs such as hospital aides and park attendants are typical of public-service employment.

The basic legislation creating public-service jobs is the Comprehensive Employment and Training Act (CETA) enacted in 1973 to coordinate the Federal government's manpower and training programs. In 1976, 160,000 public service jobs were available through CETA, together with 500,000 slots in so-called "work experience" projects, 200,000 in on-the-job and classroom training programs, 40,000 in the Job Corps (a carryover from the Johnson War on Poverty to provide jobs for young people) and 1,135,000 summer jobs for teen-agers.[10] In 1977, the maximum yearly salary payable in the public-service job was $10,000, with the average actually paid estimated at $8,400.[11]

Again, the relative effectiveness of public-service jobs remains to be determined. In terms of quality, do the state and local governments maintain the jobs at standards above the leaf-raking level? Do workers "trained" in public-service jobs make a transition to productive private employment? Are grants to local governments diverted to fund jobs that such governments would have had to fill anyway, destroying the desired incremental effect of Federal funding?

Unfortunately, it is not always clear what the primary objective of public-works and public-service programs is. If it is to stimulate the economy, the highest priority should be to get people to work, without particular regard for whether the jobs will improve their employment skills. If, instead, it is to train workers so that they can graduate to the private labor force, efficiency and wise planning are more important than the immediacy of filling job slots. These two basic objectives are probably antithetical, and it should not be surprising if any given program should fail in meeting one of them.[12]

Despite all the uncertainties and the awesome gaps in our knowledge about unemployment programs, the fact remains that a commitment of the Federal government to the achievement of full employment should be the highest priority on any social agenda.

The proposed Humphrey-Hawkins Full-Employment Act has been the subject of both intensive study and extraordinarily violent criticism. William F. Buckley, Jr., for example, has termed Humphrey-Hawkins a bill "drafted in the Kingdom of Oz for the purpose of giving a jolt to Americans who mainline on liberal ideology about unemployment,"[13] and conservative columnist James J. Kilpatrick said of even the modified version worked out in November 1977 that it "embraces all the bankrupt notions of conventional liberalism" and is "the same old 'coon with another ring around his tail."[14]

As the result of hearings in 1975 and 1976, and extensive negotiations with the White House in 1977, the version of Humphrey-Hawkins up for adoption in the Congress in 1978 eliminated some of the "Oz" features to which Buckley presumably had reference. For example, a probably unworkable—or at least unwieldy—provision giving an individual who is willing and able to work the legal right to sue the Federal government for a job has been stricken. So, too, has been a requirement that Federally created construction jobs must pay locally prevailing construction union wages (as mandated by the Bacon-Davis Act of 1931)—a requirement that surely would have tempted many to leave private employment in favor of "last resort" jobs provided by the Federal government.*

The provisions of the bill "guaranteeing" a public job are now hedged to make clear that "reservoirs of federally operated public employment projects and private non-profit employment projects" are an absolute last resort available "only to the extent that Americans aged sixteen and over and able, willing and seeking work are not, and in the judgment of the President cannot be, provided with private job opportunities or with job opportunities under other programs and actions in being." Primary emphasis is to be on the expansion of private employment, "and all programs and purposes under [the] Act shall be in accord with that purpose."

As reintroduced in January 1977, Humphrey-Hawkins attempted to solve—or to mandate solutions to—virtually every economic and un-

---

* The 1977 version simply eliminated as possible "last resort" jobs those to which the Bacon-Davis standards would apply.

employment problem the country faces. The President, for example, was ordered to present to the Congress—usually within ninety days from the date of enactment—comprehensive and seemingly permanent programs for automatic countercyclical employment measures, elimination of regional, structural and youth unemployment, revenue sharing, and reformation of existing income-maintenance (welfare) programs. This was both unrealistic and silly. We simply do not have enough knowledge to formulate and enact permanent programs in these sensitive areas on such a timetable. The November 1977 version left such proposals entirely to the discretion of the President.

Walter Heller has called the debate over full employment a two-step process: "First, to crystallize and define the national will on full employment. Second, to find new ways to carry out that will."[15]

The basic principle of Humphrey-Hawkins, that our national government is committed to a policy of full employment, is a fundamental goal, and the President and Congress should be held to a high standard of performance in vindicating that policy.

The goals set by Humphrey-Hawkins, in the proposed version approved by the White House, are subject to change after three years if the President finds they cannot be met. But Humphrey-Hawkins rightly places the burden of proof on any President failing to meet the stated goal of 3 percent over-twenty unemployment (4 percent total unemployment in the work force) within five years. In that sense, the Humphrey-Hawkins mandate is hardly illusory.

In the horse trading that went on in November 1977 to revise Humphrey-Hawkins so that President Carter would support it, it was conveniently arranged that the President could revise its goals after the 1980 elections.

"We're comfortable with ambitious goals as long as people understand they're goals," an unnamed "ranking White House assistant" told *Newsweek*. "We're willing to promise to try."[16]

This is a dangerous attitude. After all the difficulties which overpromising created for the Great Society programs, it will not do for the Carter administration to give lip service to Humphrey-Hawkins. Those who elected Carter President expect and deserve more than "a promise to try."

The Humphrey-Hawkins goals must be respected, and a vigorous effort must be made to comply with them. Such an effort must include, at a minimum, greater attention by all concerned to microeconomic measures—"targeting" of the sort discussed earlier—to relieve structural and regional unemployment; imaginative and bold experiments with incentives to businesses operating or proposing to operate in distressed areas; subsidies to employers to hire and train the structurally unemployed; and monitoring the usefulness and effectiveness of public-works and public-service job programs, including the extension and expansion of those programs found to be most effective.

Armed with a legislated mandate declaring and establishing "as a national goal the fulfillment of the right of all Americans able, willing, and seeking to work full opportunities for useful paid employment at fair rates of compensation," the administration should seek to target public-works and public-service jobs to the people and areas of the country that need them the most and should aggressively combat continued disbursement of appropriate funds to all areas (and Congressional districts), regardless of need.

The administration, the Congress and the American people must share, as Senator Jacob Javits has said, "an absolute sense of outrage that the most productive society upon which the sun has ever risen must tolerate 7 million unemployed and with an enormous attitude in official circles that it is irremedial, that we can't do anything about it."[17]

Or, as the Catholic Bishops of the United States declared in 1975, "Full employment is the foundation of a just economic policy; it should not be sacrificed for other political and economic goals."[18]

Inflation

"Nothing seems to work," an anonymous economist told writer Hobart Rowen in 1977 in discussing measures to check inflation.[19]

Economists indeed seem baffled in analyzing recent inflation. Although the economy is not growing at anything like the "overheated" rate normally thought to induce excess demand and inflation, price rises continue. Despite high unemployment, traditionally thought of as a moderating influence on wage demands (and prices raised to compensate for wage increases), high wage settlements continue.

Almost any truism of economic theory, as applied to inflation, has been turned upside down by the behavior of the American economy in the 1970s. Inflation has become like the common cold: the symptoms are well understood, but the causes and cures for it simply are not.

In the absence of a wonder drug developed by the economists, politicians have been free to look to old wives' remedies—some based on superstition and quackery; some, like folk medicine, on intuitive common sense.

As with unemployment, there is an extraordinary degree of uncertainty as to what remedies will work. But, again as with unemployment, certain basic propositions should be made clear by our national leadership to provide a framework within which pragmatic and often experimental policies can be implemented.

A commitment to a national policy of full employment must in no sense be thought of as precluding an equally strong commitment to a stable level of prices. Inflation, too, produces dreadful social costs and economic uncertainty that inhibit vigorous business growth. Just in the area of housing alone, inflation threatens to make home ownership an increasingly difficult goal for many Americans.*

But, conversely, the commitment to reducing inflation must not be implemented by means of policies that either ignore, condone, or in fact encourage unemployment. Using unemployment as either a tacit or an implicit method of easing pressures on prices should not be viewed as a viable policy alternative.

Fighting inflation must not become the bloodless exercise envisioned by Professor Allan Meltzer of Carnegie-Mellon University:

> Let's consider what an increase in the unemployment rate means. Suppose the rate increases from 5 percent to 6 percent. That means an average worker spends twelve to fifteen weeks finding a job instead of nine to twelve weeks. That's a big change, that's a big loss of real income. But is that too high a price to pay to reduce the rate of inflation? I don't think so.[20]

Depersonalizing the effect of unemployment may be acceptable as a part of academic economic analysis; it is not an acceptable part of a realistic political approach to this social problem. Lyndon Johnson said in 1968:

> This Nation should not and will not accept falling profits, high unemployment, forced retirements, rising bankruptcies, and shriveling mar-

* See pp. 41–44, *infra.*

kets as a remedy for our present problems. We have to find the path which brings us to price stability without destroying prosperity.[21]

The justification for linking unemployment and inflation is the so-called "Phillips curve," so named for Professor A. W. Phillips of the London School of Economics, who in 1958 purported to find a correlation between unemployment and wages in the United Kingdom during the ninety-six-year period ending in 1957. According to Phillips, wages tended to rise as unemployment went down, and unemployment rose as wages went down.

As adapted by later economists, and as adopted by conservative politicians, the Phillips theory was modified: *prices* tend to rise as unemployment goes down and prices decline or remain stable as unemployment increases. Thus the trade-off theory dear to the hearts of conservative politicians: inflation can be contained only if unemployment is allowed to increase.

Looking at the American experience, it is difficult to see this theory as an inflexible principle of economics. In seven of the years between 1948 and 1975, inflation and unemployment moved in the same direction, either up or down.[22] In 1976, the private National Council on Employment, a panel of labor economists, including Charles Killingsworth of Michigan State University and Secretary of Labor Ray Marshall (then at the University of Texas), concluded:

> Forty-five years ago, there was general agreement among the world's leading economists that the only way to reduce unemployment was to reduce wages. One of the great achievements of J. M. Keynes was to demonstrate the fallacy of this doctrine. Cutting wages might induce some employers to hire more workers, he said, but he pointed out that that was certainly not the only way or the most effective way to reduce unemployment. Like the insistence on wage-cutting, the Phillips curve concept surely has a kernel of truth in it. Some approaches to the reduction of unemployment would be quite likely to generate upward pressure on the price level. But there is really no convincing proof of the widely-accepted belief that any reduction in unemployment, no matter how much and no matter what means are employed, will cause more inflation. It is true that few, if any, professional economists would state the doctrine quite so crudely. But many, perhaps a majority, would still accept the generalization that there is some kind of "trade-off" between inflation and

unemployment. The belief that there is such a trade-off has become an important barrier standing in the way of a substantial reduction in unemployment. We conclude that this widely held belief lacks a substantial basis in either experience or analysis.[23]

Even if the trade-off theory were acceptable economics, its implementation should not be acceptable politics. Restricting government spending and the supply of money has just this result—dampening growth in the economy and reducing job opportunities, thus making willing workers "the principal victims" of the "national disease" of inflation. As the Joint Economic Committee of the Congress has pointed out, this is a "cruel and primitive" approach to curing inflation.[24]

A realistic program to restrain inflation cannot be developed until the basic fact is recognized that unemployment, and measures that increase unemployment, are not an acceptable basis for such a program. The "respectability that lately has attached itself to the idea that society can tolerate high unemployment rates" must be shattered.[25]

A frank acknowledgment of this position has to be the first premise of anti-inflation policy. The air must be cleared and, while a commitment to full employment and a rejection of unemployment as an anti-inflationary weapon will not please conservative traditionalists, the business community and the public generally will be able to do their forward planning secure in the knowledge that the President is not going to follow a schizophrenic stop-go approach to developments in the economy—focusing on recession one month and inflation the next.

As a matter of first principles, the President should be unafraid of announcing that he will have no hesitation in imposing wage and price controls and will do so, selectively or in general, unless there is substantial adherence to announced guidelines for wage and price increases. He should also express willingness to impose controls retroactively in order to roll back wage and price increases made in anticipation of controls.

No one can be sure that such an announcement would work, but knowing that the President does not have ideological or tactical hang-ups about imposing controls may just constitute sufficient incentive for adherence to voluntary guidelines.

The President should likewise not hesitate to require prior notification of significant price increases, backed up with the power to suspend such increases until they can be publicly justified. The inhibiting effects of such a requirement deserve to be tested.

Having ruled out a "reserve army of unemployment to hold down inflation," the President should construct an overall anti-inflation program as bold and imaginative as it is committed. This may involve "articulating sophisticated public policies that go against the grain of popular prejudice,"[26] but so be it. That is what leadership is about.

For example, the President might well propose a superficially illogical plan of tax cuts and tax increases—income tax cuts to relieve the impact of inflation on the lowest income groups; unemployment and social security tax cuts to encourage hiring without driving up wage costs; and tax increases in the higher brackets to reduce consumer demand.

Federal incentives could also be given to state and local governments to reduce sales taxes in exchange for grants from the Federal government. While such grants might be subject to the objections already noted to unrestricted revenue sharing,* they would have the desirable effect of lowering effective prices to consumers without depriving state and local governments of needed revenue.

A closer look should also be taken at the way tax dollars are spent. The Federal government and state and local governments now purchase almost a quarter of the goods and services produced in the United States, making government a powerful consumer force in the marketplace with the ability to exert downward pressures on prices if there is a will to do so—pressure that has not been particularly evident in the past.

One study estimates, for example, that the unit cost of local government expenditures increased 152 percent between 1964 and 1974, compared with an increase of 83 percent in consumer prices. This does not evidence a cost-saving mentality on the part of government purchasing agents. Indeed, the use of cost-plus contracts,† favored not only in the Pentagon but elsewhere in government, exerts no downward pressure whatsoever on prices.[27]

An aggressive policy might well include systematic government stockpiling of grain and other basic commodities and raw materials that could

---

* See pp. 214–20, *supra*.

† Contracts under which the price for goods paid to a supplier is his cost to produce such goods plus a profit margin.

be released to the market in the future to check price increases that excessively inflate producer income in relation to the producer's costs. It almost certainly should include a thorough reevaluation of government regulation which serves to substitute fixed prices for competition and a refocusing of antitrust policy on price behavior rather than bigness per se.*

Early identification of supply and production bottlenecks likely to arise as the economy expands is a fact-finding job for which the Federal government is—or should be—uniquely qualified. And if the facts are properly marshaled, an alert government should then be prepared to propose and implement measures, such as low-cost loan assistance and tax incentives, to relieve the potential shortages identified.

Arthur Okun, analyzing the current "stagflation," has observed that wages (including fringe benefits and payroll taxes) and prices in recent years have tended to be in an "8-to-6" spiral—wages have gone up at an average rate of 8 percent, prices at 6 percent. As each wage increase has been reflected in employer costs, prices have been increased to cover them; and as prices have risen, wage demands have been set to outpace them. And all of this occurring without reference to labor supply or the degree to which manufacturing capacity was utilized.

The end result Okun has likened to spectators at a parade standing on tiptoe to get a better view. As a result "no individual can afford to get off his uncomfortable tiptoe stance" and "ending the discomfort requires a collective decision."

In a speech in Chicago in October 1977, Okun proposed, among other measures, pledges of the Federal government to avoid cost-increasing expenses for a year (avoiding, for example, Social Security tax increases of the type already discussed) and to provide assistance to lower the sales tax, as suggested above. Okun also proposed a third measure, under which businesses and their employees would receive tax rebates for each year in which they would make—and carry out—a commitment to keep wage increases below 6 percent and cost increases below 4 percent. In exchange, businesses making this pledge would receive a 5 percent tax rebate on domestic operating profits, and workers would receive rebates equal to 1½ percent of their salaries (up to $225 per person).[28]

The Okun proposal clearly calls for much refinement—it would be

* See pp. 36–41, *supra*.

very difficult to administer—but it offers a refreshingly concrete means of attacking inflation and is in keeping with treating inflation as a substantive issue requiring direct governmental action.*

On a longer-range basis, the Federal government should initiate technical studies of measures to ease the effects of inflation, such as the "indexing" of Federal tax payments to avoid taxing income increases that merely reflect inflation and not real gains. This is a novel and extremely complex subject and one that requires dispassionate, technical and objective study. Any concrete proposals for indexing should await full analysis; a properly conceived plan for indexing should avoid the mistake made in "indexing" Social Security in 1972† or avoid becoming the equivalent of George McGovern's $1,000-a-year income maintenance plan.

Magnifying the problem of inflation is the lack of confidence of both the consumer and the businessman in the government's ability to curb inflation. Why are individuals saving and not spending, when classical theory teaches that consumers spend dollars likely to depreciate through inflation as fast as they receive them? Why is business unresponsive to the basically conservative economic viewpoint of the Carter administration?

The principal answer is probably the traumatic combination of inflation, recession and unemployment that characterized the last years of the Nixon administration and the demonstrable uncertainty as this is written of the Carter administration as to how to attack inflation. Until the 1974 recession, businessmen, for example, had become confident that the ups and downs of the business cycle would be relatively mild—"not many of the current generation of business managers had ever experienced an economic decline of comparable severity."[29]

This crisis of confidence will not be solved by pandering on a piecemeal basis to the immediate and selfish wants of either business or labor. Leadership does not consist, as Joseph Kraft has written, of abandoning "a tough stand on inflation the minute business and labor groups [say] boo."[30]

The war against inflation is likely to consist of a series of battles and skirmishes—there is no economic fusion bomb to end the conflict—

* Okun has estimated the cost of his rebate plan at $15 billion, and his proposal for Federal grants to lower the sales tax at $6 billion. The total would thus be lower than the $25-billion tax reduction proposed by President Carter in 1978.

† See pp. 71–72, *supra*.

some of which will be victories, others of which will not. It is likely, too, to be an unrewarding war "where labor justifies the rise of wages by the preceding rise of prices, and business justifies the rise of prices by the preceding rise of labor costs."

Leadership is required. But there is every indication that the consumer is ready for such leadership. Louis Harris found in 1976 that 71 percent of American workers would be willing to accept lower wage increases if there was an assurance that prices would not outpace wage settlements. Hobart Rowen concluded in 1977:

> I suspect that the public, fed up with the inflation merry-go-round, would accept bolder innovations than the timorous leadership at both ends of Pennsylvania Avenue is willing to try.[31]

As for business, pleasing business leaders on a daily basis is simply not possible, and the fluctuating and changeable nature of such an attempt to please will increase uncertainty, not instill the much vaunted "confidence" the Carter administration so assiduously seeks.

The managers who run American business are nothing if not inventive. If they can do business at a profit in the most chaotic less-developed country, they ought to be able to do so in a reasonably well-run United States. Once they know the policy ground rules under which the anti-inflation game is being played, they will adapt and they will play. Professor James Tobin has observed:

> One could overdo the confidence point, and all these matters about uncertainty about government policy, about the club that's still in the closet. They've always been true. They're characteristic of democratic government. And they're going to be true all the time. Business has lived with those things, and invested very highly many times in the past. And the fact that if the Administration is of a different party than most businessmen has not been an obstacle to high business investment in the past, and the fact that they had a confidence in President Ford didn't mean that they went for high investment plans, while he was President. Quite the reverse.[32]

When all is said and done, if a President and his advisers manifest an ability, a will and a competence to manage the country's economy, confidence—if not necessarily agreement—will return.

Health Care

Government policy concerning health care in America must have a very high place on any agenda of social issues because of the real and immediate threat escalating health costs pose to the fight against inflation, to the size of the Federal budget and the allocation of funds thereunder and to those individuals unfortunate enough to pay from their own pockets all or part of their health-care expenses (an estimated $43 billion in fiscal 1977).

The cost of health care is not the most visible of issues to the general public. If the manufacturers of automobiles had raised their prices by 1,000 percent between 1950 and 1977, the general public would certainly have been aware of the increase. And it would have been aware that the uniformity of the increase indicated that the competitive forces of the market were not working.

The easily predictable result of such an outrageous development in automobile pricing would have been a public outcry for either breaking up or nationalizing the car manufacturers.

In fact, the cost of a day's stay in a hospital rose in America 1,000 percent between 1950 and 1977 (compared with a rise of 136 percent in the Consumer Price Index generally). In 1976 alone, the cost of a hospital stay rose 15 percent—two and a half times the 1976 increase in the Consumer Price Index and more than increases during that year in the cost of energy.[33]

Yet there has been surprisingly little consumer resistance to such price behavior. The reasons are not hard to find. Although health care is the country's third-largest industry, ranking behind only construction and agriculture, it is virtually noncompetitive. Health, Education and Welfare Secretary Califano told the American Medical Association in 1977:

> The features of the competitive marketplace that have served our people so well in other industries—to promote efficient allocation and utilization of resources—are just about nonexistent in the health care industry.
>
> The patient—the consumer—may select his family doctor, but he does not select his specialist, his hospital, the services he is told he needs, the

often expensive medical tests, to which he is subjected: The physician is the central decision-maker for more than 70 percent of health-care services. . . .

The unavailability of price and quality information keeps the consumer of health care services dependent on the decisions of the health care provider, who plays a dominant role in determining demand for health services and whose financial well-being is determined by the price charged. . . .

We must face a basic fact: There is virtually no competition among doctors or among hospitals. And, just as important, there is precious little competition among pharmaceutical companies or among laboratories. . . .

Buying an item of health service is thus quite different from buying a new family car. And there is the further rather basic difference that the consumer of medical services, unlike the buyer of a car, either will not directly pay for them at all or will pay only some part of them. In the case of hospital charges, an estimated 90 percent of such charges are paid by third parties—private insurers such as Blue Cross, or Medicare or Medicaid. Consumer agitation in this environment simply has not developed. But the whole question of health-care costs must nonetheless be faced by the Federal government. The statistics, and their implications, are truly frightening:

• Health care spending was 4.6 percent of gross national product in 1950, 5.9 percent in 1965, 8.6 percent in 1976, and if not checked is estimated to be 9.7 percent by 1983. From annual expenditures of $12 billion in 1950, expenditures grew to $25.9 billion in 1960, $69.2 billion in 1970, $162 billion in 1977. Total health expenditures are expected to double from the 1977 level by 1983.

• Current Medicare and Medicaid expenditures by Federal, state and local governments are expected to double before 1980.

• Health-care costs generally are rising at 2.5 times the cost of living.

• The Federal government spends 12 cents of each taxpayer dollar on health care—nine cents to the hospital industry alone.[34]

• When General Motors first paid for health insurance for its workers in 1950, the entire nation paid premiums to Blue Cross and Blue Shield of $450 million. Today GM alone pays $1 billion for health insurance, a figure currently increasing at the rate of $100 million a year.[35]

The practical likelihood of securing passage of a national health-care program is most unlikely until these costs are brought under control. The Carter administration has recognized this. It has also recognized the misallocation of both public and private resources resulting from such increasing costs, as evidenced by the Hospital Cost Containment Act proposed by President Carter in April 1977.

The proposed Act concentrates on hospital costs and does not try to encompass the more fiercely controversial subject of physicians' charges. It rightly rejects an approach to costs based on limiting Medicare or Medicaid payments as such—an approach that inevitably would make the recipients under these programs second-class citizens in terms of health-care delivery.

The thrust of the President's bill is, instead, to limit the amount by which reimbursements received by hospitals from all sources—Medicare, Medicaid, Blue Cross, Blue Shield, commercial insurers and individuals—can be increased, with the projected limit for the first year being 9 percent.

No attempt is made to limit specific charges, to place any limit on wage settlements, or otherwise to dictate specific hospital policies. Hospital administrators would not be restrained in how they would allocate resources to live within the reimbursement ceiling.

The President's bill also places a dollar limit on capital expenditures for new facilities and an outright ban on increasing the number of hospital beds in areas having more than four beds per 1,000 people or with an occupancy rate of less than 80 percent. As of 1977, one source estimated, there were 50,000 surplus beds in the nation's 7,000 hospitals (out of a total of 1.5 million beds) maintained at an annual cost of $2 billion.[36]

The approach of President Carter and Secretary Califano to hospital costs seems profoundly right, even if intensive lobbying efforts apparently succeeded in totally emasculating it during the course of 1978.*

---

* The most immediate lobbying efforts were by the Shriners, who succeeded in getting the Shriners' Hospitals exempted from the modified version of the President's bill approved by a subcommittee of the House Commerce Committee.

The Carter proposal goaded the American Hospital Association and other provider organizations into adopting a fifteen-point program to reduce costs by voluntary action. This voluntary program became the basis of an at least temporarily successful strategy to block the President's bill. In February 1978, the House Ways and Means Committee approved a hospital-cost bill that would have converted the proposed mandatory controls into a stand-by measure to be invoked only if voluntary efforts proved ineffective. In July 1978, the House Commerce Committee went further and scrapped the President's control proposals altogether by a vote of 15 to 12, in favor of legislation endorsing voluntary cost-cutting and authorizing appointment of a Federal study commission if voluntary efforts were not successful.

With its hand strengthened by new enforcement legislation passed in October 1977,[37] the administration has announced plans for rooting out the fraud and abuse of Medicare and Medicaid. In 1977, HEW conducted a survey of Medicaid payments and estimated that $1 billion annually was being paid for ineligible recipients and an additional $1 billion was being paid as the result of fraud and abuse by the providers of services—somewhat lower estimates than those made by the Moss Subcommittee in the Senate in 1976. Based on its own investigations, the Moss Subcommittee estimated that between 25 and 50 percent of Medicaid payments, which then totaled $15 billion a year, were being wasted through fraud, poor quality of care and the provision of services to ineligible persons.[38]

Adequately enforcing existing laws, and especially controlling health-care costs, would seem a prerequisite to increased Federal participation in paying for health care. But this does not mean that the Executive Branch or the Congress should not press forward in resolving the issues presented by a national health-care program. These issues are troubling and difficult and must be faced if any plan ultimately enacted is to work:

1. What services should be covered? Should insurance or payments by government apply only to relatively serious illnesses and health problems, or are preventive services, such as dentistry, vision care and periodic physical examinations, to be included? What of abortions and family-planning services? What of care for the elderly in their own homes, as opposed to institutionalized nursing homes?

2. What should the individual recipient pay? A minimum amount of annual expenses before benefits are received (deductible)? A percentage of all expenses (coinsurance)? A flat fee for each service (co-payment)? Or none of these? Are the costs of the plan to be financed from general revenues of the Federal government or a combination of general revenues and additional payroll taxes?

3. How are reimbursable charges of health-care providers to be determined? Would the government require providers to adhere to prices set by it? Or would charges be set privately? Or within some limits or guidelines established by the government?

4. How would the plan be administered? Directly by the Federal government? By state governments under Federal supervision? By private insurance carriers under Federal supervision?

5. If national health insurance is to be administered by the Federal

government, what happens to the estimated 500,000 employees in the private medical insurance industry?

The difficulty of such policy questions was obliquely confirmed on July 29, 1978, by President Carter, who issued a "directive" on that date to HEW Secretary Califano to formulate a national health plan for introduction in Congress. The President set forth some ten basic principles to guide Califano; these principles did not touch, or barely touched, the questions raised above.

Nor did the President's guiding principles cover the resolution of such problems of health-care delivery as are presented by the development of expensive new technology, such as the computerized axial tomography (CAT) scanner—a sophisticated device linked to a computer which can do instant and painless scans of the human brain. The device costs between $325,000 and $700,000, with an annual operating cost running up to $300,000.

The CAT scanner has been called the most significant diagnostic tool developed since the X-ray. But when and where should such devices be introduced? Dr. Howard H. Hiatt, Dean of the Harvard School of Public Health, has posed the problem this way:

> It's gotten to the point where, if the patient enters with a headache, the first order of business for many doctors is a brain scan. There are 6,000 people a year who turn out to have brain tumors, and of those 6,000 probably we can't do much about 5,800, no matter when we diagnose them. Then the question is, do we look for those 6,000 or do we look at the 16 million people who consult doctors with headaches each year? I think it's terribly critical that we introduce into medicine a much more rigid kind of evaluation approach than we have before.[39]

In resolving these questions the President and the Congress must be prepared to do battle with the medical profession and the hospital establishment. President Roosevelt considered making health care a feature of Social Security in 1935, but was deterred because of potential opposition from the American Medical Association.[40] The AMA, the Health Insurance Association and the American Hospital Association are powerful lobbies and have prevented enactment of comprehensive health insurance for over forty years, let alone such lesser measures as President Carter's proposed Hospital Cost Containment Act. Their opposition will not die easily, and their cooperation may prove elusive.

The President and the Congress will also have to contend with less visible pressures from the powerful hospital establishment, which, through its trustees and directors, includes the most articulate movers and shakers in communities of any size, all, as dedicated trustees and directors, committed to the unquestioned rightness of private hospital administration as it exists. And, of course, nursing-home proprietors, often politically well-connected entrepreneurs in their local Congressional districts, will have to be reckoned with as well.

The leaders in the fight for a national health-care program might do well, as already suggested, to reach out beyond the groups with the most rigid and doctrinaire positions to younger doctors and administrators less tied to the hidebound traditions of the AMA and similar groups.

Medical professionals must obviously participate in the policy debates over health insurance. Whether that role is a constructive one or is surrendered by default to politicians is really a question the professionals themselves must answer. And very soon at that.

Energy

With hyperbole worthy of his penultimate predecessor, Mr. Nixon, President Carter in April 1977 called the adoption of a national energy policy an imperative which represented the "moral equivalent of war" and "the greatest domestic challenge that our nation will face in our lifetime." In the 1976 campaign, he was right in declaring that the United States was the only major industrial country without such a policy. But neither the Congress nor the public has shared his estimate of the seriousness of the problem.

Carter's program was built on the initiatives of 1975,* but with important modifications. Where President Ford had originally called for immediate deregulation of natural gas prices and decontrol of domestic oil prices, Carter called for deregulation of "new" natural gas so that both interstate and intrastate supplies would be sold at the same price as crude oil, and decontrol of oil prices over three years to the prevailing world price. But decontrol of oil prices would be accompanied by a wellhead tax that would return "windfall" profits to oil producers to the

---

* See Chapter Six.

Federal government and be rebated to voters. Carter also adopted the proposal advanced by the Ways and Means Committee in 1975 to increase consumer gasoline taxes up to 50 cents a gallon, based on consumption levels. (In other words, the tax would only be imposed if consumers failed on a voluntary basis to stay within targeted annual goals for keeping gasoline usage down.) "Gas guzzler" automobiles, if produced, would also have been subjected to high excise taxes for failing to meet specified miles-per-gallon standards.

A multitude of other proposals completed the President's program: mandated conversion to coal by industries and utilities; Federal control over cheap utility rates designed to attract business to the utilities' market areas; an industrial user tax for oil and gas (as opposed to coal) utilization; tax credits for home insulation, weatherization and the installation of solar-energy capabilities; rebates to purchasers of small and gasoline-efficient automobiles; and efficiency standards for home electrical appliances.

The President's program was not a terribly imaginative one, but it did strike a balance among the four factors he considered essential for an overall policy: "First, conservation; second, production; third, conversion; fourth, development; and, of course, fairness or equity, which is a primary consideration in all our proposals."[41]

Then Congressman Edward Koch observed in connection with the 1975 legislature debacle over energy that the Congress simply did not "have the will to demand from the gasoline consumer or from the auto industry even modest sacrifice" and that "we have shirked our responsibilities by taking the teeth out of every key provision of the [House leadership] bill."[42]

The same could be said of Congressional reaction to the Carter proposals; the Congress indeed played the dentist in extracting the teeth from them. The House, while passing the President's program rather much intact, nonetheless rejected the stand-by tax on gasoline geared to future consumer use. The Senate effectively killed the crude-oil tax, which was an essential offset to the President's proposal for decontrolling oil prices. And a fierce deadlock developed between the House and the Senate over deregulation of natural gas prices, the House supporting higher, but nonetheless regulated, prices, the Senate supporting out-and-out decontrol.

As of this writing, the "moral equivalent of war" had degenerated into an unseemly squabble in the trenches between the two legislative bodies. The only thing clear was that a precariously balanced national energy policy, as the President's proposal was, would not be passed and that "fairness or equity" would not describe the end result.

The unhappy reality seems to be that, in lieu of a balanced energy policy, a series of *ad hoc* programs will be the substitute. The result will be to increase uncertainty and decrease the effectiveness of the "policy" measures adopted.

The fact is that uncertainty would almost certainly be present in any event. To put a good face on the current situation, the tentative nature of the energy-policy "solutions" reached will probably prevent the complacency and self-congratulation that would most likely have followed the adoption of a truly comprehensive energy policy.

Uncertainty is inevitable, given the woeful state of our knowledge about energy resources. The President has proposed administrative measures to improve the quality and quantity of data available about oil and gas reserves, and the Energy Policy and Conservation Act of 1975 empowered the General Accounting Office to audit the books of the major oil companies and selected smaller companies.

Concentration on this task of gathering accurate, credible data is important—important as a means of doing intelligent planning and determining the full dimensions of our problems (or lack of them), and important also as a basis for explaining to the public actions that are taken.

"By far the most frustrating aspect of the energy crisis is that nobody knows enough to take its measurement," the *Washington Star* editorialized in 1974. "The government's information about oil supply comes mainly from the petroleum industry, and projections have gone up and down like a roller coaster during the past year."[43]

Little has changed since. Industry reports and geological surveys still make up the hard core of available data on reserves. Without in any way impugning the accuracy of industry sources—though there has been more than a little reason to do so—the fact remains that the President should not and must not administer an ongoing energy policy on the basis of data—often of a very subjective kind—furnished by the oil and gas industry. Until objectified data are available, the job of conditioning the American people to sacrifices will be extremely difficult, and government planning will simply not be as effective or as intelligent as it might be.

Even with adequate data, fine-tuning of the energy program will inevitably be necessary. We know, for example, that consumer demand for gasoline is relatively "inelastic"—i.e., people will continue to buy gasoline, just as they continue to buy cigarettes and whiskey, despite advances in price. Will the same be true in the face of substantial increases in price? (In other words, will significant price hikes make the demand for gasoline more "elastic"?) We do not know the answer, but if the answer is negative, price and tax disincentives to consumption may have to be reappraised.

Finally, a truly comprehensive energy program must look to both the short-run and long-run effects—the nation must "fix the roof and build a new house at the same time."[44] Emphasis to date has been largely on the short-run problems. What will be needed to fill out and complete an energy program is an imaginative, far-reaching—but at bottom sensible—plan for developing nuclear, thermal, solar and even more exotic energy sources.

The President, as a former nuclear engineer, demonstrated great credibility in the 1976 campaign in discussing the issue of nuclear power. His engineering experience, and his announced propensity for cutting bureaucratic red tape, could combine effectively to create a rational and efficient plan for nuclear development, and one in keeping with the safety standards that the public quite evidently desires.

With a near-term program in place, such as it may be, the administration must turn to reinforcing it by paying attention to long-range problems and long-range solutions.

Welfare

Secretary Califano has called welfare "the Middle East of U.S. politics. It is the most complicated political and economic problem I have ever dealt with."[45]

It is difficult to quarrel with the objectives of welfare reform set forth by President Carter in August 1977—"to abolish our existing welfare system and replace it with a job-oriented program for those able to work and a simplified, uniform, equitable cash-assistance program for those in need who are unable to work by virtue of disability, age or family circumstances."

Such a commitment on the part of the national government is needed to preserve the fiscal integrity and even the existence of state and local arms of the Federal system and to stem rising tides of discontent at welfare inequities on the part of recipients and taxpayers alike.

The most refreshing aspect of the President's approach is the evident belief on both his and Secretary Califano's part that the welfare "mess" is capable of solution, even though the President had to admit that analysis of the welfare system after he took office had shown it to be "worse than I expected."[46] The President summarized the daunting problems which must be faced in welfare reform in his August 1977 message to Congress:

> The defects of the current system are clear:
> It treats people with similar needs in different fashion with separate eligibility requirements for each program.
> It creates exaggerated difference in benefits based on state of residence. Current combined state and Federal A.F.D.C. benefits for a family of four with no income vary from $720 per year in Mississippi to $5,954 in Hawaii.
> It provides incentives for family breakup. In most cases two-parent families are not eligible for cash assistance and, therefore, a working father often can increase his family's income by leaving home. In Michigan, a two-parent family with the father working at the minimum wage has a total income, including tax credits and food stamps, of $5,922. But if the father leaves, the family will be eligible for benefits totaling $7,076.
> It discourages work. In one Midwestern state, for example, a father who leaves part-time employment paying $2,400 for a full-time job paying $4,800 reduces his family's income by $1,250.
> Efforts to find jobs for current recipients have floundered.
> The complexity of current programs leads to waste, fraud, red tape, and errors. H.E.W. has recently discovered even Government workers unlawfully receiving benefits, and numbers of people receive benefits in more than one jurisdiction at the same time.[47]

The President, as campaigner and as incumbent, has made his commitment to welfare reform. Carrying out that commitment will be a formidable task, requiring firm leadership to prevent both crippling and distorting alterations in an overall plan; imagination in combining existing programs and phasing in reforms; a sharp ability to articulate and explain the complexities of what is proposed; and administrative skill in carrying out and managing a reformed system.

President Carter's August 1977 proposal would abolish Aid to

Families with Dependent Children (AFDC), Supplemental Security Income (SSI)* and Food Stamps in favor of a single cash-assistance program that the President characterized as a "complete and clean break with the past."

The President's proposal has served the useful purpose of providing a focus for debate on and analysis of the welfare problem, though it is not now clear whether reform will involve a wholly new approach, as recommended by the President, or less comprehensive amendments to such existing programs as SSI and Food Stamps. Whatever direction reform takes, as important an element as any will be continued supervision of the new legislation to see clearly where it is going wrong in practice —to identify, and to correct for, unforeseen results and social consequences before they create new crises and budgetary surprises.

Attentive and concerned supervision must replace inattention and indifference, whether such inattention and indifference arise from a complacent sense that the welfare problem has been solved or from a cynical desire to see the system work itself out of control as a prelude to reactionary cutbacks.

Such supervision will be required not only from the administrators charged with making the system work, but also from Congressmen who will almost assuredly be asked to legislate adjustments as experience teaches its lessons. One can hope that both administrators and legislators can be spared reactionary ambushes, reopening the whole range of welfare issues, each time such adjustments are proposed.

IMPACT ISSUES

Recognizing that the appropriate approach to an issue may change over time, three areas of problems stand out as "impact" issues today: the environment, race relations and the family.

The Environment

The concept of dealing with an issue in terms of its impact on other problems really originated with the National Environmental Policy Act of 1969 (NEPA). Like the Employment Act of 1946, NEPA

* See p. 73 fn., *supra.*

dealt not with specifics but with a national commitment to a policy objective:

> The Congress, recognizing the profound impact of man's activity on the interrelations of all components of the natural environment, particularly the profound influences of population growth, high-density urbanization, industrial expansion, resource exploitation, and new and expanding technological advances and recognizing further the critical importance of restoring and maintaining environmental quality to the overall welfare and development of man, declares that it is the continuing policy of the Federal Government, in cooperation with State and local governments, and other concerned public and private organizations, to use all practicable means and measures, including financial and technical assistance, in a manner calculated to foster and promote the general welfare, to create and maintain conditions under which man and nature can exist in productive harmony, and fulfill the social, economic, and other requirements of present and future generations of Americans.[48]

NEPA recognized that this lofty statement of policy was unlikely to be of much force in and of itself; environmental questions were too fragmented, and the pursuit of other policy objectives—increasing oil supplies from offshore drilling, for example—might actually be inimical to environmental considerations. As the House report accompanying NEPA noted, there was "no independent source of review of the total environmental situation" in the government and no forum for advising either the President or Congress "with an estimation of the priorities" that should be assigned to different aspects of the environmental issue.[49]

The result was a directive in NEPA to government agencies to administer the laws and regulations applicable to them with environmental problems in mind and a requirement that "every recommendation or report on proposals for legislation and other major Federal actions significantly affecting the quality of the human environment" be accompanied by what became known as an "impact statement." This statement, to be prepared on the basis of expertise wherever it might reside in the government, was to assess the environmental impact of the proposed action, adverse environmental effects, alternatives to the proposed action with lesser adverse consequences and "any irreversible and irretrievable commitments of resources that would be involved" in implementing the proposed action.

Administration of the "impact statement" requirement has been much criticized because of delays and bureaucratic snarls. Under the threat of legal action to review the adequacy of impact statements—some 650 such cases having been brought in the first seven years of NEPA—executive departments have tended to produce massive, verbose statements designed less to outline environmental issues than to withstand judicial review. The impact statement of the Department of the Interior regarding the proposed natural-gas pipeline from Alaska to the lower forty-eight states, for example, was a seventeen-volume document containing 9,570 pages and weighing forty pounds.[50]

Administrative reform of the impact statement procedure is clearly in order. But the concept, in a very short period of time, has without question heightened public and governmental awareness of environmental considerations. Indifference and ignorance have been replaced with an administrative mechanism that appears to have been reasonably successful in ensuring that often subtle and not readily perceivable environmental factors are weighed in the decision-making process. The environment is an "impact" issue which policy-makers in other areas can no longer conveniently ignore.

Race Relations

In 1944, the same year that FDR outlined his "self-evident" Economic Bill of Rights, Gunnar Myrdal advanced a proposition that was not perhaps then self-evident and, unfortunately, has not become so in the minds of many even today:

> White prejudice and discrimination keep the Negro low in standards of living, health, education, manners and morals. This, in its turn, gives support to white prejudice. White prejudice and Negro standards thus mutually "cause" each other. . . . Such a static "accommodation" is, however, entirely accidental. If either of these factors changes, this will cause a change in the other factor, too, and start a process of interaction where the change in one factor will continuously be supported by the reaction of the other factor.[51]

The Federal government at all levels should be unalterably committed to a policy of racial justice designed to break the vicious cycle sketched by Myrdal and the irrational ravages of discrimination.

In 1979, this again is a problem best dealt with on an impact basis—that is, by judging policies in other fields for their effects on race relations and discrimination.

That race relations is an impact issue rather than a substantive one illustrates the progress that has been made in recent years: the Supreme Court's desegregation decision and its implementation and the Civil Rights Acts of the 1960s changed the nature of the struggle for racial justice.

Lest it be thought that regarding race relations as an "impact" issue is somehow the equivalent of "benign neglect," it is perhaps worth a moment to dispel that notion.

If problems of race and discrimination are taken seriously by the national government—if their impact is properly assessed—it is hard to see how the government can do less than make a firm commitment to full employment, given the economic status of American blacks; enforce strictly the nondiscrimination standards applicable to Federal school aid; and abandon the use of revenue sharing, or at least tighten the standards for its administration.

Such a commitment would also involve giving form and content to the Equal Employment Opportunity Commission—an unfortunate handmaiden of the Civil Rights Act of 1964. The EEOC was charged with the mission of wiping out employment discrimination. Prior to 1977, the EEOC had had six chairmen in twelve years and was characterized by what *The New York Times* called "administrative chaos and an ugly lack of professionalism."[52] This should be changed.

There is nothing of benign neglect about strict enforcement of antidiscrimination standards in either education or employment.

The Family

Our politicians have treated the institution of the family much like kindness to animals. When they have wished to view with alarm, the decline of the family and lack of respect for our furry friends have been favorite subjects. When they have wished to scale Mount Flatulent, the virtues of family and pet have been extolled. In spite of all the oratory, there has not been enough content to constitute a family policy.

The question of a national family policy is a delicate one. The family relationship is basically private. Americans, in leading—or not leading—family lives are today mercifully free from active government interference in that private relationship. We have avoided totalitarian attempts to use the family as an instrument of national policy, as a means of improving either the blood lines or the numbers of our children. Legislation and judicial decisions in recent years have also brought government to a more fully realized secular position of neutrality on moral questions affecting the family, such as divorce, contraception, abortion and even shopping on Sunday.

This is not to say that government policy and legislation have not affected the family. Amendments to the income-tax law have penalized marriage. The institutional nursing home has been favored over the family residence as the situs for treating the aged. And, in the most widely cited example, the traditional ground rules for welfare eligibility have discouraged the presence of the father in the home.

Family policy is an impact issue. Affirmative government policy interfering in the family relationship will almost always be unacceptable, particularly when any consensus as to the form and content of family life upon which to base an active family policy is probably impossible to achieve.*

But the government can and should avoid actions that are antifamily, that discourage or prevent the individual family unit from working out its own existence and future.

In 1977, the Carnegie Council on Children, after four years of study, reached a twofold conclusion that illustrates the importance of the family as an impact issue. First, that concern for children must go beyond thinking in terms of day care, education and health care to a broader concern for the family. "We believe families—and the circumstances of their lives—will remain the most critical factors in determining children's fate," the Council stated.

And second, that creating jobs for parents is essential to the wellbeing of both children and the family:

* The author may be wrong in this. He recently attended his twenty-fifth highschool reunion in Lowville, New York, a small upstate farm community. If zero population growth is a widely supported objective, and if motherhood is less than the worthiest of occupations for the liberated woman, there was precious little evidence of it among his classmates. For most of them, male and female, having been a parent has been a source of enormous pride. None seemed the worse for this traditional attitude, specifically including the women, whose charm, good looks and exuberant cheerfulness seem to have been heightened by the lives they have led as mothers, and often grandmothers. The reunion also cast doubt on another currently popular social myth—that the whole nation now drinks only white wine instead of whiskey.

The single most important factor that stacks the deck against tens of millions of American children is poverty. Other things being equal, the best way to ensure that a child has a fair chance at the satisfactions and fulfillments of adult life is to ensure that the child is born into a family with a decent income.

The traditional American view . . . is to see the excluded as ultimately to blame for their exclusion, and to place our hopes for a more just society on reforming and changing individuals, especially through schooling. But unless we also confront the economic deprivation that we now know to lie behind much of this exclusion, many of the billions of dollars we today spend on remedial, corrective, or compensatory programs for those who bear its scars will treat the symptoms, not the cause, of a deeper disease. We must also attack the causes of the deprivation—the lack of jobs for those who can, should, and want to work, and the lack of a minimal income for those who cannot work, or should not have to, and even for many who do. *If our society is determined that the family is to remain the basic institution for rearing children, and if all children are to have a chance to develop and use their potential, then it is necessary for the economic status of American families to be more secure.*[53]

The Carnegie Council seems clearly right in recognizing that the schools cannot solve many problems of children and of families. The schools cannot be expected to cope with such ugly statistics as the million children (mostly middle-class) who run away each year, the prevalence of suicide as the second most common cause of death among fifteen- to twenty-four-year-olds, the one of nine youths who end up in juvenile court by the age of eighteen[54] or the 28 percent of teen-agers who are considered to be problem drinkers.*

Vice President Mondale, who devoted much of his time as a Senator to the problems of the family, has said that, no matter what social problem he might have been studying, "I always seemed to get back to the family."[55]

In a statement in 1973, Mondale raised a series of questions that can still serve as a basis for analyzing the impact of programs on families:

- How does unemployment affect family stability? Do part-time or flexible work opportunities enhance the lives of families and children?

---

* This is the estimate of the National Institute on Alcohol Abuse and Alcoholism. A teen-ager is a "problem drinker" in the Institute's view if he has been drunk four times in a year or gotten into trouble twice within a year as the result of drinking. *Congressional Quarterly,* November 29, 1975, p. 2595.

Should children and youth be provided with more work opportunities, and more opportunities to observe and participate in the work experiences of their parents and other adults?

- To what extent has family dissolution been caused by unnecessary institutionalization of children; premature removal of children from their families for placement in foster care; unnecessary incarceration of juvenile offenders; and requirements of hospital treatment for illness in order to qualify for insurance benefits? Do we provide enough alternatives such as day care, homemaker services, community-based corrections programs or outpatient medical coverage? To what extent do these offer more promising results for children and families?
- How does mobility—particularly forced mobility—affect families? Are there ways to deal more successfully with whatever problems result from mobility decisions?
- How do welfare policies affect families and children? Do they provide a disincentive to stable families?
- What is the impact of the tax system on families and children? Does it contain incentives or disincentives for family stability? Does it provide adequate deductions for the cost of raising children?
- What has been the impact of urban renewal on families and children? What has been the impact of public-housing regulations that require families to move once they earn above a certain income? Do zoning practices unnecessarily restrict the location of community-based programs such as nursing homes in residential areas?[56]

Mondale has proposed that "Family Impact Statements" be required in connection with new legislation. This is an overly ambitious proposal, but at a minimum there should be a modestly staffed executive agency charged with the mission of publicizing the effect on families of major executive and legislative actions. Given the Vice President's long-standing interest in family problems, it would seem most appropriate to establish such an office under his direct control.

PROCEDURAL ISSUES

Broadly speaking, procedural issues are those concerned with how government transacts its business, how it regulates conduct and how it delivers services.

Congressman Lee Herbert Hamilton (Democrat, Indiana) has succinctly described the basic procedural problem:

The sheer size of the Government has done much to foster negative attitudes and beliefs among the American people. After all, a political establishment which has 5 million employees, spends over $400 billion annually, owns one-third of the Nation's land, occupies 433 million square feet of office space and administers some 1,000 aid programs through 11 Cabinet departments, 59 independent agencies, and 1,240 advisory boards can hardly be as intelligible and efficient as the Founding Fathers intended it to be. Of course, intelligibility is an important factor in the public's perception of Government: if agencies and activities are so varied that even the seasoned public servant is ignorant of most of them, then how can the average citizen be faulted if he complains that he does not know where to take a problem?

Efficiency is also an important factor in the public's perception of Government; while no one expects an immense not-for-profit-institution to function as smoothly as a profit-oriented small business, how can the average citizen be faulted if he complains that routine responses to his inquiries are delayed for months?

Beyond the sheer size of the Government—with its obvious implications for intelligibility and efficiency—there is the matter of rising expectations. The American people think the Government unresponsive and distant partly because their standards of performance are more strict now than ever before. In both the public and private sectors, the demand for more services of higher quality is outstripping the capabilities of the providing institutions and businesses. Naturally, there is disappointment when expectations are not met. The disappointment is especially acute when unsatisfactory services are tax-supported.

Nonetheless—and in stark contrast to their conservative tendencies of the past—the American people now look to the Government to solve increasing numbers of problems in increasingly efficient ways. The proliferation of regulatory agencies in the last few decades—nearly 50 such agencies have been created since 1960—is ample evidence of the new trend. Whether the Government has provided services of high quality is another question. Millions of Americans would say that it has not.[57]

There is nothing fixed about the procedural category, just as there is not with substantive or impact issues. The questions of welfare reform and national health insurance, for example, are now substantive issues; but if and when a welfare-reform program or a national health policy are written into law, these issues thereafter are likely to be procedural, the focus of concern changing to the way in which government administers payment mechanisms, delivers services itself and monitors the performance of services by private parties.

Speaking of his welfare-reform proposals, President Carter termed their administration a "major challenge" to government, providing "a valuable opportunity to demonstrate that government can be made to work, particularly in its operation of programs which serve those in our society most in need."

One can be moderately optimistic that if legislation with respect to our major substantive issues is passed, their procedural execution by the Carter administration will be competent and efficient. The President himself has given the impression of being more comfortable with questions of organization than with the politics of substantive issues. If this interest is translated into action, and if the administration takes heed of the lessons learned from carrying out the Great Society programs, we may be treated to the unusual spectacle of seeing government administering intelligently conceived programs in an efficient manner. Jimmy Carter may just have the opportunity to improve "the quality of American government" as Lyndon Johnson did not in 1967.*

Already we have seen efforts by the administration to reduce waste and fraud in Medicaid, Medicare and other social-service programs and to make a passing attempt at reforming the Civil Service. The administration has also acknowledged the existence of waste in Federal programs. A report of the Inspector General of the Department of Health, Education and Welfare, released in April 1978, estimated that up to $7.4 *billion* is lost annually through "fraud, inefficiency and waste" in all programs administered by HEW.†

Such frank acknowledgment is refreshing; even more refreshing would be a concerted effort to reduce fraud, inefficiency and waste, for continued public acceptance of both new and old social programs simply cannot be expected in the face of such mismanagement of resources.

Lyndon Johnson's observations in his Budget Message of January 21, 1964, are still relevant:

> I have been guided by the principle that spending by the Federal Government, in and of itself, is neither bad nor good. It can be bad when it involves overstaffing of Government agencies, or needless duplication of functions, or poor management, or public services which cost

* See p. 194, *supra.*
† A *New York Times* study in April 1978 estimated that fraud losses in all Federal programs exceed $12 billion a year. See Anthony Marro, "Fraud in Federal Aid May Exceed $12 Billion Annually, Experts Say," *New York Times,* April 16, 1978, p. 1.

more than they are worth, or the intrusion of government into areas where it does not belong. It can be good when it is put to work efficiently in the interests of our national strength, economic progress, and human compassion.

Public acceptance of social programs depends almost as much on a belief that waste and fraud are under control as on any other single factor. It is encouraging to have an administration that recognizes this.

Another "procedural" issue worthy of inclusion in any social agenda is the matter of deregulation—the question of what the Federal government's role ought to be, for example, in overseeing the drugs we take, the planes we fly and the securities we purchase.

Deregulation is not the mindless exercise envisioned by President Ford, who in 1975 set as an objective getting the Federal government "as far out of your business, out of your lives, out of your pocketbooks, and out of your hair as I possibly can."[58] It is a much more subtle process than that, testing whether the precepts that buttress government regulation are legitimate or merely devices for protecting the inefficient or the rapacious.

Deregulation involves a weighing of competing values and the result of that exercise is likely to be different in each instance. The degree to which Federal agencies should regulate commercial interest rates is far different from the degree to which it should regulate dangerous and unproven drugs. More regulation may be the order of the day in some cases, less in others.

Pursuing the matter of deregulation will be difficult—the folklore supporting regulation is often awesome and the power of special interests affected is great. Yet it is a task that must continue if government is to function in the optimum manner, if the public and not special interests are to be served, and if inflation is not to be fed by prices set at noncompetitive levels through regulatory action.

Three days before he died in July 1965, a tired and weary Adlai Stevenson told Eric Sevareid that "for a while, I'd really just like to sit in the shade with a glass of wine in my hand and watch the people dance."[59]

Stevenson's yearning is appealing. After the trauma of assassination, Vietnam and Watergate and with "intractable" the only adjective commonly applied to the greatest problems in our domestic affairs, it would be nice if all of us, from the President on down, could sip our wine and watch the dancing.

It would be nice if the greatest effort required of our Congressmen were to send copies of the Department of Agriculture's booklet on baby care to new mothers; if our President could spend the greatest part of his time celebrating the accomplishment of American creative and performing artists at tasteful White House gatherings; if family life were without challenge or hardship and our neighborhoods unassuming models of racial brotherhood; if our air were clean and health care cheap and competent; if there were no poor people—not only in West-chester County and Beverly Hills, but everywhere else; if the farmer, the businessman and the worker all prospered; if the great economic issues of the day were those of jam and jelly, not bread and butter[60]; if Roosevelt's Economic Bill of Rights were taken for granted.

With a traditional American spirit of optimism and idealism, bruised and tarnished though that spirit may be, we must—all of us—continue to seek the attributes of a more perfect and more tranquil Union. But with an equally American sense of realism and practicality we must—all of us—realize that such idyllic social conditions cannot even come close to realization without leadership, without statesmanship, without a thoughtful and realistic set of priorities, and without a concerned voting public prepared to rise above bigotry, greed, cynicism and, above all, indifference.

Emblazoned above the Speaker's rostrum in the House of Repre-sentatives are words of Daniel Webster from our first century which are equally applicable to the beginning of our third:

> Let us develop the resources of our land, call forth its powers, build up its institutions, promote all its great interests, and see also whether in our day and generation we may not perform something worthy to be remembered.

Appendix

TAX EXPENDITURE ESTIMATES BY FUNCTION, 1979*
(in millions of dollars)

Description	Corpo-rations	Indi-viduals
National defense:		
Exclusion of benefits and allowances to Armed Forces personnel	......	1,370
Exclusion of military disability pensions	......	120
International affairs:		
Exclusion of income earned abroad by U.S. citizens	......	385
Deferral of income of domestic international sales corporations (DISC)	1,335	....
Deferral of income of controlled foreign corporations	665	....
Special rate for Western Hemisphere trade corporations	15	....
General science, space, and technology:		
Expensing of research and development expenditures	1,520	30
Energy:		
Expensing of exploration and development costs	965	300
Excess of percentage over cost depletion	1,210	370
Capital gains treatment of royalties on coal	15	60
Natural resources and environment:		
Exclusion of interest on State and local government pollution control bonds	265	130
Exclusion of payments in aid of construction of water and sewage utilities	10	....
5-yr amortization on pollution control facilities	—45	....

* See footnote at end of table.

TAX EXPENDITURE ESTIMATES BY FUNCTION, 1979—Cont.
(in millions of dollars)

Description	Corpo-rations	Indi-viduals
Natural resources and environment—Continued		
Tax incentives for preservation of historic struc-tures	5	5
Capital gains treatment of certain timber income	230	65
Capital gains treatment of iron ore	10	10
Agriculture:		
Expensing of certain capital outlays	75	460
Capital gains treatment of certain ordinary in-come	10	365
Deductibility of noncash patronage dividends and certain other items of cooperatives	525	—185
Commerce and housing credit:		
Dividend exclusion	......	505
Exclusion of interest on State and local industrial development bonds	270	135
Exemption of credit union income	90	....
Excess bad debt reserves of financial institutions	790	....
Deductibility of mortgage interest on owner-occupied homes	......	5,530
Deductibility of property tax on owner-occupied homes	......	5,180
Deductibility of interest on consumer credit	......	2,350
Expensing of construction period interest and taxes	525	90
Excess first-year depreciation	50	155
Depreciation on rental housing in excess of straightline	70	290
Depreciation on buildings (other than rental hous-ing) in excess of straightline	130	115
Asset depreciation range	2,640	135
Capital gains (other than farming, timber, iron ore and coal)	575	7,990
Deferral of capital gains on home sales	......	980
Capital gains at death	......	8,975
Corporate surtax exemption	3,540	....
Investment credit	12,320	2,725
Credit for purchase of new homes	......	....

TAX EXPENDITURE ESTIMATES BY FUNCTION, 1979—Cont.
(in millions of dollars)

Description	Corpo- rations	Indi- viduals
Transportation:		
Deductibility of nonbusiness State gasoline taxes .	......	840
5-yr amortization on railroad rolling stock	−40	....
Deferral of tax on shipping companies	85	....
Community and regional development: 5-yr amortization for housing rehabilitation	5	5
Education, training, employment, and social services:		
Exclusion of scholarship and fellowship income..	......	330
Parental personal exemption for students age 19 or over	......	790
Exclusion of employee meals and lodging (other than military)	......	325
Exclusion of contributions to prepaid legal ser- vices plans	......	15
Investment credit for employee stock ownership plans (ESOPs)	305	....
Deductibility of charitable contributions (educa- tion)	285	645
Deductibility of charitable contributions to other than education and health	350	4,855
Maximum tax on personal service income	......	800
Credit for child and dependent care expenses ...	......	575
Credit for employment of AFDC recipients and public assistance recipients under work-incen- tive programs	20	....
Jobs credit	1,035	860
Health:		
Exclusion of employer contributions for medical insurance premiums and medical care	......	7,225
Deductibility of medical expenses	......	2,655
Expensing of removal of architectural and trans- portation barriers to the handicapped	10	....
Deductibility of charitable contributions (health) .	175	970
Income security:		
Exclusion of social security benefits:		
Disability insurance benefits	......	605

TAX EXPENDITURE ESTIMATES BY FUNCTION, 1979—Cont.
(in millions of dollars)

Description	Corpo-rations	Indi-viduals
Income security—Continued		
OASI benefits for retired workers	......	4,700
Benefits for dependents and survivors	......	1,040
Exclusion of railroad retirement system benefits .	......	280
Exclusion of workmen's compensation benefits ..	......	970
Exclusion of special benefits for disabled coal miners	......	50
Exclusion of unemployment insurance benefits ..	......	1,135
Exclusion of public assistance benefits	......	360
Exclusion of sick pay	......	60
Net exclusion of pension contributions and earn-ings:		
Employer plans	......	11,335
Plans for self-employed and others	......	1,920
Exclusion of other employee benefits:		
Premiums on group term life insurance	......	955
Premiums on accident and disability insurance.	......	80
Income of trusts to finance supplementary un-employment benefits	......	10
Exclusion of interest on life insurance savings	......	2,225
Exclusion of capital gains on home sales for per-sons age 65 and over	......	70
Additional exemption for elderly.............	......	1,215
Additional exemption for the blind	......	20
Excess of percentage standard deduction over minimum standard deduction	......	....
Deductibility of casualty losses	......	395
Tax credit for the elderly	......	255
Earned income credit:		
Nonrefundable portion	......	265
Refundable portion	......	900
Veterans benefits and services:		
Exclusion of veterans disability compensation ..	......	830
Exclusion of veterans pensions	......	40
Exclusion of GI bill benefits	......	170
General government: Credits and deductions for political contributions	......	75

TAX EXPENDITURE ESTIMATES BY FUNCTION, 1979—Cont.
(in millions of dollars)

Description	Corpo-rations	Indi-viduals
General purpose fiscal assistance:		
Exclusion of interest on general purpose State and local debt	3,865	2,150
Deductibility of nonbusiness State and local taxes (other than on owner-occupied homes and gasoline)	......	9,440
Tax credit for corporations doing business in U.S. possessions	520	....
Interest: Deferral of interest on savings bonds	......	670

All estimates are based on the tax code as of December 31, 1977.

Source: Special Analyses: Budget of the United States Government Fiscal Year 1979 (1978), Table G-1, pp. 158–60.

Notes

A Note on Sources

Presidential speeches, statements and the like are footnoted herein only to their date, since the texts are usually available in a number of sources—the annual government compilations of Presidential papers, the *Weekly Compilation* of Presidential documents, and often the *Congressional Record* and major newspapers.

Unless otherwise noted, government publications cited were published by the Government Printing Office.

Preface

1. Jonathan Schell, *The Time of Illusion* (New York: Knopf, 1975), p. 52 (hereinafter cited as "Schell").
2. "A Time for Action," in *A Selection from the Speeches and Writings of Lyndon B. Johnson 1953–64* (New York: Atheneum, 1964), p. 7.

Chapter One

1. Campaign Address at Soldiers' Field, Chicago, Illinois, October 28, 1944.
2. *Selected Literary and Political Papers and Addresses of Woodrow Wilson,* Vol. 1 (New York: Grosset, 1926), p. 122.
3. Characterization made by Harold L. Ickes, quoted in *Time,* October 18, 1948, p. 25.
4. The title of President Carter's book of 1976 campaign speeches (New York: Simon and Schuster, 1977).
5. First Campaign Debate, September 23, 1976.
6. *Gallup Opinion Index,* No. 131, June 1976, p. 25.
7. Quoted in Joseph Kraft, "Carter's Problems Are at Home," *Washington Post,* February 10, 1977, p. A15.
8. See, for example, Tom Braden, "When Innocence Is Past," *Washington Post,* May 14, 1977, p. A11.

Chapter Two

Principal sources for the statistical data in this chapter and Chapter Three were the very helpful biennial edition of *Facts and Figures on Government Finance* (1977 edition), published by the Tax Foundation, Inc. (hereinafter cited as "Tax Foundation"); the annual survey of social-welfare expenditures made by the late Alfred M. Skolnik and Sophie R. Dales, the most recent being "Social Welfare Expenditures, Fiscal Year 1976," appearing in the January 1977 *Social Security Bulletin* (hereinafter cited as "Skolnik and Dales"); the Office of Management and Budget *Special Analyses* of the 1978 and 1979 budgets (hereinafter cited as "Special Analyses..."); U.S. Department of Commerce, *Social Indicators, 1973,* and *Social Indicators, 1976* (hereinafter cited as "Social Indicators...").

1. Special Message to the Congress, September 6, 1945.
2. Bill No. S. 380 (79th Congress, 1st Session, 1945).
3. Statement on Signing Employment Act of 1946, February 20, 1946.
4. 121 *Cong. Rec.* (1975), p. S1134.
5. Statement by the President Upon Signing Bill Extending the Agricultural Trade Development and Assistance Act of 1954. September 21, 1959.
6. P.L. 95–113.
7. Barry M. Blechman, Edward M. Gramlich and Robert W. Hartman, *Setting National Priorities: The 1976 Budget* (Washington: Brookings Institution, 1975), p. 58 (hereinafter cited as "Blechman 1975").
8. 95th Congress, 1st Session, House Report No. 95-348 (1977), p. 55 (hereinafter cited as "Agricultural Act Report").
9. See Senate Report No. 1091 (1946) in *Cong. and Admin. News* (1946), p. 2407.
10. P.L. 95-113.
11. See House Conference Report No. 95-1103 (1978), p. 14.
12. Agricultural Act Report, pp. 1713–14.
13. Quoted in Alexander Cockburn and James Ridgeway, "Promises, Promises: Will a Democrat Change Anything?" *Village Voice,* December 8, 1975, p. 25.
14. Quoted in Timothy D. Schellhardt, "The Rising Tide of Price Fixing," *Wall Street Journal,* July 30, 1976, p. 4.
15. J. K. Galbraith, "Economics," *New York Times Book Review,* June 5, 1977, p. 24.
16. See Richard A. Posner, *Antitrust Law: An Economic Perspective* (Chicago: University of Chicago Press, 1976).
17. Henry J. Aaron, *Shelter and Subsidies: Who Benefits from Federal Housing Policies?* (Washington: Brookings Institution, 1972), p. 108.
18. Bernard J. Frieden and Arthur P. Solomon, *The Nation's Housing: 1975 to 1985* (Cambridge: Joint Center for Urban Studies of M.I.T. and Harvard, 1977), p. 93 (hereinafter cited as "Frieden").
19. See Aaron, *op. cit.,* pp. 74–90.
20. 92 *Cong. Rec.* (1946), p. 619.

21. See Frieden, pp. 119, 125, 130.
22. See Special Analyses 1978, pp. 205–6; Special Analyses 1979, p. 246.
23. Marjorie Smith Mueller, "Private Health Insurance in 1975: Coverage, Enrollment, and Financial Experience," *Social Security Bulletin*, June 1977, p. 3. (hereinafter cited as "Mueller").
24. William E. Leuchtenburg, *Franklin D. Roosevelt and the New Deal* (New York: Harper Torchbooks, 1963), p. 132.
25. Quoted in Arthur M. Schlesinger, Jr., *The Coming of the New Deal* (Boston: Houghton Mifflin, Century Ed., 1958), pp. 308–9 (hereinafter cited as "Schlesinger, New Deal").
26. Arthur Okun, *Equality and Efficiency: The Big Tradeoff* (Washington: Brookings Institution, 1975), pp. 107–8 (hereinafter cited as "Okun, Equality").
27. Blechman 1975, p. 169.
28. Quoted, 92 *Cong. Rec.* (1946), p. A2766.
29. Statistics quoted by Senator George D. Aiken, 93 *Cong. Rec.* (1947), pp. 5648–49.
30. *Time*, November 12, 1945, p. 91.
31. "These Are the Facts About: The Crisis in Education," *New Republic*, October 7, 1946, p. 434 (hereinafter cited as "Crisis in Education").
32. 93 *Cong. Rec.* (1947), p. 4477.
33. 94 *Cong. Rec.* (1948), p. 3386.
34. 92 *Cong. Rec.* (1946), p. 10619.
35. See, generally, Ralph W. Tyler, "The federal role in education," in Eli Ginzberg and Robert M. Solow, eds., *The Great Society: Lessons for the Future* (New York: Basic Books, 1974), pp. 164–87 (hereinafter cited as "Ginzberg and Solow").
36. *Presidential Papers* (1965), p. 811.

Chapter Three

1. Remarks to Members of the Business Council, December 4, 1968.
2. See Lindley H. Clark, Jr., "Speaking of Business—Out-of-Date Indexes," *Wall Street Journal*, June 21, 1977, p. 22; Bureau of Labor Statistics, *Escalation and the CPI: Information for Users* (1978).
3. Crisis in Education, p. 434.
4. *Gallup Opinion Index*, No. 157, August 1978, p. 30.
5. *Gallup Opinion Index*, No. 129, April 1976, p. 24.
6. 108 *Cong. Rec.* (1962), p. 10221.
7. Special Message to Congress on Sharing Federal Revenues with the States, August 13, 1969.
8. Arthur Okun, "The Costs of Inflation," in Okun, ed., *The Battle Against Unemployment* (New York: Norton, 1972), pp. 12–13.
9. Employment statistics are from U.S. Department of Labor Statistics, *Employment and Earnings*, January, June and July 1978.
10. Source: National Association for the Advancement of Colored People.

11. *To Secure These Rights* (1948).
12. Remarks to Members of the President's Committee on Civil Rights, January 15, 1947.
13. Quoted in Eric F. Goldman, *The Tragedy of Lyndon Johnson* (New York: Dell, 1974), pp. 204–5 (hereinafter cited as "Goldman").
14. Social Indicators 1973, Tables 3/16 and 3/2.
15. Social Indicators 1976, Table 7/2.
16. "Black College Enrollment Held Equal to Population Proportion," *New York Times,* December 4, 1975, p. 33.
17. "Economic developments in the black community," in Ginzberg and Solow, pp. 151, 148.
18. "Black College Enrollment Held Equal to Population Proportion," *loc. cit.*
19. Bureau of the Census, "Population Profile of the United States: 1977," *Current Population Reports,* Series P–20, No. 324, April 1978, p. 21.
20. Frieden, p. 89.
21. Social Indicators 1973, pp. 67, 72; Warren Brown, "Murder Is Found No. 1 Killer of Nonwhite Males," *Washington Post,* September 9, 1977, p. 1.
22. See Deborah Pisetzner Klein, "Women in the Labor Force: The Middle Years," *Monthly Labor Review,* November 1975, p. 15. The comparable percentages for high-school graduates: 25–34 years, 60.3%; 35–44 years, 54.6%; 45–54 years, 56.4%.
23. See June Kronholz, "Though More Women Work, Job Equality Fails to Materialize," *Wall Street Journal,* July 6, 1976, p. 1.
24. Klein, *op. cit.,* p. 10.
25. Stuart H. Garfinkle, "Occupations of Women and Black Workers, 1962–74," *Monthly Labor Review,* November 1975, pp. 28–29.
26. See *Presidential Papers* (1953), p. 744.
27. Special Analyses 1979, pp. 262ff.
28. Gayle B. Thompson, "Blacks and Social Security Benefits: Trends, 1960–73," *Social Security Bulletin,* April 1975, p. 40.
29. George F. Break and Joseph A. Pechman, *Federal Tax Reform: The Impossible Dream?* (Washington: Brookings Institution, 1975), p. 106 (hereinafter cited as "Break and Pechman").
30. The characterization of James Morgan, quoted in Juanita M. Kreps, "Social Security in the Coming Decade: Questions for a Mature System," *Social Security Bulletin,* March 1976, p. 22.
31. *Ibid.,* p. 27.
32. Preston C. Bassett, "Social Security's Weak Underpinning," *New York Times,* December 14, 1975, Section 3, p. 14.
33. Department of Health, Education and Welfare, *Summary of 1977 Annual Report of Trustees of Social Security Trust Funds,* May 9, 1977.
34. Break and Pechman, p. 107.
35. Statement Upon Signing Social Security Financing Bill, December 20, 1977.
36. Quoted at 123 *Cong. Rec.* (1977), p. H12856.
37. Letter of Transmittal Regarding Social Security Financing Proposals, May 9, 1977.

38. George Melloan, "Drifting Toward 'National Health,'" *Wall Street Journal*, November 17, 1975, p. 12.

39. Karen Davis, *National Health Insurance: Benefits, Costs, and Consequences* "Davis").

40. Department of Health, Education and Welfare, *Goals of a National Health* (Washington: Brookings Institution, 1975), p. 2 (hereinafter cited as *Program* (1978) (hereinafter cited as "HEW Goals").

41. Mueller, p. 19.

42. HEW Goals.

43. Davis, pp. 2, 34–35.

44. See Davis, pp. 31–55, for a comprehensive survey of disparities in Medicare and Medicaid benefits.

45. Leonard A. Lecht, *Dollars for National Goals: Looking Ahead to 1980* (New York: Wiley, 1974), p. 7.

46. Nancy L. Worthington, "Expenditures for Hospital Care and Physicians' Services: Factors Affecting Annual Changes," *Social Security Bulletin*, November 1975, p. 3; and Worthington, "National Health Expenditures, 1929–74," *Social Security Bulletin*, February 1975, p. 10.

47. Herbert E. Klarman, "Major public initiatives in health care" in Ginzberg and Solow, pp. 110–11.

48. 121 *Cong. Rec.* (1975), p. 4660.

49. John L. Hess, "Nursing Homes Show Progress," *New York Times*, January 12, 1976, p. 32.

50. Quoted in *Congressional Quarterly*, November 29, 1975, p. 2618.

Chapter Four

1. Quoted by J. Powell, in *San Antonio School District v. Rodriguez*, 411 U.S. 1 at 49 (1973).

2. Reinhold Niebuhr, *The Children of Light and the Children of Darkness* (New York: Scribner's, 1944), p. 9.

3. 92 *Cong Rec.* (1946), p. 1465.

4. Quoted, 108 *Cong. Rec.* (1962), p. 922.

5. Senator Lister Hill, quoted in "Taft and the Schools," *Newsweek*, April 12, 1948, p. 27.

6. 92 *Cong. Rec.* (1946), pp. 10619–20.

7. "Crisis in Education," p. 435.

8. *Everson v. Board of Education*, 330 U.S. 1 (1947); *McCollum v. Board of Education*, 333 U.S. 203 (1948).

9. Quoted, 94 *Cong. Rec.* (1948), p. 3957.

10. "Taft and the Schools," *loc. cit.*

11. 92 *Cong. Rec.* (1946), p. 10620.

12. 94 *Cong. Rec.* (1948), p. 3348.

13. January 5, 1949.

14. Quoted, *Federal Role in Education*, Washington: Congressional Quarterly Service, 1965, p. 22.

15. "Aid Squabble," *Newsweek,* July 4, 1949, p. 70.
16. "The Churches Kill Aid for the Schools," *New Republic,* March 27, 1950, pp. 5–6.
17. See Lister Hill, "A Bonanza for Education," *Harper's,* March 1952.
18. 98 *Cong. Rec.* (1952), p. 2914.
19. "Schools: Hungry Teachers," *Newsweek,* February 3, 1947, p. 25.
20. Benjamin Fine, "We Are Starving Our Teachers," reprinted in 96 *Cong. Rec.* (1950), p. 6314–15.
21. Benjamin Fine, *New York Times,* January 9, 1950, p. 1.
22. Office of Education projections, quoted 98 *Cong. Rec.* (1952), p. 2907. The Hill quote is at p. 2905.
23. Benjamin Fine, quoted 98 *Cong. Rec.* (1952), p. 2923.
24. Budget Message to the Congress, January 21, 1954.
25. Special Message to the Congress Concerning Federal Assistance in School Construction, February 8, 1955.
26. Earl J. McGrath, "American Education in Crisis," *School and Society,* January 22, 1955, p. 20.
27. Stevenson address of July 8, 1955, reprinted in 101 *Cong. Rec.* (1955), p. 10141.
28. The characterization by Senator Richard Neuberger, 101 *Cong. Rec.* (1955), p. 1371.
29. 100 *Cong. Rec.* (1954), p. 7255.
30. 102 *Cong. Rec.* (1956), p. 2784.
31. Quoted, 102 *Cong. Rec.* (1956), p. 12147.
32. *Ibid.*
33. *Ibid.,* p. 10161.
34. Drew Pearson, "Russia Pulls Up to Us on Schools," reprinted in 103 *Cong. Rec.* (1957), pp. 13061–62.
35. News Conference, July 31, 1957.
36. Quoted, 103 *Cong. Rec.* (1957), p. 2018.
37. "Today and Tomorrow—The School Crisis," *Washington Post and Times Herald,* February 5, 1957.
38. House Report No. 2157 in *Cong. and Admin. News* (1958), p. 4772.
39. According to Admiral Lewis Strauss, then Chairman of the Atomic Energy Commission, quoted 103 *Cong. Rec.* (1957), p. 990.
40. January 30, 1961.
41. Special Message to the Congress on Education, February 20, 1961.
42. Hugh Douglas Price, quoted in Philip Meranto, "The Politics of Federal Aid to Education in 1965: A Study in Political Innovation" (Syracuse: Syracuse Univ., 1967), p. 2.
43. Special Message to the Congress: "Toward Full Educational Opportunity," January 12, 1965.
44. 89th Congress, 1st Sess., U. S. Senate Subcommittee on Education, Committee on Labor and Public Welfare, *Hearings on S. 370* (1965), p. 87.
45. Committee for Support of the Public Schools, "Changing Demands on

Education and Their Implications," excerpted in 109 *Cong. Rec.* (1963), p. 5063.

46. Quoted, 110 *Cong. Rec.* (1964), p. 3691.
47. 111 *Cong. Rec.* (1965), p. 5729.
48. *Ibid.*, p. 5759.
49. Samuel Halperin, "The Great Education Act: ESEA 10 Years Later," reprinted in 121 *Cong. Rec.* (1975), p. H3322 (hereinafter cited as "Halperin, Ten Years").

Chapter Five

1. Quoted in Samuel Halperin, "ESEA: Five Years Later," reprinted in 121 *Cong. Rec.* (1975), p. H3318 (hereinafter cited as "Halperin, Five Years").
2. Sec. 2, P.L. 89–10 (1965).
3. House Report No. 93-805 in *Cong. and Admin. News* (1974), p. 4095.
4. Quoted in Bernard L. Weinstein, "Why Texas Outdraws New York for Business," *Empire State Report,* October–November 1976, p. 335.
5. Based on 1959–60 figures. Tax Foundation, p. 260.
6. 111 *Cong. Rec.* (1965), p. 6001.
7. See Alan K. Campbell, "Inequities of School Finance," *Saturday Review,* January 11, 1969, p. 44.
8. 115 *Cong. Rec.* (1969), p. 6107.
9. House Report No. 93–805 in *Cong. and Admin. News* (1974), pp. 4100–4102.
10. *Ibid.*
11. Statement of National School Boards Association, reprinted in 122 *Cong. Rec.* (1976), pp. E3831–32.
12. A finding reported in Peat, Marwick, Mitchell & Co., *Final Report: A Study of Late Funding of Elementary and Secondary Education, Office of Planning, Budgeting, and Evaluation* (Washington: National Institute of Education, 1976), p. V–10.
13. *Ibid.*, Appendix A.
14. E.g., Testimony of William Webster, Assistant Superintendent, Oakland, California. U. S. Cong., 92nd Cong., 2nd Sess., "Oversight Hearings on Elementary and Secondary Education," Hearings before Committee on Education and Labor, House of Representatives (1972), pp. 2–3.
15. P.L. 89–10, Sec. 205(a)(5).
16. House Report No. 93–805, in *Cong. and Admin. News* (1974), p. 4097.
17. Halperin, Ten Years, p. H3322.
18. Quoted in Robert Bendiner, *The Politics of Schools: A Crisis in Self-Government* (New York: Harper, 1969), p. 173.
19. Statement of AFL–CIO Executive Council, quoted 113 *Cong. Rec.* (1967), p. 12073.
20. "School Aid Diversions" (Editorial), quoted 113 *Cong. Rec.* (1967), p. 12074.
21. Andrew J. Biemiller testimony, 93rd Cong., 1st Sess., General Subcommittee

on Education, Committee on Education and Labor, House of Representatives, *Elementary and Secondary Education Amendments of 1973* (1973), Part 2, p. 2416.

22. Special Message to the Congress on Special Revenue Sharing for Education, April 6, 1971.
23. The President's Message to the Congress Proposing Reform Legislation, March 1, 1976.
24. 111 *Cong. Rec.* (1965), p. 6131.
25. 114 *Cong. Rec.* (1968), p. 21254.
26. 120 *Cong. Rec.* (1974), p. 14579.
27. Sec. 208, P.L. 94–439.
28. See Senate Report No. 95–283 (1977), p. 130.
29. See Senator Eagleton's statements in the Senate, 123 *Cong. Rec.* (1977), pp. S10897–10906, and the table at p. S10898.
30. See 120 *Cong. Rec.* (1974), p. 14823.
31. See William K. Stevens, "5 Years of Busing in Pontiac, Mich.: Gains and Losses," *New York Times*, December 3, 1975, p. 30; Reginald Stuart, "Schools in Louisville Are Calmer in 2d Year of Desegregation Plan," *New York Times*, September 11, 1976, p. 48; Tom Wicker, "The Myth of Busing: Some Contradictory Evidence," *New York Times*, September 19, 1976, Section 4, p. 15.
32. 118 *Cong. Rec.* (1972), p. 4577.
33. Quoted, 102 *Cong. Rec.* (1956), p. 2786.
34. Robert J. Harris, "The Constitution, Education, and Segregation," 29 Temple Law Q. 409 (1956), quoted in A. T. Mason, *The Supreme Court From Taft to Warren* (Baton Rouge: Louisiana State, 1958), p. 191.
35. 163 U.S. 537. The statistics are quoted in A. T. Mason and W. M. Beaney, *The Supreme Court in a Free Society* (Englewood Cliffs: Prentice-Hall, 1959), p. 261.
36. 339 U.S. 629. The leading case was *Missouri ex rel. Gaines v. Canada*, 305 U.S. 337 (1938). See also *McLaurin v. Oklahoma State Regents*, 339 U.S. 637 (1950), decided the same day as *Sweatt*.
37. *Brown v. Board of Education*, 349 U.S. 294 (1955).
38. 102 *Cong. Rec.* (1956), pp. 4515–16.
39. See *Jackson v. Rawdon*, 235 F.2d 93 (Fifth Cir. 1956).
40. Brennan, J., in *Green v. County School Bd. of New Kent Co.*, 391 U.S. 430 at 437–39 (1968).
41. *Alexander v. Holmes County Board of Education*, 396 U.S. 19 at 20 (1969). Emphasis supplied.
42. 402 U.S. 1 at 28, 30 (1971).
43. *North Carolina State Bd. of Educ. v. Swann*, 402 U.S. 43 (1971).
44. *Richmond School Board v. State Board of Education*, 412 U.S. 92 (1973).
45. 413 U.S. 189.
46. 418 U.S. 717.
47. 487 P.2d 1241.
48. 411 U.S. 1 (1973).

49. 303 A.2d 273 (1973).
50. *New York Times,* July 9, 1970, p. 1.
51. *Serrano v. Priest,* 557 P.2d 929 (1977).
52. Edward B. Fiske, "How Fair Are Schools Paid For by Taxes on Property?," *New York Times,* November 21, 1976, Section 4, p. 5.
53. Quoted, 95 *Cong. Rec.* (1949), p. A4029.

Chapter Six

1. 121 *Cong. Rec.* (1975), p. 18415.
2. Letter to the Congress, February 19, 1939.
3. Carroll L. Wilson, "A Plan for Energy Independence," *Foreign Affairs,* July 1973, p. 657 (hereinafter cited as "Wilson").
4. Address to the Nation About Policies to Deal with the Energy Shortages, November 7, 1973.
5. Quoted in *Congressional Quarterly,* December 20, 1975, p. 2766.
6. State of the Union Message, January 15, 1975.
7. *Phillips Petroleum Co. v. Wisconsin,* 347 U.S. 672 (1954).
8. See, generally, James W. McKie, "The United States," and Joel Darmstadter and Hans H. Landsberg, "The Economic Background" in *Daedalus* (Fall 1975). (The McKie article is hereinafter cited as "McKie.")
9. See the testimony of Charles L. Schultze in "The Economic Impact of Forthcoming OPEC Price Rise and 'Old' Oil Decontrol," Hearings Before U.S. Congress, Joint Economic Committee, Subcommittee on Consumer Economics, 94th Congress, 1st Sess. (July 10, 1975) (1976), p. 65.
10. 121 *Cong. Rec.* (1975), p. S7264.
11. "My Case for National Planning," *Fortune,* February 1977, p. 102.
12. 121 *Cong. Rec.* (1975), p. H10004.
13. The characterization of Representative Barber B. Conable, Jr., 93rd Congress, 1st and 2d Sess., Joint Economic Committee, Subcommittee on Priorities and Economy in Government, "Energy Statistics (1974)," p. 112 (hereinafter cited as "Energy Statistics").
14. Quoted in McKie, p. 85.
15. Energy Statistics, p. 122.
16. On the subject of depletion generally, see the statement of Senator Ernest Hollings, 121 *Cong. Rec.* (1975), pp. S4232 ff.
17. "Breaking Up Big Oil," *New York Times Magazine,* October 3, 1976, p. 90.
18. See William Greider, "Oil Industry Stakes Out Role for the Future," *Washington Post,* May 22, 1977, p. 1.
19. 121 *Cong. Rec.* (1975), pp. 19777–78.
20. "A Major Presidential Mistake" (Editorial), *Wall Street Journal,* December 26, 1975, p. 4; "Right on Energy..." (Editorial), *New York Times,* December 24, 1975, p. 20.
21. 121 *Cong Rec.* (1975), p. H5131.

Chapter Seven

1. Frank E. Smith, *Congressman from Mississippi* (New York: Pantheon Books, 1964), p. 127.
2. See Martin Tolchin, "Senate Approves a Plan to Revamp Committee Setup," *New York Times,* February 5, 1977, p. 1.
3. Howard E. Shuman, "Canonizing 'Pork,' " *New York Times,* November 19, 1976, p. A27.
4. P.L. 93–344.
5. "New Budget System Survives First Year Intact," *Congressional Quarterly,* December 27, 1975, p. 2864.
6. Blechman 1975, p. 243.
7. See Stanley S. Surrey, "The Federal Tax Legislative Process," 31 *Record of the Association of the Bar of the City of New York,* November 1976, p. 531.
8. Adam Clymer, "Budget Watching Is a Strain on Congress," *New York Times,* May 15, 1977, Section 4, p. 3.
9. Warren Weaver, Jr., "2 Polls Provide Support for Congressional Reforms," *New York Times,* February 4, 1977, p. A11.
10. Hamilton or Madison, Federalist No. 57, *The Federalist* (New York: Modern Library, 1937), p. 372.
11. See John A. Ferejohn, "On the Decline of Competition in Congressional Elections," *American Political Science Review,* March 1977, p. 166.
12. See Morris P. Fiorina, "The Case of the Marginals: The Bureaucracy Did It," *American Political Science Review,* March, 1977, p. 177.
13. Alan L. Otten, "Politics and People—Errand Boys," *Wall Street Journal,* August 18, 1977, p. 18.

Chapter Eight

1. Remarks, Springfield, Illinois, October 19, 1962.
2. *Gallup Opinion Index,* No. 131, June 1976, p. 25. The results total more than 100 percent because of multiple responses.
3. Quoted in Clayton Fritchey, "A Republican Drift," *New York Post,* December 26, 1975, p. 36; 44 percent felt the Democrats were "competent" and 45 percent felt they were "trustworthy."
4. Quoted in *Time,* July 5, 1948, p. 20.
5. The phrase is President Eisenhower's. Address at a Rally in the Public Square, Cleveland, Ohio, October 1, 1956.
6. Tax Foundation, pp. 65–66.
7. Remarks at the Luncheon of the Republican Women's Spring Conference, April 24, 1953.
8. Veto of Bill to Reduce Income Taxes, June 16, 1947.
9. John Kenneth Galbraith, *Money: Whence It Came, Where It Went* (Boston: Houghton Mifflin, 1975), p. 284.
10. *Ibid.,* p. 300.

11. Veto Message, January 26, 1970.

12. Remarks, 50th Anniversary Convention of the United States Jaycees, St. Louis, Missouri, June 25, 1970.

13. *The Memoirs of Herbert Hoover, The Great Depression 1929–1941* (New York: Macmillan, 1952), pp. 132–34.

14. Announcement of Appointment of Members, National Commission on Productivity, July 10, 1970.

15. P. L. 94–136.

16. Address to the Nation on Economic Policy and Productivity, June 17, 1970.

17. News Conference, January 21, 1975.

18. See Remarks Concluding the Summit Conference on Inflation, September 28, 1974.

19. State of the Union Message, January 22, 1970.

20. Adlai E. Stevenson, *Putting First Things First: A Democratic View* (New York: Random House, 1960), p. 65.

21. Statement by the President on Signing Bill to Extend and Improve the Unemployment Insurance Program, September 1, 1954. Emphasis supplied.

22. Veto of Economic Opportunity Amendments of 1971, December 10, 1971.

23. Remarks, Luncheon of the All America Council of the Democratic National Committee, October 27, 1968.

24. See Herbert Stein, " 'Full Employment' Once More," *Wall Street Journal*, November 10, 1975, p. 10.

25. "The Human Costs of Unemployment," in Okun, ed., *The Battle Against Unemployment, supra*, p. 7.

26. See Arthur F. Burns, "The Real Issues of Inflation and Unemployment," address at Blue Key Honor Society Annual Awards Dinner, Athens, Georgia, September 19, 1975 (Federal Reserve Board press release).

27. Quoted in *Time*, October 25, 1968, p. 24.

28. Social Indicators 1973, Table 2/1; *Time*, June 30, 1975, p. 13.

29. "Committee Probes Drug Enforcement Effort," *Congressional Quarterly*, July 5, 1975, pp. 1427–28.

30. *The Challenge of Crime in a Free Society* (1967).

31. Statement by the President Upon Signing the Omnibus Crime Control and Safe Streets Act of 1968, June 19, 1968.

32. U.S. Congress. House Committee on the Judiciary, Subcommittee No. 5. Law Enforcement Assistance Administration Hearings (1973), p. 133 (hereinafter cited as "1973 Hearings").

33. Testimony of former Congressman John S. Monaghan, Hearings, 1973, p. 133; 122 *Cong Rec.* (1976), p. H9278; Victor S. Navasky, "Background Paper," in *Law Enforcement: The Federal Role, Report of the Twentieth Century Fund Task Force on the Law Enforcement Assistance Administration* (New York: McGraw-Hill, 1976), p. 27.

34. Special Message to the Congress on Special Revenue Sharing for Law Enforcement, March 2, 1971.

35. Statement of Sidney J. Weinberg, Jr., 1973 Hearings, p. 274.

36. 1973 Hearings, p. 341.
37. Statement of M. Carl Holman, President, National Urban Coalition, quoting the U.S. Commission on Civil Rights, 1973 Hearings, p. 325.
38. General Accounting Office, *Long-Term Impact of Law Enforcement Assistance Grants Can Be Improved* (1974).
39. Schell, pp. 44–45.
40. Quoted in *Congressional Quarterly Almanac* (1974), p. 274.
41. Farewell Address, January 18, 1961.
42. Characterization by Senator (then Congressman) Lee Metcalf, 105 *Cong. Rec.* (1959), p. 3079.
43. See William V. Shannon, "Eisenhower as President: A Critical Appraisal of the Record," *Commentary,* November 1958, pp. 390, 398.
44. Daniel P. Moynihan, *Coping: On the Practice of Government* (New York: Random House, 1973), p. 8.
45. News Conference, November 4, 1966.
46. Schell, p. 140.
47. Schell, p. 6.
48. Inaugural Address, January 20, 1969.
49. Schell, p. 185.
50. Statement About Policy on Abortions at Military Base Hospitals in the United States, April 3, 1971.
51. 410 U.S. 113 (1973).
52. Schell, p. 183.
53. William V. Shannon, "Politics," *New York Times Book Review,* June 5, 1977, p. 27.
54. John Hersey, *The President* (New York: Knopf, 1975), p. 44.
55. News Conference, September 5, 1956.
56. May 19, 1953.
57. Foster Rhea Dulles, *The Civil Rights Commission: 1957–1965* (Lansing: Michigan State Univ. Press, 1968), p. 11.
58. Barry Goldwater, *The Conscience of a Conservative* (Louisville: Victor Publishing, 1960), p. 34.
59. Address to the Nation on Busing, March 19, 1972.
60. See "The Administration's Proposed 'Anti-busing' Legislation," *Record of the Association of the Bar of the City of New York* (December 1972), p. 749. (Report of the Committees on Federal Legislation and Civil Rights of the Association.)
61. See U.S. Commission on Civil Rights, *Title IV and School Desegregation* (1973).
62. Message to the Congress Transmitting the Proposed School Desegregation Standards and Assistance Act of 1976, June 24, 1976.
63. *Ibid.;* Philip Shabecoff, "Ford's Busing Stance," *New York Times,* June 22, 1976, p. 25.
64. U.S. Commission on Civil Rights, *Desegregation of the Nation's Public Schools* (1976), pp. 300–301.

65. Quoted in B. Drummond Ayres, Jr., "Racism in U.S. Southern Schools Takes Subtle New Forms," *International Herald Tribune,* September 10, 1975, p. 5.
66. State of the Union Message, January 22, 1970.
67. Quoted in *Time,* September 29, 1952, p. 13.
68. News Conference, April 12, 1961.
69. Address to Conference of the Federal Council of Churches, Columbus, Ohio, March 6, 1946.

Chapter Nine

1. *Who Needs the Democrats and What It Takes to Be Needed* (New York: Doubleday, 1970), p. 4.
2. Radio and TV Address Opening Campaign, September 19, 1956.
3. Quoted in Samuel and Dorothy Rosenman, *Presidential Style: Some Giants and a Pygmy in the White House* (New York: Harper, 1976), p. 428.
4. Barton J. Bernstein and Allen J. Matusow, eds., *The Truman Administration: A Documentary History* (New York: Harper, 1966), p. 86.
5. *Presidential Papers* (1966), Document 524.
6. Quoted in Goldman, p. 395.
7. Goldman, p. 616.
8. Special Message to the Congress: "The American Promise," March 15, 1965.
9. Okun, Equality, p. 117.
10. State of the Union Message, January 8, 1964; Letter to the President of the Senate and to the Speaker of the House, February 17, 1965; and Address in Boston, October 27, 1964.
11. State of the Union Message, January 17, 1968.
12. Seymour E. Harris, *Economics of the Kennedy Years and a Look Ahead* (New York: Harper, 1964), p. 203.
13. Ginzberg and Solow, pp. 213–214.
14. Remarks to Key Officers of the Internal Revenue Service, February 11, 1964.
15. First Press Conference, December 7, 1963; Statement to Cabinet on Manpower Utilization and Control, December 11, 1963.
16. Okun, Equality, p. 116.
17. See George McGovern, "On Taxing and Redistributing Income," *New York Review of Books,* May 4, 1972.
18. This is the unconfirmed account of Kristi Witker in her book *How to Lose Everything in Politics Except Massachusetts* (New York: Mason & Lipscomb, 1974), pp. 88–94. Theodore H. White's account is not dissimilar; see *The Making of the President 1972* (New York: Bantam Books, 1973), pp. 165–67.
19. George McGovern, *An American Journey: The Presidential Campaign Speeches of George McGovern* (New York: Random House, 1974), p. 158 (hereinafter cited as "McGovern").
20. McGovern, p. 137.

21. "McGovern Takes Major Share of Blame for His 1972 Defeat," *New York Times,* October 26, 1975, p. 41.
22. White, *op. cit.,* p. 156.
23. Okun, Equality, pp. 48–49.
24. Break and Pechman, pp. 111, 116.
25. McGovern, pp. 37, 145; Tax Foundation, p. 109.
26. Hubert H. Humphrey, *The Political Philosophy of the New Deal* (Baton Rouge: Louisiana State, 1970), p. 51.
27. See Robert J. Donovan, *Conflict and Crisis* (New York: Norton, 1977), p. 113.

Chapter Ten

1. Quoted in Alan L. Otten, "Defender of the Faith," *Wall Street Journal,* March 25, 1976, p. 14.
2. Eugene McCarthy, *The Hard Years* (New York: Viking, 1975), p. 13.
3. Quoted in Lee Lescaze, "Mixed Reviews on Officials' Openness," *Washington Post,* February 20, 1977, p. A2. The "subterfuge" characterization by President Carter two paragraphs below the Powell quote was also taken from this article.
4. News Conference, January 22, 1948.
5. Remarks at a Meeting with the American Society of Newspaper Editors, April 17, 1947.
6. Paul K. Conklin, *FDR and the Origins of the Welfare State* (New York: Crowell, 1967), pp. 70–71. Emphasis supplied.
7. See "Capital Formation: New Tax Incentives Needed?" *Congressional Quarterly,* August 9, 1975, p. 1751; Lindley H. Clark Jr., "Speaking of Business—Capital Shortage?", *Wall Street Journal,* November 10, 1975, p. 10; Barry Bosworth, James S. Duesenberry and Andrew S. Carron, *Capital Needs in the Seventies* (Washington: Brookings Institution, 1975).
8. "Mr. Murphy Takes the Blame," *New York Times,* October 10, 1976, Section 3, p. 16.
9. Commencement Address at Yale University, June 11, 1962.
10. Adlai E. Stevenson, quoted 103 *Cong. Rec.* (1957), pp. 994–95.
11. See M. H. Waterfield, *Federal Grants: The Need for Reform* (New York: Tax Foundation, 1973); Walter W. Heller, "A Sympathetic Reappraisal of Revenue Sharing," in Harvey S. Perloff and Richard P. Nathan, eds., *Revenue Sharing and the City* (Washington: Resources for the Future, 1968, p. 3 (hereinafter cited as "Perloff and Nathan").
12. Walter W. Heller, *New Dimensions of Political Economy* (Cambridge: Harvard University Press, 1966), especially pp. 117–121, 145.
13. Statement About the General Revenue Sharing Bill, October 20, 1972.
14. Department of the Treasury, Office of Revenue Sharing, *Reported Uses of General Revenue Sharing Funds 1974–1975* (1976), pp. 6–11.
15. Presidential Campaign Debate, October 22, 1976.
16. The National Revenue Sharing Project of the League of Women Voters

Education Fund, National Urban Coalition, Center for Community Change and Center for National Policy Review, *General Revenue Sharing in American Cities: First Impressions* (Washington: National Clearinghouse on Revenue Sharing, 1974).

17. See Morton H. Sklar, "The Impact of Revenue Sharing on Minorities and the Poor," *Harvard Civil Rights-Civil Liberties Law Review*, Winter 1975, p. 113.
18. "Nixon and Neo-Jeffersonianism," in Irving Howe and Michael Harrington, eds., *The Seventies: Problems and Proposals* (New York: Harper, 1972), p. 422.
19. Remarks on Signing the General Revenue Sharing Bill, October 20, 1972.
20. "Approaches to Staffing the Presidency: Notes on FDR and JFK," *American Political Science Review*, December 1963, p. 856.
21. Nathan Glazer, "The Limits of Social Policy," *Commentary*, September 1971, p. 52.
22. Ginzberg and Solow, p. 212.
23. Leonard Reed, "Firing a Federal Employee: The Impossible Dream," *Washington Monthly*, July/August 1977, p. 15.
24. "HEW's Califano: Reflections on a Changing Bureaucracy," *Washington Post*, March 29, 1977, p. A6.
25. This is the characterization of Lyle C. Fitch in Perloff and Nathan, p. 88.
26. Quoted in Peter Lisagor, "Fuzzy Strategy," *New York Post*, October 20, 1975, p. 31.
27. *The New America* (New York: Harper, 1957), p. 87.
28. "National Economic Planning: Pro," *New York Times*, December 21, 1975, Section 3, p. 12. The quote of Senator Humphrey which follows is also from this article.
29. "National Economic Planning," *Newsweek*, July 14, 1975, p. 71.
30. Annual Message to the Congress: The Economic Report of the President, February 2, 1970.

Chapter Eleven

1. 94th Cong., 1st Sess., H.R. 50, Section 2.
2. The Ph.D. estimate is that of the National Board on Graduate Education, quoted in Gene I. Maeroff, "Teaching Job Prospects for Graduates With Doctorates Reported to Be Growing Worse," *New York Times*, January 21, 1976, p. 32.
3. See William L. Shirer, *The Rise and Fall of the Third Reich* (New York: Simon and Schuster, 1960), p. 251.
4. "Social Dynamite in Our Large Cities," quoted in 107 *Cong. Rec.* (1961), p. 8998.
5. Quoted, 122 *Cong. Rec.* (1976), p. E2920.
6. Quoted, Tom Wicker, "Bigger, Not Better," *New York Times*, January 28, 1977, p. A23.
7. Title I of the Public Works Employment Act of 1976, P.L. 94–369 (1976).

8. James C. Hyatt, "The Public Works Controversy," *Wall Street Journal,* February 14, 1977, p. 14; "Public-Works Grants Help Baltimore a Bit, the Jobless Very Little," *Wall Street Journal,* July 21, 1977, p. 1.

9. P.L. 95–28.

10. Special Message of the President on Youth Employment Programs, March 9, 1977.

11. Hobart Rowen, "Despite Some Misgivings, Hill is Backing Carter Jobs Plan," *Washington Post,* February 15, 1977, p. A4.

12. See testimony of Alice Rivlin, director of the Congressional Budget Office, at hearings on the "Full Employment and Balanced Growth Act of 1976," before the Subcommittee on Manpower, Compensation and Health and Safety of the House Education and Labor Committee, April 8, 1976, p. 225.

13. "What Carter's Critics Are Disillusioned About," *New York Post,* August 25, 1977, p. 36.

14. Quoted, 123 *Cong. Rec.* (1977), p. E7168.

15. 94th Cong., 2d Sess., Joint Economic Committee Hearings, *Thirtieth Anniversary of the Employment Act of 1946—A National Conference on Full Employment* (1976), p. 270 (hereinafter cited as "Full Employment Hearings").

16. " 'Year of the Economy,' " *Newsweek,* November 21, 1977, p. 41.

17. Full Employment Hearings, p. 172.

18. Full Employment Hearings, p. 30.

19. Hobart Rowen, "Nothing's Working in the Inflation War," *Washington Post,* June 2, 1977, p. A19.

20. "A Plan for Subduing Inflation," *Fortune,* September 1974, p. 212.

21. Remarks to Members of the Business Council, December 4, 1968.

22. Social Indicators 1976, Chart 8/12b.

23. National Council on Employment, "How Much Unemployment Do We Need?" quoted, 122 *Cong. Rec.* (1976), p. S11236.

24. U.S. Congress, Joint Economic Committee, *1977 Midyear Review of the Economy* (September 1977).

25. Hobart Rowen, "What Humphrey-Hawkins Would Do," *Washington Post,* November 17, 1977, p. A23.

26. Joseph Kraft, "A Carter Loss in Economic Round One," *Washington Post,* April 19, 1977, p. A19.

27. "Local Governments Must Lift Efficiency to Fight Recession, Inflation, Study Says," *Wall Street Journal,* March 4, 1976, p. 19.

28. "The Great Stagflation Swamp," Address to the Economic Club of Chicago, October 6, 1977, *Vital Speeches,* December 1, 1977, p. 120.

29. Statement of Arthur F. Burns to Joint Economic Committee Hearing on the Economic Situation, February 23, 1977.

30. Kraft, *loc. cit.,* note 26.

31. Rowen, *loc. cit.,* note 19.

32. Transcript, MacNeil-Lehrer Report, reported in *American Banker,* April 21, 1977, p. 10.

33. HEW Fact Sheet on Proposed Hospital Cost Containment Act of 1977, released April 25, 1977.

34. Joseph A. Califano, Jr., "What's Wrong with U.S. Health Care," *Washington Post,* June 26, 1977, p. B3; statement of Alice Rivlin, Director, Congressional Budget Office, reprinted at 122 *Cong. Rec.* (1976), p. H4989; HEW Goals.

35. Eliot Marshall, "What's Bad for General Motors," *New Republic,* March 12, 1977, p. 22.

36. Statement of Leonard A. Woodcock before Joint Hearing of Health Subcommittees of House Ways and Means and Interstate and Foreign Commerce Committees (March 3, 1977).

37. P.L. 95–142.

38. "Ineligibles Get $1 Billion Yearly From Medicaid," *Washington Post,* April 30, 1977, p. A2; Richard D. Lyons, "Fraud and Waste in Medicaid Found In Senate Report," *New York Times,* September 30, 1976, p. 1.

39. Lawrence Meyer, "New Machines Send Costs Soaring," *Washington Post,* May 8, 1977, p. 1.

40. Richard J. Margolis, "National Health Insurance—The Dream Whose Time Has Come?" *New York Times Magazine,* January 9, 1977, p. 12; Schlesinger, New Deal, p. 307.

41. "National Energy Program, The President," Address Delivered Before a Joint Session of the Congress, April 20, 1977.

42. 121 *Cong. Rec.* (1975), p. 19779.

43. "Getting the Energy Facts" (Editorial), *Washington Star-News,* January 17, 1974.

44. Wilson, p. 670.

45. "Something Less Than the Millennium," *Time,* August 15, 1977, p. 7.

46. News Conference, August 6, 1977.

47. Welfare Message to Congress, August 6, 1977.

48. See 101 (a), P.L. 91–190 (1970).

49. 91st Cong., 1st Sess., House Report 91–378 (1969).

50. Margot Hornblower, "The Cumbersome Ways of Bureaucracy—Impact Data: What's Wrong?" *Washington Post,* February 13, 1977, p. 1.

51. *An American Dilemma* (New York: Harper, 1944), pp. 75–76.

52. "The Equal Employment Mess" (Editorial), *New York Times,* February 12, 1977, p. 20.

53. Kenneth Keniston and The Carnegie Council on Children, *All Our Children: The American Family under Pressure* (New York: Harcourt, 1977), pp. xiv, 83–84. Emphasis supplied.

54. "As Parents' Influence Fades—Who's Raising the Children?" *U.S. News and World Report,* October 27, 1975, p. 41.

55. Nadine Brozan, "Mondale: Family's Man in the Senate," *New York Times,* February 26, 1974, p. 32.

56. Statement of Senator Walter F. Mondale, in press release, September 24, 1973.

57. 123 *Cong. Rec.* (1977), pp. H9809–10.

58. Remarks to the American Hardware Manufacturers Association, August 25, 1975.
59. Quoted in John Bartlow Martin, *Adlai Stevenson and the World: The Life of Adlai E. Stevenson* (New York: Doubleday, 1977), p. 861.
60. The metaphor, optimistically premature, is from *Time*, July 11, 1960, p. 17.

Index

About the Author

James Duffy, a graduate of Princeton University and Harvard Law School, is a partner in a New York law firm. He and his wife, Martha, live in Manhattan.